CULTURAL DIFFERENCE, MEDIA MEMORIES

For LIFE
and for, truth
& justice

Gina Owens

July, 1997.

CULTURAL DIFFERENCE, MEDIA MEMORIES

ANGLO-AMERICAN IMAGES OF JAPAN

Edited by
Phil Hammond

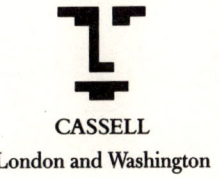

CASSELL
London and Washington

Cassell
Wellington House
125 Strand
London WC2R 0BB

PO Box 605
Herndon
VA 20172

First published 1997

British Library Cataloguing-in-Publication Data
A catalogue record for this book is available from the British Library.

ISBN 0 304 70110 6 (hardback)
         0 304 70111 4 (paperback)

Typeset by JP Graphics Ltd, London

Printed and bound in Great Britain by Biddles Ltd, Guildford and King's Lynn

CONTENTS

ACKNOWLEDGMENTS

This volume is, more than most, a collective effort, since it grew out of the *Images of Japan* project undertaken by the London International Research Exchange. I would like to thank all those—far too numerous to mention individually—who freely gave their time, energy and creativity to the research during its various stages. My particular thanks to Joan Hoey and Daniel Ben-Ami, whose visit to Japan in the summer of 1994 provided the initial inspiration for the project; and to Sharon Kinsella for her editorial advice and support.

On behalf of the Exchange, I would like to thank the Daiwa Anglo-Japanese Foundation, who kindly allowed us to use their facilities for the duration of the project, and who generously supported the writing up of the research.

Although the credit for this volume should be widely shared, the responsibilty for any errors or inaccuracies which remain, of course, is mine.

Phil Hammond
February 1997

Note

Japanese names are given throughout in Japanese name order.

INTRODUCTION: QUESTIONING CULTURAL DIFFERENCE

Phil Hammond

During the Second World War the director Frank Capra made a film for the American government, called *Know Your Enemy— Japan*. Released on 9 August 1945—the day Nagasaki was atom-bombed—the film was withdrawn from circulation before the month was out. Short as its life was, however, *Know Your Enemy* is an interesting piece of propaganda because of the history of its making. First drafted in June 1942, the film took three years to come to the screen. The chief cause of the delay was, ironically, the fact that the film-makers did not 'know their enemy'. As one of the scriptwriters, Irving Wallace, recounted:

> From [President Franklin Roosevelt] to General Marshall down, no one knew what to tell the troops about who their real enemy was. Some felt that the only good Jap was a dead Jap and condemned the whole race of people as the enemy (as Colonel Capra believed). Others felt the enemy was the Emperor. Still others believed Tojo and the military clique were the real enemy.[1]

The first producer of *Know Your Enemy—Japan*, the Dutch film-maker Joris Ivens, thought that Japan should be treated in the same way that Germany had been treated in US propaganda, whereby military and political leaders were the main villains. He came into conflict with Capra and the Pentagon, who insisted that the whole Japanese people as a race were the enemy. Since Japan was a non-white power, a racial double standard was applied. As John Dower notes in his discussion of the film, there was no room for the 'good Japanese' as there was for the 'good German'.[2]

This differential treatment of the Japanese and Germans was again apparent fifty years later on the occasion of the anniversary of the end of the Pacific War. The British government announced in January 1995 that, while for the anniversary of Victory in Europe 'the theme is reconciliation, a celebration of fifty years of peace in Europe and hope for the future', the anniversary of Victory over Japan Day 'will have quite a different theme'.[3] The different tone of the two occasions reflected the decision not to invite any Japanese representative to August's sombre commemoration of VJ-Day, in contrast to the invitation extended to German Chancellor Helmut Kohl to attend the celebratory festivities marking VE-Day in May. The *Daily Mail* positively delighted in this decision, declaring that: 'there is a huge difference in the way we are treating these once mortal enemies. Rightly so.'[4] The *Mail*—which ran this story as a front-page item, placed it at the top of its editorial column, and carried a feature article on it—argued that 'John Major had no choice but to snub Japan'.

Though the *Mail* may have been singularly enthusiastic, it was not alone in taking its cue from the government. In the months that followed, virtually all sections of the British press were relentless in their demand that Japan apologise for its wartime conduct, and vociferous in their justification of the atomic bombings of Hiroshima and Nagasaki. A similar mood existed in the United States, although there the priorities were reversed, and the primary focus of the media was on defending the decision to use the bomb. In this volume, Uday Mohan and Leo Malley III describe the coverage of the Pacific War anniversaries in America, while Paul Stirner and I provide an equivalent analysis of the British press, and John Knight illustrates the impact which the anniversaries made in the Japanese media. As Mohan and Malley demonstrate, despite a past legacy of dissent over the bomb decision, in the 1990s, media reporting has closed down public discussion, curtailing historical investigation in favour of an uncritical commemoration of the past.

Occasionally, a dissenting voice would be heard, and sometimes official initiatives went too far for the media. For instance, when the US government proposed issuing a special postage stamp to celebrate the bombing of Hiroshima—bearing a picture of a mushroom cloud and the slogan 'Atomic bombs hasten war's end, August 1945'—one American commentator pointed out that it would be hard to imagine an equivalent Japanese stamp, depicting a sinking battleship and captioned: 'Japanese aviators achieve surprise at Pearl Harbour, December 1941.'[5] Yet in general the sense of Anglo-American moral superiority over the Pacific War was so ingrained that it was echoed even by those writers who tried to take a distance from the anniversary fever. In Britain, for example, the *Guardian's* Political Editor, Michael White, rightly set the obsession with the war in the context of 'a backward-looking, heritage-minded society...where the past offers more comfort than the future'. Yet even as he described Britain's attempt to monopolise the 'trade in moral superiority', White referred to the atomic-bombing of Hiroshima as 'a cost-effective life-saver'.[6] It seemed evident, to any reader of the British or American press, that 'they' commit atrocities and never apologise, while 'we' save lives (and cheaply) by atom-bombing them.

During the Second World War Allied propaganda portrayed the Japanese as a sub-human species. American and British newspaper cartoonists routinely depicted them as rats, lice, and, most commonly, as apes or monkeys.[7] Fifty years later, the commemorations of the end of the Pacific War became the occasion, in Britain and the United States, for a media deluge of anti-Japanese chauvinism and self-righteousness. The continuity appeared to be striking, particularly in the way in which racial thinking underpinned the contemporary view of Japan. Why were apparently similar attitudes still surfacing in the media half a century after the end of the war? This question was the starting point for the research presented in this book.

Continuity and Change

Some argued that the Japan-bashing of 1995 was simply a hangover from the past. Scott Lucas and Richard Hope, for example, observing that the British attitude was worse than that of America or Australia, explained this perceived difference by reference to the legacy of wartime propaganda:

> Behind this British portrayal there is a history, not only of the treatment of prisoners of war or the cost of the Pacific conflict, but also of the propaganda of the second world war. Long before the first battles in Asia, the British government was producing a vision of Japanese fanaticism, unthinking loyalty, and even barbarism, which still continues today.[8]

Quite apart from the fact that, in terms of the hostile and racist depiction of Japan in wartime and earlier, there is little to distinguish Britain from the United States, this explanation cannot stand. It strains credibility to assert that the news coverage of 1995 was determined by the propaganda of the 1930s and 1940s. Certainly, there were remarkable continuities. In a judicious synthesis, Gina Owens' chapter in this volume traces the pre-war history of Western perceptions of Japan. Themes which emerged in the thinking of the Anglo-American élite in the nineteenth century are still strikingly evident in today's discussion of Japan. Yet these echoes are present in the 'normal', routine reporting of the country—and were not simply prompted by the wartime anniversaries stirring old memories.

A truism about British media reporting of Japan is that there is not much of it. Despite being one of the most economically powerful and technologically sophisticated countries in the world—and despite being a major investor in both Britain and America—Japan is generally rather under-reported. Yet during 1995 Japan was a highly newsworthy country, experiencing a major earthquake, a poison gas attack on the Tokyo subway, a hijacking, and a trade war with the United States. As against all these extraordinary stories, however, the wartime anniversaries provided the longest-running news event of the year. In one sense, of course, it was the most exceptional story: catastrophes and disasters, though rare, may happen any time; fiftieth anniversaries, by definition, happen only once. But in another sense the war commemorations were the most typical events—

not just because the Second World War is central to British political cul-ture,[9] but also because, as Paul Stirner and I demonstrate in our chapter, the loud proclamation of Western moral superiority which accompanied the anniversaries of the Allies' atomic bombings and ultimate victory was simply a full-throated version of the prejudices and double standards which are voiced routinely the rest of the time in more muted tones. This is a point developed in this volume by Tessa Mayes and Megan Rowling, who present the results of a survey of British Japan correspondents and Foreign Editors.

On the occasion of the wartime anniversaries, one could perhaps be forgiven for thinking that anti-Japanese chauvinism was a throwback to earlier attitudes. Yet we had been there before, without the prompt of a victory commemoration. As David Morley and Kevin Robins note:

> An outburst of 'Japan bashing' flared up around 1987, and it did so as an immediate consequence of the thawing relations between the West and the Soviet bloc. It is the transformation to the so-called New World Order that is now changing American and European attitudes to Japan. Now there is a growing hostility to what is seen as its ruthless and dedi-cated economic expansionism, anger at a corresponding insensitivity to global concerns (the environment, famine) and resentment about its lack of political solidarity (the Gulf War).[10]

In 1991 the French Prime Minister, Edith Cresson, notoriously described the Japanese as 'ants'. These 'little yellow men', she said, have 'a strategy of world conquest', and 'stay up all night thinking about ways to screw the Americans and Europeans. They are our common enemy'.[11] As Morley and Robins rightly observe, it was the growing power of Japan relative to America, in the context of a changing framework of inter-national relations, which prompted outbursts such as Cresson's. In other words, the causes of contemporary anti-Japanese sentiment are contem-porary, rather than a throwback to an earlier era.

However, Morley and Robins suggest that this argument is insufficient to explain the outburst of Japan bashing in recent years:

> In 1989, the Japanese overtook the Russians in opinion polls as the nation which Americans fear most. The 'official' explanation of this is in economic terms....It is, however, not simply a matter of economic hegemony.[12]

In one sense, of course, this is true: economic rivalry is not explanation enough on its own, although it is important. By the early 1990s, the USA had gone from being the world economy's lender of last resort, the world's largest creditor, to being in hock to an economic rival and the world's largest debtor. While Japan financed American borrowing it also bought up American businesses and the USA began to complain bitterly of Japan's 'unfair' trading policies. Yet these economic tensions have to be set in the context of, first, a thaw in US-Soviet relations, and then the end of the Cold War. Though noting this context, in practice Morley and Robins tend to underestimate its significance. American hegemony was not simply a matter of the economic pre-eminence enjoyed in the early post-war period. Increasingly, as its economic power declined, the United States came to rely on the stable framework of international politics provided by the Cold War as a means to assert its global leadership. With the fall of the Berlin Wall, America's established position as leader of the free West against the Soviet Evil Empire also collapsed.

Western triumphalism over 'winning' the Cold War was muted and short-lived. The political élites of London and Washington have come to miss an international order in which challenges from the relatively dynamic economies of Germany and Japan could be offset by the balance of military power and political influence established through the Cold War. Perhaps the most useful point of historical comparison to be made today is with the pre-war period, when, as now, Japan was seen as upsetting the world order. In a world dominated by white colonial powers, the growing strength of Japan was perceived as a threat not just to the economic and political interests of Europe and America, but to the ideology of racial superiority through which they justified their domination of the globe. Whereas in the past such concerns were expressed explicitly as a fear for 'white prestige' in the Far East, today's commentators are more likely to frame the problem in terms of Japan's *moral* inferiority and *cultural* difference.

This is not to suggest that contemporary Japan-bashing is purely a matter of international politics and world economic rivalry. Rather, the British crusade for apologies, American sanctimony over the bomb, and French name-calling are designed primarily for domestic consumption. This is why, in his chapter in this volume, Uday Mohan locates the controversy over the Smithsonian Institution's planned Hiroshima exhibition in the context of the 'culture war'. He argues that the conservative reaction against critical history in 1995 was as much an attack on the legacy of 1960s liberalism as it was an attempt to enforce the official interpretation of the decision to use the atomic bomb. Similarly, in Britain commemoration of wartime anniversaries provided a rare opportunity for an unpopular government to generate a 'feelgood factor'. Berating the Japanese for their war record afforded politicians and journalists a comforting sense of moral superiority in an uncertain present. Anti-Japanese chauvinism in the 1990s, then, is a product of contemporary Western problems and concerns. This point deserves emphasis because it has important consequences for how one understands the significance attributed to Japanese 'cultural difference'.

The West and No 'Other'

Morley and Robins draw on the work of Edward Said and Robert Young to supply what they perceive to be missing from what they call the 'official' explanation of contemporary anti-Japanese chauvinism:

> Our interest here is in tracing a set of discursive correspondences that have been, and still are being, developed in the West between 'Japan', the 'Orient' and the 'Other'. More specifically, we want to explore why, at this historical moment, this particular Other should occupy such a threatening position in the western imagination.[13]

Despite an avowed intention to be historically specific, viewing Japan as the 'Other' of the West inexorably leads to an ahistorical and ultimately mystifying perspective. Since the approach Morley and Robins adopt towards Japan is representative of much of today's thought about the West and its 'Others', it is worth examining in some detail.

The concept of the Other refers to the way in which what Said calls the 'universalising discourses of modern Europe and the United States' silence the rest of the world.[14] The universalism of Enlightenment thought, it is argued, is ultimately oppressive—a form of intellectual imperialism. As Young puts it:

> The appropriation of the Other as a form of knowledge within a totalising system can thus be set alongside the history (if not the project) of European imperialism, and the constitution of the Other as 'Other' alongside racism and sexism.[15]

The West can only construct its own sense of identity by excluding the non-Western world. The discourse of the conscious, rational, acting subject exists only at the expense of silencing an objectified Other. This radical critique of Enlightenment rationalism, which traces its roots to the phenomenology of Edmund Husserl, suffuses much contemporary critical thought, and, Morley and Robins contend, provides a useful framework for examining the West's relationship with Japan. The latter is the West's mysterious Orient; a 'traditional' culture of inscrutable irrationality counterposed to the rationalism of Western modernity. Accordingly, Morley and Robins argue that contemporary outpourings of anti-Japanese sentiment should not be understood as an expression of economic rivalry, but rather as a reaction against Japan's refusal to be the West's Other:

> Western anxieties about Japan are an expression of resentment at this emergence of a threat to what has been seen as the West's natural and proper claim on universalism.[16]

Thus, Japan's refusal to toe the Western line—as exemplified in Ishihara Shintaro's 1989 polemic, *The Japan That Can Say No*—should be understood as a fundamental challenge to the West's very sense of self.

However, to say that Japan has been constructed as the West's Other is to lose sight of the specific historical conditions which have determined the country's relationship to the West. Just such an ahistorical approach is evident when, for example, Morley and Robins state that: 'For nearly five centuries now, Japan has been among the West's Others.'[17] This telescopes five hundred years of history into one 'discursive practice'. Similarly, they suggest that:

> The image of "Japan Inc." can readily be seen as an echo of the West's age-old fear of "Oriental Despotism"—a phrase first used by the ancient Greeks to describe the Persians, but one which still provides the inherited script according to which the West now imagines (post)modern Japan.[18]

What are we to make of such a statement? Can it be that contemporary Western fears of Japanese industrial strength are not at root a matter of economic and geopolitical rivalry, but are really the playing out of an ancient Greek script? This is a particularly peculiar claim to make since elsewhere in their essay Morley and Robins point to the 'arbitrary annexation of Hellenic culture to Europe' as part of the very universalising Enlightenment tradition they criticise.[19]

At best, such an approach may illuminate the continuities of racial thinking—though tracing these ideas back to ancient Greece is decidedly unhelpful. But even when this is achieved, it is at the expense of understanding the specificity of how the ideology of race has been reworked and reformulated in changing historical circumstances. A key argument running through many of the contributions to the present volume, presented initially in Daniel Ben-Ami's chapter, is that ideas of *racial* difference have been re-thought, in the post-war period, in the language of *cultural* difference. It may be tempting to say that nothing has changed in the West's view of Japan, and in one sense this is true: there is still an underlying racist attitude. Yet if we focus exclusively on the element of continuity we lose sight of the specificity of the contemporary discussion of cultural difference. It is not a question of an inherited script, but of a different script—one appropriate to the times. Edith Cresson's 1991 remarks prompted an outcry for exactly this reason. It is not the same to portray Japanese as racially different—a nation of rats, monkeys or ants— and to portray them as culturally different. Today the one causes a furore, while the other is likely to draw nods of assent.

For those who criticise the universalism of Enlightenment thought, the alternative must be an endorsement of difference. When Morley and Robins describe the 'fear that Japan's irreducible difference will remain aloof from, and impenetrable to, western reason and universalism',[20] they are not challenging the notion that Japan is 'irreducibly different' but agreeing with it. If a universalist perspective is a 'totalising' and ultimately 'totalitarian' one, the answer is a celebration of particularism. The goal, as Young puts it in discussing the work of Michel Foucault and Jean-François Lyotard, must be to construct 'a form of knowledge that respects the other without absorbing it into the same'.[21] Despite the good intentions evident in this statement, assuring respect and de-capitalising the 'other' provide no solution. The notion of cultural difference, after all, promises precisely to 'respect' difference, but in practice equates difference with inferiority. As Ben-Ami and other contributors to this book argue, despite the subjective intentions of the liberal proponents of cultural difference, 'culture' turns out on closer examination to be very similar to the concept of race. Where once European élites classified the peoples under their colonial rule, and the classes at the bottom of their own societies, as biologically different, their contemporary counterparts now speak of cultural difference as the cause both of savagery abroad (for example, in Rwanda or the former Yugoslavia), and of the persistence of an 'underclass' at home.

Take, for example, the work of the American social scientist Charles Murray, whose 1994 book, *The Bell Curve,* written with Richard Herrnstein, was greeted by many with outrage. Murray and Herrnstein sought to explain the inequalities of American society through IQ, the supposedly objective measure of inherited, innate intelligence:

'the wages earned by people in high-IQ occupations have pulled away from the wages of low-IQ occupations, and differences in education cannot explain most of this change.'[22]

The alleged link between IQ test scores and differences in income is thus supposed to prove that the inequalities of society are not social, but natural. As Murray and Herrnstein put it: 'the evidence presented here should give everyone who writes about ethnic inequalities reason to avoid flamboyant rhetoric about ethnic oppression.'[23] In other words, if blacks are at the bottom of US society, this is not the result of racism, but the natural consequence of their lower intelligence. The reason *The Bell Curve* was such a controversial book is that it used old-fashioned genetic, or racial theories to naturalise social divisions. However, in earlier works Murray employed the more contemporary idiom of cultural difference to make essentially the same point. In a 1990 pamphlet for the British conservative think-tank the Institute of Economic Affairs, he explained the existence of an 'underclass' not in genetic, but in cultural terms. The underclass, he argued, are the product of a 'culture of poverty'. They have a distinctive 'mindset'. They have different 'values' which are 'contaminating the life of entire neighbourhoods'. Such an underclass develops, Murray contended, not as a result of the socio-economic system, but not as a result of inherited biological traits, such as innate intelligence, either. Rather, it is as a result of the socialisation of children by underclass parents; the passing on of cultural values and attitudes, rather than genes.[24]

In one sense it makes little difference whether one explains social inequality as a result of culture or nature. The concept of cultural difference fixes human characteristics just as much as the concept of race. Whether the argument is posed in terms of a biological inheritance or a cultural one, people are seen to be as they are, not as a result of their own actions and ideas, but as a result of an inheritance from the past. This is why an ahistorical notion such as that of the West and its Others is so problematic. Differences between societies are not seen as the product of human social activity in changing historical circumstances; rather, culture constructs people differently according to its own trans-historical discursive logic. It is not just that racial thinking underlies the liberal discussion of cultural difference. The latter is also far more dangerous because, to view differences between and within societies in terms of culture is generally deemed acceptable, even sympathetic and sensitive, while the outmoded language of race is condemned.

Modernity and Self-loathing

The conclusion of Morley and Robins' essay is that contemporary fear of the Japanese Other may reveal a disenchantment with the Western self. They speculate:

> ...we might suggest that the resentment expressed against Japanese technology (rationality, development, progress) reflects an unconscious and primal hatred of this aspect of western maturity. There is perhaps a (delirious) refusal, rejection, detestation of that modernity into which our own culture has been transformed; of that (totalitarian) element of modernity that threatens some deep-seated aspect (or cultural monad) in western society.[25]

Hatred of the Other, it is argued, belies a repressed self-loathing. Since contemporary anti-Japanese chauvinism is often expressed as a fear of Japanese technological advancement, perhaps the real object of attack is not so much the Oriental Other, but Western 'modernity' itself. This is something that Morley and Robins see as positive:

> Japan is significant because of its complexity: it is non-western, yet refuses any longer to be our Orient; it insists on being modern, yet calls our kind of modernity into question. Because of this Japan offers possibilities.[26]

Thus, a hostility to universalism implies a critique of 'modernity'. If universalism, reason and progress are seen as characteristic of a totalising Eurocentric discourse, then its rejection must entail the disparagement of all these Enlightenment ideals.

Some recent thinking on the concept of race has questioned the equation being made here. This critique of 'modernity', as we have seen, implicates certain ideas or discourses—of progress, reason, universalism—in the history of imperialism. Yet pitching the argument against a certain discourse—that which constructs the Other—entails an ahistorical approach. As Kenan Malik writes:

> By conflating the social relations of capitalism with the intellectual and technological progress of "modernity", the product of the former can be laid at the door of the latter. The specific problems created by capitalist social relations became dehistoricised....In this way the positive aspects of capitalist society—its invocation of reason, its technological advancements, its ideological commitment to equality and universalism—are denigrated while its negative aspects—the inability to overcome social divisions, the propensity to treat large sections of humanity as "inferior" or

"subhuman", the contrast between technological advance and moral turpi-
tude, the tendencies toward barbarism—are seen as inevitable or natural.[27]

Evidently, the intention of critics such as Said, Young, Morley and Robins
is not to provide an apologia for racial division, but to challenge it. Yet the
approach adopted cuts the ground from under their own critique. As
they rightly observe, the Western claim to universalism is false. However,
what is criticised, from this perspective, is not a *false* universalism, but
false *universalism*. In other words, the criticism is not that the ideal of
universalism is betrayed in practice; rather, what is rejected is universalism *per se*. Universalism is therefore abandoned in favour of a celebration
of particularism and difference. As Frank Füredi puts it in discussing the
New Left of the 1960s:

> The New Left was not in its origin motivated by a conservative impulse,
> but by rejecting universalism in general—because it confused the univer-
> salist form in which Western capitalism presented itself with the concept
> itself—it uncritically ended adopting a particularist epistemology.
> Unconsciously, the New Left reaction to post-war Western capitalism
> copied the methods and arguments of the conservative reaction to the
> Enlightenment.[28]

Yet a universalist outlook does not imply that differences, divisions or
inequalities should be denied, but rather locates these as products of
society and history. By contrast, where racial thinking explains inequality
as the inevitable outcome of innate biological characteristics, the celebration of cultural difference understands divisions as the product of inherited cultural values. Instead, the target ought to be the inability of capitalist
society to live up to its universalist ideals and to deliver on its promised
freedom and equality.

It may seem odd to criticise the celebration of culture for fixing identities, since it often appears to offer a view of cultural identity as something
infinitely fluid and malleable. Where racial thinking rigidly ordered
human being according to biological traits, culture is an 'anti-essentialist'
concept. As I have argued, in practice what amounts to a cultural essence
is substituted for a biological one, but in theory this should not be the
case. If subjectivity is understood as the product of various discourses,
there simply is no 'essential' self; we can reinvent ourselves. In relation to
Japan, this perspective is adopted by the contributors to a recent volume
on consumerism which suggests that: 'in a changing Japan, what people
consume may be as important as what they produce in shaping a sense of

self'.[29] One of the essays in the collection, for instance, addresses Japanese drinking etiquette:

> ...the reason mixed drinks have not done well in the past is not that people did not like the taste or found the drinks too heavy or prohibitively expensive, but rather that Japanese social drinking traditionally emphasises the sublimation and unification of individuals into community. Mixed drinks, by definition, are mixed and thus require special preparation that focuses undesirable attention on the individualistic demands of the drinker's order. Japan is a culture in which diners frequently seek consensus as to what they should order, a culture in which guests are automatically given sugar and cream in their coffee so as to save them from socially awkward decisions and the expression of individual demands.[30]

In many ways this passage simply reiterates established clichés about Japanese cultural difference, whereby ordering a whisky and soda supposedly precipitates an agony of embarrassment at an act of such rampant egoism in a conformist, 'group' society. The point being made, however, is that consumption—drinking, eating, shopping—is the means by which we construct our sense of self and through which social identities are transformed. Accordingly, the essay concludes that the situation regarding beverages is now more fluid than might be expected: 'In sum, one finds that there are more drinking contexts and more ways to drink, making drinking a more individualised, less ritualised experience.'[31] Culture, in this respect, appears not as a fixed and rigid phenomenon, but as something which can change through the act of consumption.

The example of drinking etiquette may seem a trivial one, but it is symptomatic of a tendency to promote consumption as a potentially liberating sphere of human activity. As Stuart Hall argues, consumption involves the 'pluralisation' of social life, since it 'expands the roles and identities open to ordinary people (at least in the developed world)'.[32] Even overlooking the fact that we are obliged to write off most of the world's population in order to sustain this theory of progressive consumerism, it implies a highly limited view of human potential.

If we understand the human subject as the product of an inherited script, who can only sustain a sense of self through oppressive objectification of the Other, human subjectivity itself is degraded. This is not simply an unfortunate by-product of the notion of the Other, it is central to the hostility towards Enlightenment rationalism. This is the hidden danger which underlies the celebration of cultural difference: not only is it a coded, liberal expression of racial thinking; it also ultimately denigrates purposeful human activity and the project of social change. Even when culture is understood as a fluid and manipulable phenomenon, our capacity for social action is limited. Though the re-invention of the self through culture may appear as an active process, it is essentially passive: human potential and control is constrained within the limits of shopping, or ordering drinks.

It is, in a sense, ironic that Morley and Robins should understand Japan bashing as a reaction against a challenge to Western claims of universalism. In her chapter in this book, Lynn Revell examines the way in which Anglo-American commentators have often viewed Japan as exceptional and different precisely because of its particularism; its refusal to conform to a universal standard. They point to Nihonjinron—the theory of 'Japaneseness'—as confirmation that not only are the Japanese different, they also see themselves as different. Japanese expressions of particularism do not challenge the Western world-view, but confirm it. As Revell argues, the notion of cultural difference is of European origin, and the emphasis on Japanese cultural difference is a product of American thought. While the European emphasis on culture and tradition traces its roots to the nineteenth-century reaction against the Enlightenment, the post-war adoption of the language of cultural difference was the product of the Nazi experience: after the Holocaust, the ideology of racial superiority was discredited, and had to be re-thought in cultural terms. In either case, there is nothing progressive or challenging in the celebration of difference or the denigration of universalist values.

'Cultural' explanations of all sorts of social phenomena are increasingly popular today.[33] As I hope to have indicated here, at the same time as having a very specific focus on the Anglo-American media portrayal of Japan, this book also raises broader issues and engages a number of wider debates which preoccupy scholars working in several disciplines. One of the aims of the book is to interrogate the concepts of culture and cultural difference, and the first three chapters do this by exploring the history and contemporary nuances of Western images of Japan. The second section of this volume continues these arguments, taking a detailed look at how the discussion of difference was expressed in the media coverage of Japan in 1995, and examining the role of the media in constructing history and popular memory.

NOTES

1. Quoted in W.J. Blakefield, 'A War Within: The Making of *Know Your Enemy—Japan*', *Sight and Sound*, Spring 1983, p130.

2. John Dower, *War Without Mercy*, London, Faber & Faber, 1986, p322n.

3. Downing Street Press Office, 11 January 1995.

4. *Daily Mail*, 6 January 1995.

5. *International Herald Tribune*, 7 December 1994.

6. *Guardian*, 14 January 1995.

7. See Dower, op. cit., pp181-190, for some representative examples.

8. *Guardian*, 19 August 1995.

9. See: Phil Hammond and Joan Hoey, *History As News*, London, LIRE, 1994.

10. David Morley and Kevin Robins, 'Techno-Orientalism: Futures, Foreigners and Phobias', *New Formations*, No. 16, spring 1992, p151. In relation to their point about criticism of Japan on 'environmentalist' grounds, it is perhaps also worth noting the long-running press story of the same period concerning Japanese whaling. See: Arne Kalland, 'Whale Politics and Green Legitimacy', *Anthropology Today*, Vol. 9, No. 6, December 1993.

11. Quoted in Morley and Robins, op. cit., p136.

12. Ibid., p144.

13. Ibid., p136.

14. Edward Said, *Culture and Imperialism*, London, Chatto & Windus, 1993, p58.

15. Robert Young, *White Mythologies: Writing History and the West*, London, Routledge, 1990, p4. This is a passage which Morley and Robins quote approvingly, op. cit., p147.

16. Morley and Robins, op. cit., p150.

17. Ibid., p136.

18. Ibid., p142.

19. Ibid., p143.

20. Ibid., p148.

21. Young, op. cit., p10.

22. Richard J. Herrnstein and Charles Murray, *The Bell Curve: Intelligence and Class Structure in American Life*, New York, Free Press, 1994, p91.

23. Ibid., p340.

24. Charles Murray, *The Emerging British Underclass*, London, Institute of Economic Affairs, 1990.

25. Morley and Robins, op. cit., p155.

26. Ibid., It is interesting to compare Morley and Robins' own invocation of Japan's supposed 'complexity' here with their earlier observation that: 'Its difference has been contained in the idea of some mysterious ambiguity. Japan is both "the chrysanthemum and the sword"....It is this complexity and ambiguity in the image of Japan that has given it a particular resonance in western fantasies. But, if it has been complex, it has always been possible symbolically to control this image of Japan.' (pp136-7) They draw attention to the past mystification of Japan as 'mysteriously complex' only to reiterate the idea themselves.

27. Kenan Malik, *The Meaning of Race*, London, Macmillan, 1996, pp246-7.

28. Frank Füredi, *Mythical Past, Elusive Future: History and Society in an Anxious Age*, London, Pluto, 1992, p227.

29. Joseph J. Tobin, 'Introduction: Domesticating the West', Joseph J. Tobin (ed.), *Re-Made in Japan*, New Haven, Yale University Press, 1992, p8.

30. Stephen R. Smith, 'Drinking Etiquette in a Changing Beverage Market', in ibid., pp153-4.

31. Ibid., p156.

32. Stuart Hall, 'Brave New World', *Marxism Today*, October 1988.

33. For an illuminating discussion of this trend see Lynn Revell, 'The Cultural Apology', *Confrontation*, Vol. 2, No. 1, 1996.

PART ONE:
CULTURAL DIFFERENCE

1 IS JAPAN DIFFERENT?

Daniel Ben-Ami

The aim of this chapter is to refute the idea of 'cultural difference' as a way of understanding modern Japan. We will argue that the notion of culture, as used by many writers, conceals what is at root a racial conception of Japan. First, we examine the 'revisionist' school of commentators which has emerged (particularly in writing on the Japanese economy) in recent years. The assumption that Japan is culturally different from other industrialised societies is now widespread. Commentators do not all agree on the precise characteristics that distinguish Japan from Western societies, but the premise of Japanese cultural difference runs through much of the contemporary literature. Indeed, some writers have recently extended the notion of cultural difference to other East Asian societies.

Second, the chapter traces these ideas of cultural difference back to the influence of Cultural Anthropologists, particularly Ruth Benedict, on today's discussion of Japan. We will argue that the notion of cultural difference is a barrier to developing a rational understanding of Japan. Indeed, it is precisely because the notion of cultural difference is so pervasive that it needs to be made explicit and challenged. A method which centres on the question of cultural difference is fundamentally ahistorical, irrational, and mystifies what it purports to explain. In conclusion, after looking briefly at how notions of cultural difference have influenced discussion within Japan itself, we outline an alternative approach to understanding Japanese society.

The Revisionist School

The assumption of Japanese cultural difference came to prominence in the late 1980s when the emergence of a distinct 'revisionist' school on Japan precipitated a broader discussion in the American media.[1] Revisionist writers argued that the Japanese state behaved differently from its Western counterparts—particularly in its relationship to the market. Underlying the discussion was a core assumption of cultural difference. The leading figures in this discussion were Karel van Wolferen (a Dutch journalist based in Japan), James Fallows (Washington editor of *The Atlantic Monthly*), and Clyde Prestowitz (a former US trade representative).

Key features often seen as characteristic of 'Japan Inc.' included the notion of the developmental state, the role of MITI (the Ministry of International Trade and Industry), the system of *keiretsu* (inter-locking share ownership) and the system of lifetime employment for a section of the Japanese work force. Writers on management tended to emphasise such factors as: lean production methods such as the *kanban* (just in time) system for controlling stock inventories, worker involvement, goal setting and a commitment to quality. Underlying these notions is the idea of Japan as a form of communitarian society where loyalty to the group is paramount.[2]

The intellectual godfather of the revisionist movement, although not as prominent in the media debate, was Chalmers Johnson. His *MITI and the Japanese Miracle*, which emphasised the importance of the developmental state in Japan, informed the work of more prominent commentators. As Kent Calder argued in 1993: 'the developmental state contentions...have dominated analysis of the Japanese political economy for a decade.'[3] Nor was Johnson's influence restricted to the USA. Sakakibara Eisuke's *Beyond Capitalism* (which includes an introduction by Clyde Prestowitz) put forward a similar argument from the point of view of a senior Japanese Ministry of Finance official.[4]

For Johnson, the key point was not that the Japanese state intervened in the economy: as he notes, all states practice economic intervention to some extent.[5] However, in the USA, for example, the state is primarily concerned with regulation rather than economic planning. In contrast, the developmental state is 'plan rational'—in other words, élite bureaucrats organise the economy to meet 'substantive social and economic goals'.[6] Johnson also compares Japan to the USSR, which he labels as 'plan ideological', where the principle of planning was a fundamental value in itself. In ideological terms he sees Japanese political economy as 'located precisely in the line of descent from the German Historical School—sometimes labelled "economic nationalism", Handelspolitik, or neomercantalism'.[7]

More recently, an attempt to link the Japanese experience more broadly to the notion of Asian values has come into vogue. The argument here is that 'Confucian' values—particularly those related to strong family ties—have somehow contributed to the economic success of Japan and of East Asia more generally. As David Howell, the Chairman of the House of Commons Foreign Affairs Committee, argues:

> ...the sobering thought has to be faced that not only are the Asian nations, or at least growing regions within them, now better equipped economically and technically to succeed in the information age, but that their underlying philosophies of life, duty and work, reflected in personal, family and community behaviour, may be more suited to support this success—indeed may actually account for it.[8]

This latest twist in the argument clearly owes much to the relative slowdown of the Japanese economy compared to its East Asian neighbours.

While the Japanese economy has virtually stagnated since 1990, many of the East Asian economies have continued to exhibit strong growth. Western writers have naturally sought to explain why the East Asian region has been experiencing by far the strongest economic growth in the world.

Perhaps the baldest statement of cultural difference by a mainstream commentator in recent years is Samuel Huntington's essay, 'The Clash of Civilizations', published in a leading American foreign policy journal, in the summer of 1993. Huntington's argument is that with the end of the Cold War, and the consequent end of the division between the Soviet Bloc and the West, the main divisions in the world will be civilisational:

> It is my hypothesis that the fundamental source of conflict in this new world will not be primarily ideological or primarily economic. The great divisions among humankind and the dominating source of conflict will be cultural.[9]

Unlike some writers, Huntington draws a clear distinction between Confucian societies and Japan. But he shares with the majority of commentators the view of Japan as culturally distinct from Western societies.

While the emergence of the revisionist school is relatively recent, the ideas which inform such contemporary commentary on Japan have their origin in an earlier period. Specifically, today's widespread assumption of cultural difference owes much to post-war anthropology, initially to the work of the American Cultural Anthropologist Ruth Benedict.

From Race to Culture

Ruth Benedict, who spent her whole academic career at Columbia University, came to the study of Japan relatively late in life. She was assigned to the study of Japan by the US Office of War Information (OWI) in June 1944, and died in 1948. Yet her work has had an enormous and enduring influence on Japanese Studies. Until her Japan study, Benedict was best known for her field work among native Americans and her general works on culture. Her *Patterns of Culture*, first published in 1934, played an important role in popularising the idea that culture, rather than race, was the main driving force behind human behaviour. In her general work on cultural anthropology she was influenced by contemporaries such as Margaret Mead and by predecessors such as Franz Boas, one of the most influential anthropologists this century.[10] On Japan specifically, her influences included E. H. Norman, the leftist economic historian, and John Embree, whose earlier anthropological field study of a Japanese village she described as 'invaluable'.[11]

Although Ruth Benedict's *The Chrysanthemum and the Sword* was first published in 1946, it still retains great influence both on academic studies of Japan and on popular journalism. In the USA it has sold 350,000 copies, a huge number for a work of anthropology. In Japan it has sold over one million copies despite its origins as a study for the OWI.[12] Benedict's work is still the model for Western writing on Japan, and the assumptions it voices have set the standard for over fifty years. Many of the core concepts used in today's discussions of Japan can be traced back to Benedict. For example, the concept of 'groupism'—the idea that Japanese society is based on the group rather than the individual—is central to her argument. Although she does not use the term herself, the idea of groupism is implicit in her famous distinction between 'shame cultures' and 'guilt cultures'. She believed that in 'guilt cultures', as in the USA, behaviour is regulated by individual conscience. By contrast, in shame societies, such as Japan, people are worried mainly about looking bad in front of the group: 'True shame cultures rely on external sanctions for good behaviour, not, as true guilt cultures do, on an internalised conviction of sin.'[13]

Benedict's method is simply to draw attention to the cultural differences between Japan and the USA. She draws attention to these differences from the opening sentence of the book: 'The Japanese were the most alien enemy the United States had ever fought in an all-out struggle.'[14] The rest of the book is an examination of the differences between the two nations. So, in Japan great emphasis is placed on hierarchy, while in the USA equality is a key value; in Japan the state is the supreme good, while in the USA it is always seen as a potential threat to liberty.

Benedict's core assumption of cultural difference has permeated Japanese Studies since the Second World War. Most writers on Japan have accepted that it is useful to see Japan as embodying fundamental differences from the West. This premise applies equally to anthropologists, economists, historians, political scientists and sociologists. Journalists, in turn, have drawn on these works in their writings and helped to popularise their core assumptions. There are, naturally, disagreements between authors on what constitutes the defining characteristics of Japanese society. Different writers attach varying degrees of importance to cultural factors, socio-economic factors, the unusual character of the Japanese labour market, and the 'developmental state'.[15] But the importance of difference is assumed.

Ruth Benedict's influence also lives on in her own field of anthropology. For example, *Understanding Japanese Society,* by Joy Hendry, a professor of Social Anthropology at Oxford Brookes University, whose work is discussed in more detail below, is essentially an attempt to update *The Chrysanthemum and the Sword* for a modern audience. Like Benedict, she is concerned with examining the differences between Japanese society and the West, only in Hendry's case the cultural differences that she points to are sometimes different from Benedict. For instance, Hendry sets great store by the distinction between *uchi* and *soto*—roughly translated as those 'inside' and those 'outside' a particular group. Yet the assumption of groupism runs through the work of both authors.

What, then, is wrong with the notion of cultural difference? It would be clearly absurd to deny that there are any differences between Japan and the USA or Britain. It would also be foolish to contend that such differences are unworthy of study. As Benedict says, in 1940s terminology:

> These protagonists of One World have staked their hopes on convincing people of every corner of the earth that all the differences between East and West, black and white, Christian and Mohammedan, are superficial and that all mankind is really like-minded. This view is sometimes called the brotherhood of man. I do not know why believing in the brotherhood of man should mean that one cannot say that the Japanese have their own version of the conduct of life and that Americans have theirs.[16]

The problem does not arise from the recognition of differences between societies, which is a truism, but from the implicit assumption that these differences reflect the innate characteristics of different peoples. Few writers today would be so crass as to pose such arguments in biological or explicitly racial terms. Instead, the discussion is framed in terms of cultural difference.

Nowhere is the assumption of fixed, innate difference clearer than in the discipline of Cultural Anthropology (or Social Anthropology, as it is called in Britain).[17] To understand what is wrong with the anthropologists' view of Japan it is necessary to examine the methods they use. Both Benedict and Hendry say that their first aim is to reconstruct the view of Japan as held by its own citizens. According to Benedict: 'The ideal authority for any statement in this book would be the proverbial man in the street. It would be anybody.'[18] While for Hendry: 'The aim is to introduce the world as it is classified and ordered by the Japanese people.'[19] So far there is not a problem. It is legitimate to examine how people perceive themselves; this would only be problematic if such perceptions were taken at face value. However, both authors state that they are keen to go beyond appearances. Benedict defined the aim of her study as: 'to describe deeply entrenched attitudes of thought and behaviour.'[20]

For Hendry: 'it is one of the aims of an anthropological approach to penetrate the deeper levels of operation behind the familiar façade.'[21]

Yet this is where the problem arises. Both Benedict and Hendry take a deeply ahistorical view of Japan. For both authors, 'deeply entrenched attitudes' means ideas that have essentially existed since time immemorial. This is not some aberration peculiar to these two authors, but is in fact implicit in the method and approach of the anthropologist. Ruth Benedict's avowed aim is to make sense of Japanese cultural difference. She says that, despite the popular American belief that the Japanese are so different that 'whatever we do they do the opposite':

> Such a conviction of difference is dangerous only if a student rests content with saying simply that these differences are so fantastic that it is impossible to understand such people. The anthropologist has good proof in his experience that even bizarre behaviour does not prevent one's understanding it.[22]

Yet Benedict does not illuminate difference, but mystifies it. Her argument reduces itself to the idea that Japanese society can be understood through looking at the toilet-training of Japanese infants. In 'The Child Learns', the climactic chapter of her book, she says, for example, that:

> It is true that a Japanese baby must find diapers unpleasant, not only because they are heavy but because custom does not decree that they be changed whenever he wets them. The baby is nevertheless too young to perceive the connection between nursery training and getting rid of uncomfortable diapers. He experiences only an inescapable routine implacably insisted upon. Besides, the mother has to hold the baby away from her body, and her grip must be firm. What the baby learns from the implacable training prepares him to accept in adulthood the subtler compulsions of Japanese culture.[23]

The proposition that customs relating to nappies hold the key to Japanese culture may seem ridiculous. Yet Benedict insists on the central explanatory importance of child-rearing:

> The contradictions which all Westerners have described in Japanese character are intelligible from their child rearing. It produces a duality in their outlook on life, neither side of which can be ignored....It gives them an assertiveness and a certain self-confidence. It underlies their frequent willingness to tackle any job, no matter how far above their

ability it may seem to be....On occasion, it gives them a capacity for mass megalomania.[24]

Although the leap from child-rearing to mass megalomania may seem highly implausible, Benedict's argument rests on a key idea of social sciences, that of socialisation.

Joy Hendry poses the same argument in a fashion that sounds more familiar to modern ears:

> Socialisation is the means by which an essentially biological being is converted into a social one, able to communicate with other members of the particular society to which it belongs. A child learns to perceive the world through language, spoken and unspoken, through ritual enacted, and through the total symbolic system which structures and constrains that world. Through socialisation a child learns to classify the world in which it lives, and to impose a system of values upon it.[25]

Accordingly, Hendry attributes a similar importance to child rearing, citing, for example, the way that Japanese infants are taught to change their shoes when entering or leaving the house as an explanation of the importance of *uchi* and *soto* (in-group and out-group) to Japanese social organisation.[26]

This concept of socialisation is central to the anthropological explanation of cultural difference. Yet it only makes sense if we examine, not society, but the experience of the individual. For an individual Japanese child, culture is indeed a given: something to be learned, assimilated, and passed on. Yet if we ask where this culture came from, the anthropological method can provide no answer. Instead, the process of 'socialisation' stretches back in an endless chain through the generations. It is this individual-centred method which gives rise to the ahistorical character of cultural explanations. To understand a phenomenon such as the regimentation of Japanese society, one would have to examine various aspects of Japanese social history: the experience of military dictatorship, world war and rapid industrialisation. Failure to do this means that cultural explanations are inevitably ahistorical and cannot explain the differences to which they point.

An approach which starts from the individual makes culture appear, not as a human product, a product of society, but as a something external to and bearing down upon people, determining the way they behave. In this sense, the notion of culture is not unlike the idea of race: we 'inherit' culture; differences are fixed. The anthropological conception of culture is racial since, although culture may be modified over time, its essence remains unaltered. In pre-war racial theories the differences between nations were seen as being fixed by biology. After the Second World War such discredited theories were recast to rely on an ahistorical notion of culture. As a result, the significance of hugely important social changes is often downplayed. Thus, Benedict could argue in 1946—after half a century of dramatic social transformation—that 'Japan has not changed so fundamentally since the 1890s'.[27] This is also the view presented routinely in introductory textbooks on Japan.[28]

Benedict and Hendry both avoid using any racially-loaded language. The only time they come close is in comparing Japan with other non-white societies. For Benedict: 'There are many social arrangements and habits of life in Japan which have close parallels even in the primitive tribes of the Pacific islands.'[29] Hendry is more explicit: 'much of the effectiveness of mechanisms of social control relies, in the Japanese case, on principles which are more commonly found in small communities of Africa and South America than in the industrial societies with which Japan is usually compared.'[30] Both Benedict and Hendry would undoubtedly recoil from any overtly racial language to describe the Japanese. Indeed, Benedict followed the tradition of 'scientific anti-racism' associated with Franz Boas, which explicitly rejected the notion of fixed biological differences between different ethnic groups. It should also be remembered that while Benedict was writing American newspapers were routinely portraying the Japanese in terms of animal images—apes, monkeys, termites and so on.[31] Yet both Benedict and Hendry use the language of cultural relativism to present the same essential idea: of fixed differences between peoples. This is the key contribution of liberal Cultural Anthropology to mainstream thought: it puts the ideas of racial superiority that were discredited through the experience of the Nazi gas chambers into politically correct language.[32]

Rejecting Difference

Let us now turn to look at the legacy of anthropology for the broader contemporary debate about Japanese difference. Writers in other disciplines are rarely as clear about their assumptions as the Cultural Anthropologists. Indeed, a frustrating characteristic of Anglo-American writing on Japan—and more generally—is its empiricist character. Both American and British writers tend to concentrate on listing facts, rather than making their assumptions explicit. This practice means that intellectual debts are rarely acknowledged. It is common for the prevailing assumptions to be woven directly into the text and to inform the choice of subjects studied.

In attempting to challenge the arguments of today's British and American commentators on Japan, disputing incorrect facts is straightforward, but mounting a broader challenge is more complex. The first step must be to tease out core assumptions often left unstated by the authors concerned. There are four characteristics common to much contemporary writing on Japan: its lack of historical specificity; its use of culture as the starting-point for explanation; its irrationality; and its application of a double standard.

Lack of historical specificity

Much writing on Japan, as has already been noted, is ahistorical. Rather than examining how particular characteristics of Japanese society have developed, the assumption is that they are somehow innate. For example, the notion of Japan as a group society, a common theme in much of the literature, is assumed rather than explained. Other characteristics, such as lifetime employment, are also often seen as typically Japanese. Yet this practice is of relatively recent origin and only applies to a minority of Japanese workers.[33]

Another example is the often-quoted distinction between *honne* (inner feelings or intentions) and *tatamae* (the way things are presented or ostensible motives). Many Western writers are happy to use this distinction to make sweeping observations about Japanese society. For Karel van Wolferen, for example, it 'provides a frame of reference in which many forms of deceit are socially sanctioned'. He goes on to argue that the dichotomy allows the Japanese to 'be honest about their fakery to a degree that Westerners could not possibly be. They are allowed to pretend honesty without fear of being chided for dishonesty'.[34] There is no clear explanation in van Wolferen's work as to why the Japanese should be any more dishonest than Westerners. After all, Americans and British people also, in practice, distinguish between what they say and what they think. Even if one assumes that the distinction is more important in Japan, it is simply asserted that it exists as a cultural trait rather than explained.

Culture as a starting point

Ahistorical explanations of Japanese society generally start from supposed cultural characteristics of the Japanese. As we have seen, Joy Hendry discusses the Japanese custom of removing shoes before entering a house as a way of teaching children the distinction between a clean inner domain and an unclean outer one. For Hendry this is far more than a simple question of hygiene. Instead, she is quick to draw sweeping conclusions about how the Japanese learn distinctions between public behaviour and their true feelings.[35] In reality, such questions as what one does with one's shoes on entering a house have little social significance. The study of Japanese behaviour must consider broader economic, political and social questions.

On a grander scale, some authors have tried to use culture to explain Japan's economic success. Morishima Michio, a professor at the London School of Economics, notes that 'Japan has had its own culture from ancient times, and the ethos of the Japanese people has been formed over many years within this cultural environment'.[36] Morishima is more cautious than many when he notes that Japan's national ethos will gradually, over a long period of time, interact with material conditions. However, his conception of an essential national ethos which helps explain Japan's economic development still stands. A more fruitful approach would be to recognise that the separation of economic, political and social elements in understanding Japan is more conceptual than real. The key point is to understand how all these elements relate to each other rather than reduce analysis to what is essentially a form of cultural determinism.

Irrationality
A weakness related to ahistorical analysis is irrationalism. From a rationalist point of view, identifying particular characteristics of Japanese society must be followed by more thorough analysis. To again take the example of Japan as a group society, assuming that the description is correct, the next logical question to ask is why Japanese society takes this form. Benedict's original designation of Japan as a group society is surely based on the conformist character of Japan when she wrote her classic study in the mid-1940s. Given that the Japanese were in the midst of war, it is hardly surprising they were not in a mood to express their individuality.[37] Yet Benedict feels free to generalise from the particular experience of a period of extreme militarism to assign a supposed cultural trait to the Japanese people.

Chalmers Johnson, one of the most sophisticated and erudite Western writers on Japan, goes some way towards introducing rationality into the discussion of Japan. In his conclusion to *MITI and the Japanese Miracle* he notes that the 'priorities of the Japanese state derive first and foremost from an assessment of situational imperatives' rather than culture. For Johnson, these imperatives 'include late development, a lack of natural resources, a large population, the need to trade, and the constraints of the international balance of payments'.[38] In making this argument, he goes further in the direction of rationality than many of his disciples. But it is unfortunate that for Johnson these points seem to be more of an after-thought than the core of his analysis. In addition, many of the imperatives he identifies, though important, are seen in narrowly economic or demographic terms. The late development of Japan, as is argued in the conclusion of this chapter, had important political and social consequences.

Double standards

It is astonishing how pervasive double standards are in relation to criticisms of Japanese behaviour. In discussions of history, for example, the Japanese are frequently criticised for their barbaric behaviour during the Second World War. No doubt much of this criticism is justified, but Western commentators demonstrate a marked reluctance to apply the same standards to their own national histories. It is hard to imagine British historians attacking Britain's record in India or Malaya, or American historians discussing the Korean War or Vietnam in the same way as they discuss Japanese atrocities. In *The Wages of Guilt*, for example, Ian Buruma constantly criticises Japan for its amnesia towards its wartime atrocities. Buruma is careful to acknowledge that 'not every Japanese suffers from historical amnesia', but he does see it as a widespread trait in Japanese society. In the introduction to the book he notes that no 'Japanese politician [has] ever gone down on his knees...to apologise for historical crimes'.[39] Yet the idea that the West should even consider apologising for the bombing of Hiroshima and Nagasaki does not even strike him as worthy of consideration.[40]

Underlying the emphasis on cultural difference is a fundamentally racial conception of Japan. Ideas which were expressed in biological terms up until 1945 are now expressed in the language of culture. As a result, studies of Japan tend to be ahistorical and irrational. In many cases explicit double standards are evident.

Ironically, the emphasis on *cultural* difference means that real political differences that exist between Japan and the West are often not explored. For example, the difficulty the Japanese élite has had in inculcating a clear-cut sense of national pride in the population at large is rarely examined. In Britain and the USA the notion of being proud of one's country has generally been seen as unproblematic in the post-war period. In Japan, by contrast, nationalism was discredited by the experience of defeat in the Second World War and the post-war reconstruction of the state by the USA. For many years the Japanese tended to identify with their country's economic success, but were more circumspect about its political institutions. Perhaps the most striking example is in relation to the armed forces—or 'self defence forces' as they are euphemistically known—where Japanese have tended to support the pacifist constitution. Most American and British citizens, on the other hand, took some pride in the military power of their nations. When the key characteristics are assumed rather than explained, real economic and political differences are often missed.

The Notion of Difference in Japan

Given the underlying racial thinking in Benedict's work it is perverse that it has been so popular in Japan. The explanation of this apparent paradox is quite straightforward. As Aoki Tamotsu, a professor of Cultural Anthropology at Osaka University, has noted: 'her book was widely accepted in Japan. The reason lies in the relativist paradigm she adopted.'[41] This relativist method means that Japanese readers can identify the same cultural traits in relation to their country as Americans do, but put a different value judgement on them. In other words, the same traits that might be identified as positive by a Japanese might be seen as negative by an American. An American reading about cultural differences is likely to see the discussion as confirmation that the USA is best. But a Japanese person reading the same text may not reach the same conclusion.

Thus, there is a symbiotic relationship between Japanese proponents of *Nihonjinron* (the cult of Japanese uniqueness) and Western liberal critics of Japan. Western critics point to cultural differences, such as Japan's alleged group character, and use this implicitly to reinforce a view of Japan as inferior to the West.[42] Japanese theorists take these distinctive characteristics but interpret them differently. Where one puts a plus sign, the other puts a minus. As Ishihara Shintaro argues, the Japanese 'should turn the tables on self-righteous American critics by simply agreeing with them that our economy and society are different from theirs. *Vive la différence!*'.[43]

Nihonjinron is cited as the basis of the greatest Western myth about Japan: that the Japanese are the real racists in international affairs. Edwin O. Reischauer, who was US ambassador to Japan in the 1960s, and Marius B. Jansen, a Princeton Emeritus professor specialising in the Far East, are the authorities for the charge of Japanese racism. Interestingly, this charge is usually made with one eye on the West's own bad reputation:

> We often think of racial prejudice as being a special problem of the white race in relations with other races, but it actually pervades the world. Nowhere is it greater than in Japan and the other lands of East Asia.[44]

The sleight of hand here is breathtaking. First racism is not particularly Western, but pervasive; then it is nowhere greater than in Japan and the other lands of East Asia. Two pages later, Reischauer and Jansen dismiss the reputation of 'so-called racist America' in an aside.[45] Characterising Japan as racist is a convenient way of whitewashing the record of American and European armies in Asia, from the bombing of Hiroshima to the killing fields of the Korean and Vietnamese wars. In fact, the substance of the accusation that the Japanese are racist is, ironically, that they do not accept that whites are superior.

An Alternative Method

An alternative method for understanding Japan world start by rejecting the all-pervasive idea of historical continuity. The behaviour of any nation cannot be understood simply in terms of a legacy from the past. The Britain of today, for example, is a very different place from that of the 1950s—let alone the Britain of the Victorian era. The differences between Japan today and earlier this century are dramatic. In the space of a century Japan has emerged as a regional power, become a colonialist nation in Asia, lost a world war, been occupied by a foreign power and undergone possibly the most rapid economic transformation of all time. The differences between Japan before and after 1945 are particularly marked. In the years of occupation following the war, the USA refashioned all of Japan's political and social institutions. During the war, for example, Japan was dominated by the military; afterwards, the US-written constitution officially defined Japan as a pacifist state.

Japan's behaviour this century, which often seems peculiar to Western commentators, makes perfect sense in the context of its unique historical experience. For example, Japan's emergence as a non-white power early this century placed it in an awkward position. Japan was desperate to become a colonial power just like its US and European peers, promoting its invasion of China in the 1930s, as part of its own Monroe Doctrine.[46] However, the white powers would not let Japan play such a role, since it challenged the assumption of racial superiority through which their own empires were justified.[47] The peculiar position of Japan explains the difference between Japanese nationalism and the racial outlook of the American and European powers. While the white powers had already established a colonial division of labour between them, the Japanese latecomers were never accepted into the club.

National pride in Japan always took on the defensive character of an excluded people, reacting to the racial notions of Western imperialism. In the first half of the century, Japanese propaganda was far less concerned with denigrating other races as inferior than with building the self-image of Japan as a unique nation. As John Dower recounts:

> …to an immeasurable degree, there was a reactive cast to the anti-Western rhetoric of the Japanese during the years under discussion—a clear sense of revenge for past indignities and maltreatment which, again, has no precise counterpoint in the racism of white supremacism.[48]

Japanese military propaganda was often framed in terms of opposition to the colonialist West, however oppressive Japanese rule in East Asia eventually proved to be. After 1945, Japan, as a non-white nation defeated in a world war, could not claim superiority. Instead, the emphasis was on the distinctiveness of Japanese institutions.

Understanding this also makes possible a more rational approach towards Japan's contemporary discussion of the Second World War. Japanese politicians, far from ignoring the Second World War, were all too eager to talk about it by the 1990s. Such a stance is perfectly explainable in terms of the uncertain character of Japanese politics following the end of the Cold War in the late 1980s. A full explanation of the 'diplomacy of contrition' pursued by Japan in the 1990s is beyond the scope of this chapter, but some of the basic elements can be outlined.[49]

By the late 1980s Japan found itself in a position where many of the old certainties could no longer be counted on. First, the relative decline of the USA meant that Japan felt that, rather than relying too much on American power, it should pursue a more independent regional and global role. This trend was already apparent to Japanese thinkers over fifteen years ago. Amaya Naohiro, a leading MITI official, listed in the conservative *Bungei Shunju* journal in 1980 a litany of what he regarded as American failures:

> On top of Vietnam came the Watergate affair, the Arab-Israeli war and the oil crisis of 1973, uncontrollable inflation combined with the loss of American industry's competitive edge, the decline of the dollar, the exposure of the embarrassing gap between the promise and reality of President Jimmy Carter's human rights diplomacy, and the incredibly swift fall of the Shah of Iran. Against this backdrop there were menacing Soviet advances in Angola, Ethiopia, South Yemen and Afghanistan, the decline of US influence in Middle East peace negotiations, and the erosion of American military superiority to the point of actual inferiority in some respects.[50]

Japan's geopolitical position has, admittedly, changed considerably since Amaya wrote this piece. However, the important point is that, even by 1980, Japan's leadership was considering relying less on the USA and playing a more independent world role. This trend has continued still further with the end of the Cold War. Japan's quest for a permanent seat on the United Nations Security Council and its involvement in UN peacekeeping operations are just two examples of a more assertive Japan.[51]

Second, the demise of the Soviet Union removed the old rationale for Japanese defence policy and the US-Japan security relationship. During the Cold War period the spectre of the Soviet threat provided the rationale for the US-Japan security treaty. With the break-up of the USSR, the US-Japan relationship needs to be conceptualised in new ways.[52] Yet Japanese politicians felt it was neither possible nor desirable for Japan to revert to old-fashioned militarism to defend its interests in East Asia. Instead, Japan used the language of humanitarianism to justify playing a broader role in Asia. By 1992, following the passage of the Peace Keeping Operations Bill, Japan had sent troops on a peacekeeping operation to Cambodia, followed by dispatches of units to Mozambique and Rwanda.[53] Such moves, which would have been unthinkable if promoted in the old language of militarism, were acceptable once packaged as humanitarianism. The important point here is not the existence of a few hundred lightly armed Japanese troops in faraway places. It is rather that the Japanese government had managed to set a precedent, re-establishing its right to play a broader political and military role in world affairs.

The 'diplomacy of contrition' helped justify a broader global and regional role by redefining the meaning of the Second World War for Japan. Until the 1990s the prevalent view in Japan was that, since it had played such a destructive role in the Second World War, it should limit its concerns primarily to economic affairs. Yet the implicit assumption behind the diplomacy of contrition was that the legacy of the Second World War, far from limiting Japan's role in world affairs, meant that it had a moral obligation to play a broader global role. The war was certainly not forgotten, but its meaning was redefined. As Kono Yohei, Japan's Deputy Prime Minister and Minister for Foreign Affairs, said in a speech to the UN General Assembly in September 1994:

Reflecting with remorse upon the Second World War, Japan has never wavered from its commitment to contribute to world peace and prosperity. Japan does not, nor will it, resort to the use of force prohibited by its

Constitution. Japan will remain resolutely a nation of peace....In accordance with what I have just stated, Japan has dispatched members of its Self-Defence Forces as well as civilian personnel to several countries, including Cambodia and Mozambique, in response to requests by the United Nations.[54]

Unfortunately, the dominant mode of Western scholarship often precludes asking some of the most interesting questions about Japanese society—let alone finding the right answers. Too much attention is often given to identifying the distinctive characteristics of Japanese culture, which are often of a superficial nature, rather than explaining why such differences exist. At its worst, this approach leads to an examination of Japanese society in terms of its supposedly innate cultural traits. Even at its best it tends to become obsessed with particular features of Japan, rather than finding rational social explanations for the forms that Japanese society takes.

Western writing on Japan today may be cloaked in the sympathetic language of Cultural Anthropology, but its underlying assumption is too often the racial inferiority of the Japanese. Admittedly, few authors are willing to state explicitly that they believe the West is superior to Japan. Nor is there a discussion in respectable circles of biological differences between the Japanese and Westerners. Instead, the distinctions are framed by the notion of cultural difference. Despite its origins in the theory of 'scientific anti-racism' the idea of cultural difference embodies its own form of racial thinking. The predominant influence on human beings is seen as the culture into which they happen to be born. Such differences are then held to explain differences between societies. The notion of cultural difference takes its authority from common sense experience. It is clear to any observer that there are some differences in the behaviour of Japanese and Americans or British people. However, to make such differences the organising principle of any study of Japanese society can only lead to superficial conclusions. Two more fundamental questions need to be asked. First we need to ask how genuine and significant such differences really are. Often there is a straightforward double standard in Western writing on Japan. Second, to the extent that differences do exist, it is essential we demand a rational, social explanation of them. Only if such questions are asked is it possible to understand the complexities of modern Japan.

NOTES

1. It was rarely explained in the discussion that the 'revision' in revisionism referred to the view of the post-war modernisation theorists in relation to Japan. These writers assumed that Japan would increasingly take on the characteristics of American society. The demise of modernisation theory reflected the relative decline of American power in the world. On modernisation theory see: David Williams, *Japan: Beyond the End of History*, London, Routledge, 1994, pxvi; and Sheldon Garon, 'Rethinking Modernization and Modernity in Japanese History', *Journal of Asian Studies,* 53 (2), May 1994, p347. For a radical critique of modernisation theory, see the introduction to Gavan McCormack, and Sugimoto Yoshio (eds.), *The Japanese Trajectory*, Cambridge, Cambridge University Press, 1988.

2. Francis Fukuyama reiterates this point, referring to Japan as a high-trust society. See his *Trust: The Social Virtues and the Creation of Prosperity*, London, Hamish Hamilton, 1995. Charles Hampden-Tuner and Fons Trompenaars attempt to give the argument some empirical rigour, surveying managers from seven of the main industrial countries, including Japan and the USA. See their *The Seven Cultures of Capitalism*, London, Piatkus, 1993.

3. Kent Calder, *Strategic Capitalism,* Princeton, Princeton University Press, 1993, p17.

4. Sakakibara Eisuke, *Beyond Capitalism,* Lanham, University Press of America, 1993.

5. Calder, op. cit., p17.

6. Ibid., p19.

7. Ibid. p17. James Fallows develops this argument in *Looking at the Sun,* (New York, Pantheon, 1994), where he traces economic nationalism in Japan back to Friedrich List, the nineteenth-century German writer, and even further back to Alexander Hamilton (1757-1804), the American statesman and First Secretary of the Treasury.

8. David Howell, 'Easternisation', *Demos Quarterly,* Issue 6, 1995, p27.

9. Samuel P.Huntington, 'The Clash of Civilizations', *Foreign Affairs,* 72 (3), Summer 1993, p22.

10. John Dower, *War without Mercy,* London, Faber & Faber, 1986, p119.

11. Ruth Benedict, *The Chrysanthemum and the Sword,* London, Routledge & Kegan Paul, 1967, p4.

12. Aoki Tamotsu, 'Anthropology and Japan: Attempts at Writing Culture', *The Japan Foundation Newsletter,* XXII (3), October 1994, pp4-5.

13. Benedict, op. cit., pp156-7.

14. Ibid., p1.

15. See chapter one of Chalmers Johnson, *MITI and the Japanese Miracle* (Stanford, Stanford University Press, 1982), for a discussion of different schools in relation to explanations of the Japanese economic miracle.

16. Benedict, op. cit., p10.

17. It is sometimes argued that Social Anthropology takes a different approach from Cultural Anthropology, even if the difference is only understood as one of emphasis. Claude Lévi-Strauss, for example, suggests that there is little difference between the social and cultural approaches to anthropology, comparing the two disciplines to books which contain the same chapters, but in a different order (*Structuralist Anthropology*, Harmondsworth, Penguin, 1963, pp356-359). In its stronger form, such an argument might seem to exempt Social Anthropology from the criticisms made here of Cultural Anthropology, in that while the latter concentrates on ideas and concepts, the former studies social relationships. For a rebuttal of this view, see: Harris, Marvin, 'History and Ideological Significance of the Separation of Social and Cultural Anthropology', in Eric B. Ross, (ed.), *Beyond the Myths of Culture*, London, Academic Press, 1980. As this chapter goes on to demonstrate, the criticisms levelled at a Cultural Anthropologist such as Ruth Benedict are equally applicable to a contemporary British Social Anthropologist such as Joy Hendry.

18. Benedict, op. cit., p11.

19. Joy Hendry, *Understanding Japan*, London, Routledge, 1995 (second edition), p2.

20. Benedict, op. cit., p11.

21. Hendry, op. cit., p187.

22. Benedict, op. cit., p7.

23. Ibid., p181.

24. Ibid., p200.

25. Hendry, op. cit., p38.

26. Ibid., p40.

27. Benedict, op. cit., p213.

28. See, for example: Edwin O. Reischauer, and Marius B. Jansen, *The Japanese Today*, London, The Belknap Press of Harvard University Press, 1995 (enlarged edition).

29. Benedict, op. cit., p6.

30. Hendry, op. cit., p223.

31. See Dower, op. cit..

32. For an extended analysis of the process whereby racial thought was recast in the language of cultural difference, see: Kenan Malik, *The Meaning of Race*, London, Macmillan, 1996.

33. See Janet Hunter, 'Before Lifetime Employment: Employers and Employees in Prewar Japan', *The Japan Society Proceedings*, No. 126, Winter 1995.

34. Karel van Wolferen, *The Enigma of Japanese Power*, London, Macmillan, 1989, p235.

35. See Hendry op. cit., chapter 3. This distinction relates to the discussion of *tatamae* and *honne* above.

36. Morishima Michio, *Why Has Japan 'Succeeded'*, Cambridge, Cambridge University Press, 1982, ppvii-viii.

37. Some pre-war anthropologists, such as John Embree, did write on the group character of Japanese society, but it was through Benedict's wartime work that the notion was popularised.

38. Johnson, op. cit., p307.

39. Ian Buruma, *The Wages of Guilt*, London, Jonathan Cape, 1994, p9.

40. The idea that there the USA could have had a racial motive in dropping atomic bombs on Hiroshima and Nagasaki is dismissed in one paragraph: ibid., p98.

41. Aoki, op. cit..

42. However, in recent years the notion of groupism—often in the guise of communitarianism—has become more popular in the USA.

43. Mohammed Mahathir, and Ishihara Shintaro, *The Voice of Asia*, Tokyo, Kondansha, 1995, p109. For a more extensive discussion of *Nihonjinron,* see Lynn Revell's chapter in this volume.

44. Reischauer and Jansen, op. cit., p396.

45. Ibid., p398.

46. See, for example: Kaneko Kentaro, 'A "Japanese Monroe Doctrine" and Manchuria', *Contemporary Japan*, 1 (1), June 1932; and Kamikawa Hikomatsu, 'The American and Japanese Monroe Doctrines', *Contemporary Japan*, VIII (6), August 1939. For an American view, see: George H. Blakeslee, 'The Japanese Monroe Doctrine', *Foreign Affairs*, 11 (4), July 1933.

47. This is an area of great controversy which it is not possible to enter into here. Useful books which touch on the geo-political position of pre-war Japan include: Dorothy Borg, and Okamoto Shumpei, (eds.), *Pearl Harbor as History*, New York, Columbia University Press, 1973; and James B. Crowley, *Japan's Quest for Autonomy*, Princeton, Princeton University Press, 1966; Christopher Thorne, *The Limits of Foreign Policy*, London, Hamish Hamilton, 1972; and James W. White, et al., (eds.), *The Ambivalence of Nationalism*, Lanham, University Press of America, 1990.

48. Dower, op. cit., p204.

49. The *Economist* (17 August 1991) argues that Japan's 'diplomacy of contrition', which centred on Japan saying sorry for past transgressions, began with apologies to South Korea in May 1990. More broadly, Japanese diplomacy has centred on humanitarian themes.

50. *Bungei Shunju,* March 1980, translated as: 'Japan as a Mercantile Nation', *Japan Echo,* VII (2), 1980, p54.

51. This argument does not imply that Japan is seeking a total break from the USA. Rather, it is seeking to play a more active role in world affairs while maintaining friendly relations with the USA.

52. For useful studies of recent trends in Japanese foreign policy, see: Edward J. Lincoln, *Japan's New Global Role*, Washington DC, Brookings Institution, 1993; and Kenneth B. Pyle, *The Japanese Question*, Washington DC, American Enterprise Institute, 1992.

53. See Lincoln, op. cit.. At the time of writing it was also planned to send troops to the Israeli-occupied Golan Heights.

54. Kono Yohei, *Statement at the 49th General Assembly of the United Nations*, 27 September 1994. (Press release of speech issued by the permanent mission of Japan to the United Nations.)

2 THE MAKING OF THE YELLOW PERIL: PRE-WAR WESTERN VIEWS OF JAPAN

Gina Owens

G rowing up in 1950s Britain, it was common to hear people speak in hushed tones of the veterans of Japanese war camps. Despite the fact that only 30,000 British servicemen lost their lives in the Pacific War, compared to 235,000 in the European theatre, a virulent hatred was reserved for the Japanese.[1] The Germans had fallen from grace, but the Japanese were just 'like that'. This chapter examines the development of some of the key ideas behind this racist assumption, isolating key periods in the evolution of relations between the Western powers and Japan. Events are chosen to demonstrate how racial thinking was intimately bound-up with the maintenance of power.

The ideology of race was paramount in the attitudes of Western governments in the pre-war period. It also helps to explain the treatment meted out during the Second World War to the Japanese, who were presented as responsible for their own deaths, from the beaches of Iwo Jima to the suburbs of Hiroshima and Nagasaki. The politics of racial thinking penetrated every area of international relations before 1939. The pre-war world was characterised by the domination of vast areas of the globe by a handful of Western powers. The war in the Pacific was part of a dramatic change in this situation, catalysing resistance to former colonial masters. Japan played a central role in this, not least as the force that exposed the pretensions of white supremacy in the Far East. The Japanese people paid a terrible price.

As an 'Oriental' power, Japan focused the 'yellow peril' fears of the West: Japanese national characteristics became central to the image of the Oriental hordes. Racial stereotypes cast as 'national characteristics' were promoted by the Western powers as justification for their dominant position, forming part of the armoury of racial theories that originated in the late nineteenth century. Japan became both a victim and a proponent of such ideas. Physical racial characteristics were also identified in spurious 'scientific' theories and research, which were used to justify an ordering of humanity with the whites firmly ensconced at the top of the hierarchy. From 'yellow monkeys' to 'dwarf slaves' and 'verminous lice', the Japanese were subjected to a barrage of racial insult from the 1850s reaching a crescendo in Second World War propaganda.

Civilising Japan

In 1853 a United States naval squadron under the command of Commodore William Perry extended a forceful invitation to Japan to join the modern world. The American journal *New Monthly Magazine and Humorist* described the firepower of Perry's squadron as 'the means by which Americans proposed to themselves to bring Japan within the pale of humanity and international courtesy'.[2] One justification given for Perry's mission was the pursuit of the 'white man's common interests and feelings'.[3] Commodore Perry himself wrote that:

> It is manifest from past experience that arguments or persuasion addressed to this people unless they be seconded by some imposing manifestation of power will be utterly unavailing.[4]

Perry's comment would be echoed with awesome consequences in 1945.

The terms on which relations were established by this display of Western power were aptly described by the Japanese as the 'unequal treaties'. Treaty ports with special concessions were established by the Western powers, notably the British. Relations between Westerners in the Treaty Ports and the Japanese were characterised by an aloof disdain, and by complaints about the 'mendacity' of the Japanese with whom they traded. Mendacity, deceit, and untrustworthiness were terms often applied to 'Asiatics' in China and Japan: according to Yokoyama Toshio, the 1860s saw constant attacks on the 'insincerity' and 'irresponsibility' of Japanese officials.[5] Perry, for example, found the Japanese officials with whom he negotiated 'sagacious and deceitful',[6] while Sir Rutherford Alcock despaired of the Japanese character as 'Oriental', declaring that: 'The Japanese…still remain true to the traditions and instincts of their race.'[7]

However, the late nineteenth century Western attitude towards Japan was more complex than either Perry's imperious comments, or the imperialist terms of the unequal treaties, might suggest. The first point to grasp is the centrality of racial thinking to the West's sense of itself and the world. The Victorian imagination was obsessed with questions of race and the civilising mission of the Anglo-Saxons. Attitudes towards the Japanese were framed in racial terms, regardless of whether such attitudes were positive or negative. From the 1850s, for example, favourable impressions of Japanese life and character were reflected in a discussion of their origins. While Mongol origins would consign them to the lower levels of the human ladder envisaged by the Victorian mind, other theories were put forward suggesting that the Japanese were of Malay, Polynesian, or possibly Semitic origin.

The second key point is that, from the 1850s, the idea that there was something 'unusual' or 'singular' about Japan became increasingly common. One commentator, writing of his impressions of Lord Elgin's mission to the Far East (1857-59), was struck by the difference in the conditions of life in China and Japan. He concluded: 'of all nations in the East the Japanese are most susceptible to civilising influences.'[8]

Similarly, another contemporary writer, Alexander Knox, considered the 'racial difference' between the Chinese and Japanese to be 'of a very high degree'.[9] The idea of Japanese peculiarity encompassed both trivial cultural observations and more significant challenges to Western prejudices about Asiatic peoples. Everyday customs and the determination of the Japanese to modernise were considered singular.

Following Perry's forcible opening up of the country, Japan's attempt to modernise its society and achieve an independent status as a nation initially provoked a mixed response. There were those, such as the writer Lafcadio Hearn, who bemoaned the loss of the old Japan and eulogised its qualities. Such commentators stressed the dangers of a speedy transition to an industrial modern state. On the other hand, there were many who were impressed by developments in Japan, and who often sought to flatter themselves and the Japanese by drawing comparisons with Britain. In the process of Japan's modernisation, two key themes emerged. The first was the romantic notion of the Japanese as an emotional people with a particular sensitivity to nature. Secondly, the view developed that the Japanese had a particular philosophical and moral code handed down through the generations: Bushido, the 'soul of the nation'. Let us examine each of these in turn.

Writers who celebrated 'old Japan' displayed an antipathy towards modernity itself. A. B. Mitford, the author of *Tales of Old Japan*, 'bitterly regretted the corrupting influences of foreigners in the Open Ports'.[10] Another spoke of 'an irruption of Birmingham into Arcadia'.[11] Such preoccupations expressed a romantic reaction to industrialisation and modernity, not uncommon in the West at the end of the nineteenth century. Yet the tendency to eulogise Japan as a romantic 'elfinland' and to bemoan its corruption by modernisation was combined with the suggestion that the Japanese were limited, and unsuited to building a modern society. Lafcadio Hearn exemplifies this complex response. Of mixed race and irascible temperament, Hearn sought Utopia in Japan. 'The soul of the race', he wrote, 'comprehends Nature infinitely better than we do'.[12] He found the Japanese wanting in their social organisation, however, due to the 'despotism of collective opinion'.[13] Hearn wrote of 'soft coverings of courtesy', but suggested that underneath lay the 'primitive clay, hard as iron, kneaded perhaps with all the mettle of the Mongol, all the dangerous suppleness of the Malay'.[14] He also compared the Japanese to 'insects'.[15] In his view, the Japanese could not leap into modernity—a view he justified by reference to the racial characteristics he had noted. Others were more measured, but voiced similar concerns. Rutherford Alcock, for example, wrote in 1874 that in the acquisition of a foreign civilisation there was 'no problem in the world's previous history, which can help us to foresee the end'.[16] In general, the 'old Japan' romantics stressed the idea of a sensitive, emotional, natural, even childlike nature in the Japanese. Their own rejection of modern industrial Western society was matched by a tendency to eulogise a mythical, idyllic Japanese past.

In 1895 Japan defeated China in war, and by 1900 had overturned the unequal treaties, thereby winning national sovereignty. Japan had a modern constitution, army and national education system. In 1902, Great Britain recognised Japan's status by signing the Anglo-Japanese Alliance. Interestingly enough, as Japan became a force to be reckoned with in the Pacific, the traditions of the past were again invoked to explain this success. Henry Dyer wrote in his *Dai Nippon: The Britain of the Far East* that the Japanese drive to modernise was motivated by Bushido:

> The sense of honour which cannot bear being looked down upon as an inferior power—that was the strongest of motives.[17]

He considered Japan the wonder of the latter half of the nineteenth century. Dyer had taken his ideas directly from the work of Nitobe Inazo: arguably the most influential writer on modern Japan at the turn of the century. Nitobe argued that Japan owed its success to Bushido, the 'way of the Samurai'. This was presented as a system of moral ideas previously encoded by the Samurai and then filtered through society in the modern era. For Nitobe, Bushido was 'still the guiding principle of the transition', and 'the formative force of the new era'. As he put it: 'scratch a Japanese of the most advanced ideas and he will show a Samurai.'[18] This notion was important to Japanese conservatives like Nitobe. Bushido provided a moral force linking the past to the future, which could ensure stability and patriotism. Many British onlookers were so impressed with the spirit of the Samurai that they proposed such a code as a solution to the ailments of British society.[19]

Paradoxically, the idea of the Japanese as childlike, natural and sensitive, and the notion of the continuity of Japan's warrior code had certain common elements. Both views appealed to the notion of a distinct racial identity, and both stressed an ancestral national character. The belief that Japan's identity had a collective quality, identifying and motivating all Japanese, was implicit in the importance attributed to Bushido, with its emphasis on Confucian codes of loyalty and filial piety. This theme was destined to play a crucial role in Western perceptions of Japan. It is also interesting to see how romantic notions in Western commentary informed responses to developments in Japan. From the 1850s to around

1900 the tendency to patronise the Japanese was predominant. A racial outlook informed the arguments over whether Japan was capable of modern civilisation, but as we shall see, Japan's transition from junior Asian country to independent competitor would bring racism to the fore in international affairs.

The Emergence of the Yellow Peril

By 1900 the USA had embarked on an imperial mission, and in the Pacific, Hawaii and the Philippines came under American control. It was popular amongst the élite in Washington to see America as the inheritor of the Anglo-Saxon mantle. The idea of an inevitable Anglo-Saxon destiny figured in the outlook of John Hay, Theodore Roosevelt's Secretary of State, as well as that of the President himself. During the fight for the annexation of the Philippines, when the larger question of imperial policy was thrown open for debate, expansionists were quick to invoke the laws of progress, the inevitable tendency to expand, the Manifest Destiny of Anglo-Saxons, and the survival of the fittest. 'God has not been preparing the English-speaking and Teutonic peoples for a thousand years for nothing but vain and idle self admiration', cried Senator Beveridge before the Senate in 1899:

> No! He has made us the master organisers of the world to establish system where chaos reigns. He has made us adept in government that we may administer government among savages and senile peoples! [20]

Beveridge's remarks encapsulate the all-embracing nature of the imperial mission. The civilising role of the Anglo-Saxon peoples would bring progress to all. The virile and democratic qualities of Anglo-Saxons had been developed and transmitted through hundreds of generations. Expansion was in the blood, and, as Beveridge had proposed in 1898: 'we must obey our blood and occupy new markets, and if necessary new lands.'[21]

Élitist views of society and the promotion of nationalism sought credibility in pseudo-scientific ideas such as Social Darwinism, which reflected in a distorted form the ruthlessly competitive nature of the world economy of the late nineteenth century. That competition was seen as one in which the 'fittest' races would predominate. In *A Short History of Anglo-Saxon Freedom* (1890), for example, James K. Hosmer declared:

> Though Anglo-Saxon freedom in a more or less partial form has been adopted (it would be better perhaps to say imitated) by every nation in

Europe but Russia, and in Asia by Japan, the hopes for that freedom in the future rest with the English speaking race. By that race alone it has been preserved amidst a thousand perils....The inevitable issue is to be that the primacy of the world will lie with us.[22]

This identification of progress with the racial characteristics of white Anglo-Saxon nations found expression in the comforting idea of racial superiority as the big powers carved up the world. The domination of the peoples of Africa, Asia and elsewhere foregrounded the issue of race.

Moreover, in the closing decades of the nineteenth century the leading powers experienced prolonged economic depression and social discontent. Socialist movements burgeoned throughout Europe; trade unions expanded. The Paris Commune and France's defeat at the hands of an emerging Germany brought a crisis of confidence to French identity. The British bemoaned their loss of authority in the Boer War. Insecurity was expressed through the prism of race and the question of leadership. In 1893 one British writer, Charles Pearson, predicted that the failure of virility in the Anglo-Saxon peoples would mean 'Chinese, Hindus, Negroes will be likely to challenge the supremacy of Western civilisation'.[23] Admiral Mahan of the United States Navy saw:

...a Western world at bay, in danger of losing its momentum and facing the staggering task of assimilating millions of semi-civilised people.[24]

The theme was taken up in Japan by Lafcadio Hearn. In a piece called *The Coming Race* he foresaw the Orient wreaking vengeance on the West's 'moral laxity'.[25]

When these insecurities encountered the emergent power of Japan, 'fears of a yellow peril previously half dormant emerged in a virulent form'.[26] A cartoon which circulated at the end of the 1890s depicted the symbols of the European Nations, such as Britannia, gazing across the ocean as a huge Buddha rose ominously and inexorably over the horizon to the East. This disconcerting vision was provoked by the threat which Japan posed to Russian interests at the end of the Sino-Japanese War (1894-95), when Germany, France and Russia intervened to prevent the Japanese gaining control of the Liaotung Peninsula in Korea. The vision of the yellow peril conjured up an image of Oriental hordes, perhaps led by the Japanese, descending on Europe and bringing despotism where there had been enlightened rule. In November 1898 the American magazine *Arena* declared:

> The peoples of the Occident are face to face with a powerful Oriental competitor in the arts of war, diplomacy, industry and commerce.[27]

The imagery was of a civilisational confrontation between East and West.

The terrors raised by this vision did not exert any direct influence over the policies of the US or British governments at that time. There was without doubt an underlying shared racial sentiment, but Britain and the USA neither cared for Russian interests, nor saw Japan as an immediate threat to their own interests. Indeed, it was Russian expansion which was considered a major threat, and Britain consequently signed an alliance with Japan in 1902. The Russo-Japanese war of 1904-1905, however, transformed the situation. The notion of the yellow peril became an integral feature of US political life. As a consequence of the war US policy in the Pacific was developed in a hot-house environment involving issues of naval power, immigration and policy towards China. Contemporary commentators were astounded by Japanese success in defeating the Russian imperial forces. One, for instance, wrote that:

> Europe is baffled by the excellent students it had not expected to form. We must not be surprised if from now on we must take account of these yellow people whom we have roused from slumber and coerced out of isolation.[28]

Similarly, the Canadian Premier Wilfred Laurier remarked: 'The day is passed when we can treat Japan as we can treat China and other oriental powers.'[29]

Portrayals of the Japanese army by conservative commentators were an overt expression of the insecurity and racial contempt which characterised Western ideology. One noted French commentator, René Pinon, spoke of the 'savage races—Manchus and Mongols'.[30] The British imperialist T.W.H. Crosland claimed that Japan:

> ...beats Russia because her ranks are packed with men who would rip themselves up rather than suffer defeat, and to whom life is not a matter worth a moment's consideration.

He concluded that they were 'men in fact who believe themselves to be without souls.'[31] Baron Von Falkenegg spoke of 'the uncanny wild bravery, incomprehensible to the European mind, which sets the value of the individual at nought'.[32] In this context, reference to the code of Bushido was used to conjure up a vision of despotic Oriental hordes motivated by alien and atavistic drives. Pinon expounded:

What we see is the preparation of some mysterious destiny whose menace worries and fascinates. The inscrutable enigma of the yellow soul adds to everything we hear of the Far East something of the shudder man feels in front of secrets he cannot penetrate. The Romans must have felt something analogous before the fathomless depths of Barbarity.[33]

A spectre of decay was haunting Western society. This anxiety focused on Japan and produced a virulently racist response, as images of Oriental masses and 'stunted yellow-faced heathen' abounded.[34] Japan as a competitor with alien motivations became the focus of concern in the United States and in the white dominions of Canada and Australia. The issue was brought home when the question of immigration was raised. Archibald Cary Coolidge summed up the prevailing sentiments in his book *The United States as a World Power*. He noted that Japan's victory over Russia:

…may have given a rude blow to the complacent assumption of the peoples of Europe and America that they were called upon to rule the world; but this has not altered a whit the determination of the Californian or Australian to keep his land, at any cost, a white man's country.[35]

The *San Francisco Chronicle* had raised the issue of Japanese immigration in 1899 (the Japanese were entering American's West Coast via Hawaii), arguing that Japanese immigration 'was more serious than Chinese because Japan had attained the status of a great power'.[36] This theme was taken up and repeated in a number of ways, often stressing the idea of the Japanese worker as too virile, motivated by alien drives and consequently not open to assimilation.

The issue of immigration became an explosive one. The Canadian Premier Laurier was wooed by the US Government on the basis that Canada, the USA and Britain had 'a common interest in keeping the yellow man out'. The Canadian Conservative Party appealed to the electorate and the anti-Japanese rioters in British Columbia with the promise to 'keep British Columbia a white man's country'.[37] Although President Roosevelt was irritated by the activities of the anti-Japanese protesters on the West Coast, he considered anti-Japanese sentiment on the part of Americans, Canadians and Australians to be fundamentally proper. The course of events that began with anti-Japanese riots on the West Coast of America led to a series of negotiations on immigration between the American and Japanese governments that culminated in the so-called

'Gentleman's Agreement' of 1908. In the process, such was the virulence of racial feeling that even Japanese school children, of whom there were less than 100, were segregated in the San Francisco area. The issue of land ownership rumbled on until 1913, when the Webb Alien Land Act was passed, limiting land ownership by Japanese immigrants.

The concerns of the United States government, however, were of a higher order than simply controlling 'coolie immigration'. Japanese military success focused minds on US policy towards China and the Far East. Initially, the US government offered to host the Treaty talks in Portsmouth. They persuaded the Japanese delegation not to demand the traditional payment of an indemnity from the Russian government. There is little doubt that Roosevelt was motivated by sympathy with a white power, and by a determination to ensure that Japan did not gain too much from her victory. With Elihu Root, his Secretary of State, Roosevelt shared the view that the Japanese were 'bent upon establishing themselves as the leading power in the Pacific'.[38] While he considered the proliferation of war scares on the West Coast to be 'as foolish as if conceived by the mind of a Hottentot',[39] his administration set about expanding the US Navy. In December 1907 sixteen battleships sailed out of Hampton Roads and rounded the Cape to arrive in California in March 1908. The fleet was then despatched on a victorious 'world cruise'. Roosevelt's stated principal reason was to 'impress the Japanese with the seriousness of the situation'.[40] The 'Great White Fleet' had the desired effect. The Australian press were ecstatic when the fleet arrived on their shores. Celebrating the 'White Australia' policy, the *Melbourne Age* declared in February 1908: 'we are unfeignedly glad that America has invaded the Pacific. It is a move that cannot help but lessen our danger of Asiatic aggression.'[41] The fleet was 'invited' to Japan and duly arrived in Yokohama Bay in October 1908.

The success of the fleet was recognised throughout the world. It represented a new stage in naval authority for the USA, sending a clear signal to friend and foe alike—and in particular to Japan. Elihu Root noted that in relations between Japan and the United States:

...the tendency is towards war—not now but in a few years. But much can be done to check or divert the tendency.[42]

American policy also turned towards more overt engagement in China in the following years, evoking much fear and suspicion from the Japanese. It was clear that, with Japan and the USA both coming of age as imperialist powers, competition had given the ideology of race a central importance. In 1909 Thomas F. Millard, an adviser on US affairs, noted that: 'the ultimate issue of any war between America and Japan will be whether the ideas and genius of the white or yellow race will dominate the future of civilisation.'[43]

The Russo-Japanese War profoundly altered both Japan's status in the world and the opinions of Japan held by Western powers. In the space of a decade (1895-1905) Japan became the primary focus for Western fears. Racial ideology was the means through which the West justified to itself and to others its domination of millions. Japan's precipitous rise threatened the very core of the West's self-perception and its precarious position of rule. 'The echoes of that yellow triumph over one of the great white powers', wrote the American author Lothrop Stoddard, 'reverberated to the ends of the Earth'.[44] The importance of the explosive issue of race was to be raised still further in the next phase of Japan's relations with the West.

The Demand for Racial Equality.

At Versailles in 1919 the Japanese proposed that a clause on racial equality should be written into the declaration of the new League of Nations. Despite the profound desire of the participants for a stable, peaceful world order after the horrors of the First World War, they were unable to agree to such a proposition. The United States played a leading role in the peace talks at Versailles. President Woodrow Wilson chaired the session at which the Japanese made their final attempt to include some reference to the equality of peoples, and was widely blamed by the Japanese for its failure. There is considerable justification for this point of view, since despite a vote in favour of a mildly-worded clause, Wilson declared the vote invalid on the grounds that it was not unanimous. The whole story makes sorry reading. Undoubtedly the prejudices of particular individuals played a part, but there were far more profound issues at stake.

Yellow peril panics about the Japanese continued to be a feature of US politics. In 1913 Wilson had told his cabinet that he 'feared the yellow race getting the better of the white.'[45] The Webb Alien Land Act, passed in the same year, drew an angry response from the Japanese. Referring to the Gentleman's Agreement of 1908, when they had voluntarily agreed to control emigration to the United States, the Japanese government responded that the Act undermined 'the spirit and fundamental principles of amity and good understanding upon which the conventional relations of the two countries depend'.[46] The situation provoked further fears of war in the USA, fed by the military authorities. Admiral Fiske, for example, warned that the Japanese were a highly-strung, proud race who intended to seize Hawaii and the Philippines. When the Japanese took advantage of the First World War to take the German leasehold of Shantung in China the US became obsessed with the Yellow Peril. The press portrayed Japan as the Germany of Asia—'brutal, militaristic, grasping'[47]—and Wilson referred to the 'Prussianised militarism' of Japan. When, in 1915, Japan presented China with an overtly imperialist package of 'Twenty One Demands', US resolve to contain Japan was strengthened. Forced to concede that Japan had a 'special interest' in China, if only by virtue of geographical contiguity, the Americans remained adamant that this must not entail Japanese expansion in China. The British government was now embarrassed by their alliance with Japan.

Such was the situation when the powers met in Paris: the issues of race, and competition between powers were a potent brew. However, the issue of race was of wider international significance. Each of the leading white powers at the table had many reasons for objecting to a declaration of racial equality. For the USA, unequal treatment of their black population was a prime concern, and the delegation was warned of domestic repercussions by Secretary of State Elihu Root. Furthermore, discriminatory immigration laws were in place in all the major metropolitan powers, as well as in the Dominions. No power would countenance the challenge to its immigration policies which would surely flow from such a proclamation, and therefore the white powers roundly defended their national sovereignty. This defence was ironic, since a major consideration for these powers was their ability to deny the peoples of Asia and Africa any right to national sovereignty. As Colonel House of the US Army remarked to Wilson: 'The trouble is that if this Commission should pass it, it would surely raise the race issue throughout the world'.[48] Informal discussion with the US delegation had prompted the suggestion, taken from the Declaration of Independence, 'that all men are created equal'. The British delegate, Balfour, was direct:

> Mr. Balfour said that was an eighteenth century proposition that he did not believe was true. He believed that is was true in a certain sense that all men of a particular nation were created equal, but not that a man in Central Africa was created equal to a European.[49]

Indeed, on this conviction rested the right of the European powers and the USA to control vast areas of the globe.

Much discomfort and dirty-dealing accompanied the attempts to jettison the Japanese proposal. The major powers had never been confronted on this central issue before, since no non-white power had ever held sufficient international prestige to demand equality of treatment.

The Japanese had called their bluff. The Japanese government summed up the situation in the instructions issued to its delegates in December 1918:

> The Imperial Japanese Government considers the League of Nations the most important organisation of peace and agrees to its purpose. However, the racial discrimination still prevailing in international relations would endanger the very purpose for which the League of Nations was constituted. This situation may bring considerable disadvantages to our nation.... You are instructed to exert your utmost effort in order to obtain as far as possible the necessary guarantee against any possible disadvantage that may be caused by this racial prejudice.[50]

The utmost efforts and compromises made by the Japanese delegation were to be no avail. Many Japanese drew pessimistic conclusions. A future Prime Minister, Yoshida Shigeru, remarked that: 'we gained the impression that the high hopes of a new international order were doomed to disappointment.'[51] The failure to include a statement on racial equality in the declaration of the League of Nations exposed the double standards of the Western powers. The democratic rights which they so loudly claimed as their inheritance were reserved for those who they deemed fit.

In the period that followed World War One, social instability in the West and national uprisings in the colonies proliferated. The issue of race became central to the insecurities experienced in Western régimes. Racist ideology was the hallmark of reactionary regimes in Europe; immigration a central concern.

The Road to War

The Covenant of the League of Nations, with its framework of 'essentially Western assumptions, values and preoccupations at a time of declining Western supremacy',[52] was to be severely tested by the Japanese in September 1931. In a context of world and domestic economic crisis, and assertive Chinese nationalism, Japan moved to protect her interests in Manchuria. By early 1932 Japan had established a puppet regime, and proceeded to recognise the 'independent' state of Manchukuo. The Japanese refused to back down on terms presented by the League of Nations, and in 1933 walked out of the League. Western responses were driven by a confusion of concerns in the Far East. Initial responses from the key powers—Britain and the USA—expressed frustration at their own failure to contain Chinese nationalism and the accompanying instability in China. Moreover, they were concerned about Soviet influence in the region. As a consequence, there was some sympathy in Washington and London for Japanese authority in the region.

As tension increased with Japanese refusal to accept terms framed by the status quo powers of the West, assumptions of Western superiority became more explicit. The response of the leading US official, Henry Stimson, was indicative. In October 1931 he declared that:

> …the peace treaties of modern Europe made out by the Western nations of the world no more fit the three great races of Russia, Japan and China than…a stovepipe hat would fit an African savage.[53]

American actions in Asia were, Stimson later claimed, a product of:

> …humanitarian idealism…which had turned our colonial adventure in the Philippines into a far sighted attempt to train an Oriental people in the art of self-government according to the American model.[54]

Joseph Grew, US Ambassador to Tokyo (1932-41), rewrote history: 'our action [in Cuba in the 1890s] was basically humanitarian while Japan's action was expediency pure and simple.'[55] Stanley Hornbeck, Head of the US State Department's Far Eastern Division, considered peace treaties to be 'an idealism in advance of the thought of the great majority of human beings and for all practical purposes an ideal of a few Occidental states'.[56] By the 1930s, according to this self-flattering vision, the USA had shouldered the civilising mission of the Anglo-Saxon race. The White Man's Burden was being taken up in the corridors of power in Washington DC.

As Britain experienced a loss of authority in Asia, the question of white prestige came to dominate tensions in the Far East. Crude biological theories of race proliferated in the USA and Europe: Nazi Germany was not the only proponent of 'scientific racism'. In the United States, compulsory sterilisation programmes were introduced to prevent the poor and blacks from breeding:

> In the Great Depression years about twenty five hundred individuals underwent this radical procedure annually. Germany was one of the few other nations to follow the American example in adopting legislation providing for mandatory sterilisation of groups designated as defective.[57]

President Roosevelt was to advocate German methods of sterilisation to control population in Puerto Rico. Theories for and against 'miscegenation', the mixing of races, abounded. It should be no surprise, then, that a US State Department official, John F. Carter, should record in an internal memorandum on Manchuria:

> For at least twenty five years the people of this country have regarded Japan as a natural and inevitable enemy of the United States. We are afraid of Japan as a people and hence...apt to hate the Japanese....We have a very deep-seated colour prejudice in this country, based...upon our own negro problem. The fact that the Japanese are coloured is a major element in our relations with Japan and serves to poison those relations.[58]

These remarks may seem an unusually blunt expression of how presumptions of Western racial superiority informed responses to Japan's imperial ambitions in the 1930s, but they are by no means an isolated example.

In 1931 George Sansom framed a discussion of Japan in terms of civilisation. In his classic study, *Japan: A Short Cultural History,* he confirmed the idea that Japan was 'unique'. Sansom considered that:

> ...when after 1640 they [the Japanese] were cut off from the source of new learning it is not surprising that their minds turned in upon themselves and evolved nothing but elaborations and refinements of their own culture.[59]

'New learning' referred to the scientific and artistic concepts of the Renaissance, which 'in general they were unwilling or unready to receive'.[60] Sansom clarified this in a preface in 1952:

> I fear I did not succeed in showing the characteristic attitude of the Japanese towards moral and philosophical problems—their intuitive, emotional approach and their mistrust of logic and analysis....The quintessence of Japanese thought is to be found in Zen Buddhism or in other philosophical systems whose doctrines are by definition incommunicable by the written word and can be made clear only by some inner illumination.[61]

Sansom clearly felt in 1952 that his advice to the pre-war British government had underestimated the irrationality of the Japanese. In 1930s Europe, the idea that Japan had not developed in a 'continuous' way, comparable to the West, fed off and fed into the existing racial ideology of empire.

Such prejudices were only reinforced by Japanese figures such as Nitobe Inazo. In 1932 Nitobe toured the USA to mollify public opinion on the question of Japan's ambitions in Manchuria. As he laid out Japan's 'national characteristics' and racial features, his ideas found little opposition among Western thinkers of a similarly conservative nature. The characteristics he proposed were: patriotism ('well nigh a religion'); loyalty (the Emperor had been a symbol for 'twenty centuries'); self-abnegation ('absorption of a small ego in the great entity of the nation'); the sense of duty and responsibility ('*giri*'); a sense of honour (Bushido); a cheerful view of life's pathos; sentimentality; love of contact with nature; a talent for detail; and a realistic psychology.[62] Clearly, these characteristics elaborated ideas propounded at the turn of the century: the idea of a collective racial identity was reinforced and developed around national symbols. The insistence on a primal quality, ancient and 'incommunicable' as Sansom put it, was repeated by Japanese conservatives such as Nitobe. Japan's adoption of these ideas was turned against her in the West's propaganda assault during the Pacific War.

In the 1930s, the idea that the Japanese and other 'Orientals' lacked the rationality and capacity for independent thought necessary for modern society was expressed by all the key Western players. Increasingly, the conflict of US, British and Japanese interests in China was expressed through the idea that Japanese motivation was irrational and alien. Indeed, the Japanese, it was suggested, were so alien that 'the great majority of Japanese do not know they are in the wrong'.[63] Here was a flawed society not ready for the burden of modern nationhood. The general consensus was with Perry in 1853: 'only superior physical force'[64] would influence the Japanese in Manchuria. Stanley Hornbeck, for example, elaborated:

…with regard to the sanctity of treaties, the vast majority of Orientals consider that the degree of sanctity is in direct proportion to the physical rather than the moral force which lies behind.[65]

The term 'vast majority of Orientals' brought up images of the Oriental hordes envisioned at the turn of the century. All the commentators responding to the crisis in Manchuria drew on the idea of a collective Japanese identity and the Bushido code to evoke an image of a people: 'inured to regimentation' and 'inculcated with the Samurai spirit which became ingrained in the race'.[66]

The moral inferiority of the Japanese was a well-established notion in the early 1930s, well before their ruthless imperial exploits in Nanking in 1938 drew forth cries of 'Barbarians' from the Western powers. Here was a civilisation which 'aped' Western nationhood, but which was viewed as 'backward' and irrational by the white powers. Contempt for the Japanese was openly expressed by Western officials as tensions escalated towards the end of the decade. The physical stature of the Japanese was equated with their moral backwardness, in the view of Sir Alexander Cadogan of the British Foreign Office, who described the Japanese as 'yellow dwarf slaves'.[67] Such contempt for Asian peoples was common among Western élites: Winston Churchill described Asians as 'dirty baboons'. During the Second World War, the savagery of such terminology was overt. As one US marine put it:

> The Japanese made the perfect enemy. They had many characteristics that an American marine could hate. Physically they were small, a strange colour and by some standards unattractive....Marines did not consider that they were killing men. They were wiping out dirty animals.[68]

While the British Minister L. S. Amery considered an infusion of Nordic blood into the Indian population a solution to their backwardness, President Roosevelt sought the assistance of a Professor Hurdlicka of the Smithsonian Institute in determining the biological basis for Japanese evil. The startling conclusion was that Japanese craniums were at least 2,000 years less developed than those of the civilised white man. The logic of these views was expressed in 1943 by a US naval officer, Captain Pence, who advocated the 'almost total elimination of the Japanese as a race'.[69] The 'war of vengeance' launched against the Japanese in 1941 after the debacle of Pearl Harbour was savage, and defined by a ruthlessness bred of racial contempt. The determination to crush the Japanese, however, can only be understood by placing racial ideology in its proper context—the supremacy of white civilisation in Asia. It was the insecurities and fears of a collapse of white prestige which fired Western actions.

At the beginning of the 1930s British power in Asia was suffering a crisis. In the late 1920s the British Prime Minister, Baldwin, recognised that 'the unchanging East had changed': 'a wind of nationalism and freedom is blowing around the world and blowing as strongly in Asia as anywhere.'[70] The French Colonial Minister, Albert Sarrant, agreed when in 1932 he warned against 'the restless surf in the sea of progress, the counter-offensive of native energy'.[71] Sir Maurice Hankey, Secretary to the Cabinet, warned in 1931 that weak policy: 'reacts on our prestige in all Eastern countries. The result has been a great fall in our prestige throughout the world'. Clearly, a confident imperial strategy was called for if the tide of nationalism in the Far East was to be quashed. Churchill presaged:

'Once we lose confidence in our mission in the East then our presence in those countries will be stripped of every moral sanction and cannot long endure.'[72] Japan's challenge to Western authority in the Manchuria crisis underlined this problem, but sensitivity to the issue increased when threats to British and US spheres of influence became a reality with the Japanese attack on the Nanking government in 1938. While the future British Prime Minister Anthony Eden emphasised the importance of 'effectively asserting white race authority in the Far East',[73] Sir Frederick Maze described the looming confrontation as: 'the Orient against the occident—the yellow race against the white race.'[74]

On the eve of war with Japan, contempt for the Japanese was the predominant sentiment. US officials believed they could defeat Japan in six months. The British Commander-in-Chief in the Far East described seeing:

> …various sub-human species dressed in dirty grey uniforms, which I was informed were Japanese soldiers….I cannot believe they would form an intelligent fighting force.[75]

Contempt for the Japanese would soon be turned about-face with the loss of moral authority that accompanied the Japanese capture of Singapore—a defeat which Churchill described as 'the greatest disaster in our history'. White prestige was 'shattered'.[76] The US authorities, too, recognised its importance. The chief of the US State Department's Far Eastern Division described Singapore as 'a symbol of the power, the determination and the ability of the United Nations to win this war'. To lose Singapore

> …would lower immeasurably the prestige of the white race and particularly of the British Empire and the United States in the eyes of the natives of the Netherlands East Indies, of the Philippines, of Burma and of India.[77]

The yellow peril, a nightmare vision in the minds of the white powers, would take on monstrous proportions in the wartime propaganda that followed.

Conclusion

The yellow peril was a vision which represented the worst fears of the Western powers. From the end of the nineteenth century their fears were represented through the distortions of racial ideology. The domination of vast areas of the globe by a minority was inverted in the fear of 'hordes' beating at the doors of 'civilisation'. Civilised values were identified with spurious biological differences and codified as racial characteristics. The challenge to the Western powers launched by the Japanese in Asia could only be viewed through the distortions of racial ideology: power and authority had been understood through the prism of race for nearly a century. To throw out racial ideology was unthinkable, since the right to rule was justified in precisely these terms. It would take the horrors of the Nazi Holocaust to force Western ideology to adopt a new form, when the destructive logic of racial thinking was laid bare.

A grotesque irony underpins the popular mythology of embattled Allied forces at the mercy of barbarous, fanatical, inhuman Japanese troops. In a convenient amnesia of historic proportions, the Japanese are presented as the authors of their own destruction, and reality is turned on its head. In the topsy-turvy world of Western racial thinking, the Japanese were the racists who brought barbarism to the Far East. The persistence of such distortions continues to this day to justify the horrors of Hiroshima and Nagasaki.

NOTES

1. Christopher Thorne, *Allies of a Kind: The United States, Britain and the War against Japan, 1941-45,* Oxford, Oxford University Press, 1979, p155.

2. Quoted in Yokoyama Toshio, *Japan in the Victorian Mind: A Study of Stereotyped Images of a Nation 1850-1880,* London, Macmillan, 1987, p18.

3. V.G. Kiernan, *America: The New Imperialism: From White Settlement to World Hegemony,* London, Zed Press, 1978, p50. The white men in question were a group of marooned whalers captured by the Japanese. Their 'feelings' were for comfort, 'women and rum'.

4. Ibid., p51.

5. Yokoyama, op. cit., p78.

6. Kiernan, op. cit., p51.

7. Yokoyama, op. cit., p83.

8. Ibid., p61.

9. Ibid., p15.

10. Ibid., p103.

11. Commander C.A.G. Bridge of the Royal Navy, quoted in ibid., p162.

12. Lafcadio Hearn, *Writings from Japan,* Harmondsworth, Penguin, 1984, p189.

13. Ibid., p225.

14. Ibid., p140.

15. Ibid., p225.

16. Yokoyama, op. cit., p140.

17. Henry Dyer, *Dai Nippon: The Britain of the Far East,* London, Blackie & Son, 1904, p32.

18. Nitobe Inazo, *Bushido: The Soul of Japan,* London, G.P. Putnam & Sons, 1906, p171, p172.

19. See: Colin Holmes, and A.H. Ion, 'Bushido and the Samurai: Images in British Public Opinion, 1894-1914', *Modern Asian Studies,* 14 (2), 1980.

20. Richard Hofstadter, *Social Darwinism in American Thought, 1860-1915,* Philadelphia, University of Pennsylvania Press, 1945, p155.

21. Kiernan, op. cit., p86.

22. Hofstadter, op. cit., p149.

23. Ibid., p160.

24. Charles E. Neu, *The Troubled Encounter: The United States and Japan,* New York, Wiley, 1975, p28.

25. Yu Beongcheon, *An Ape of Gods: The Art and Thought of Lafcadio Hearn,* Cambridge, Mass., Wayne State University Press, 1964, p.228.

26. Neu, *The Troubled Encounter*, p45.

27. Iriye Akira (ed.), *Mutual Images: Essays in American Japanese Relations*, Cambridge, Mass., Harvard University Press, 1975, p73.

28. Jean Pierre Lehmann, *The Image of Japan from Feudal Isolation to World Power, 1850-1905*, London, Allen & Unwin, 1978, p165.

29. Charles E. Neu, *An Uncertain Friendship: Theodore Roosevelt and Japan 1906-1909*, Cambridge, Mass., Harvard University Press, 1967, p189.

30. Lehmann, op. cit., p168.

31. Ibid., p171.

32. Ibid., p174.

33. Ibid., p168.

34. Ibid., p169.

35. Iriye, *Mutual Images*, pp76-7.

36. Ibid., p76.

37. Neu, *An Uncertain Friendship*, p193.

38. Thomas A. Bailey, *Theodore Roosevelt and the Japanese-American Crisis*, Gloucester, Mass., Peter Smith, 1964, p284.

39. Ibid., p1.

40. Ibid., p223.

41. Ibid., p284.

42. Neu, *The Troubled Encounter*, p56.

43. Iriye, *Mutual Images*, p91.

44. Paul Gordon Lauren, *Power and Prejudice: The Politics and Diplomacy of Racial Discrimination*, Boulder, Westview Press, 1988, p67.

45. Kiernan, op. cit., p153.

46. Neu, *The Troubled Encounter*, p81.

47. Ibid., p90.

48. Russell H. Fifield, *Woodrow Wilson and the Far East: The Diplomacy of the Shantung Question*, Hamden, Connecticut, Archon, 1965, p166.

49. Ibid., p160.

50. Ibid., p158.

51. John Dower, *Empire and Aftermath: Yoshida Shigeru and the Japanese Experience, 1878-1954*, Cambridge, Mass., Harvard University Press, 1979, p46.

52. Christopher Thorne, *The Limits of Foreign Policy: The West, The League and the Far Eastern Crisis of 1931-33*, London, Hamish Hamiliton, 1972, p411.

53. Neu, *The Troubled Encounter*, p136.

54. Henry L. Stimson, *The Far Eastern Crisis*, New York, Harper & Bros., 1936, p155.

55. Joseph C. Grew, *Ten Years in Japan*, London, Hammond & Company, 1944, p76.

56. Justus Doenecke, 'Introduction', in Stanley K. Hornbeck, *The Diplomacy of Frustration: The Manchurian Crisis of 1931-33, as Revealed in the Papers of Stanley K. Hornbeck*, Stanford, Hoover Institution Press, 1981, p87.

57. Philip R. Reilly, *The Surgical Solution: A History of Involuntary Sterilisation in the United States*, Baltimore, John Hopkins University Press, 1991, px.

58. Hornbeck, op. cit., p129.

59. George B. Sansom, *Japan: A Short Cultural History*, London, Cresset, 1952 (revised edition), p456.

60. Ibid., p455.

61. Ibid., preface.

62. Nitobe Inazo, *Lectures on Japan*, London, Ernest Benn, 1937, p302.

63. Grew, op. cit., p81.

64. Ibid., p44.

65. Hornbeck, op. cit., p85.

66. Grew, op. cit., pp262-265.

67. John Dower, *War Without Mercy*, London, Faber & Faber, 1986, p84.

68. J. Weingartner, 'Trophies of War: US Troops and the Mutilation of Japanese War Dead, 1941-45', *Pacific Historical Review*, February 1992.

69. Iriye, *Power and Culture: The Japanese-American War, 1941-45*, Cambridge, Mass., Harvard University Press, 1981, p123.

70. Thorne, *The Limits of Foreign Policy*, p47.

71. Ibid., p40, p41.

72. Ibid., p46.

73. Ibid., p45.

74. Christopher Thorne, *The Issue of War: States, Societies, and the Far Eastern Conflict, 1941-45*, London, Hamish Hamilton, 1985, p27.

75. *Living Marxism*, No. 81, July/August 1995, p20.

76. Thorne, *Allies of a Kind*, p202.

77. Ibid., p207.

3 NIHONJINRON: MADE IN THE USA

Lynn Revell

I n the Western imagination the image of Japan has changed many times. Gilbert and Sullivan captured the late nineteenth century vision of Japan as a land where the gentlemen are 'queer and quaint'. In his nightmares Kaiser Wilhelm II dreamt the Japanese were a yellow peril ready and waiting to challenge European domination of the world.[1] During the Second World War Hitler dismissed the Japanese as 'little yellow Aryans no better than half-lacquered monkeys',[2] and at the end of the war the Supreme Commander of the Allied occupation of Japan called them children.[3] In 1962 General De Gaulle ridiculed Japan's emerging economic power when he described the Japanese Prime Minister as a transistor salesman.[4] The historian Edwin Hoyt describes the Japanese as a 'nation of anomalies'.[5] In explaining the forces shaping the Japanese economy the *Economist* could only conclude that 'Japan is different, because it undoubtedly is'.[6]

Western commentators have alternately noted that Japan is different because of its exoticism, military aggression, or economic success. A theme that runs through Western observations of Japan is that not only are the Japanese different, but *they think* they are different. Not only are the Japanese not like us, but they do not *want* to be like us. The contribution of Japanese writers to the discussion of their difference often provokes sly and caustic comments on the part of Western observers. In his account of Japanese society, the American journalist Jared Taylor claims that 'what most distinguishes them [the Japanese] from other people is their profound, agonising sense of just how different they are'.[7] In his analysis of the Japanese discussion of their language, Roy Miller argues that this interest is part of 'the apparently always fascinating question of who and what the Japanese themselves "really are"'.[8] Japanese writers have also noted the popularity of this fascinating question. Kano Tsutomu, editor of the *English Language Journal*, noted that the Japanese are obsessed with questioning themselves in an attempt to uncover what makes them unique.[9] Yoshino Kosaku argues that within Japan there is an 'endless discussion of Japanese uniqueness'.[10] Psychologist Minami Hiroshi writes in his article 'The Introspective Boom: Whither the National Character', that self-analysis and a celebration of their difference are integral to what he calls the 'Japanese experience'.[11]

It is the discussion of Japanese uniqueness that is the focus of this chapter. Both inside and outside Japan, the discussion of Japanese uniqueness is commonly called Nihonjinron—literally translated as the theory of the Japanese people. The themes of Nihonjinron—race, identity, nationalism, Japan's relationship with the rest of the world—are complex and politically sensitive. Yoshino notes that not only is there academic criticism of Nihonjinron, but that the 'discourse on Japanese uniqueness now tends to be identified as problematic not merely among scholars but on the international political scene'.[12] The bulk of this discourse concerns the validity and origins of Nihonjinron.[13] Whether the claims of Nihonjinron can be substantiated in history and fact, and whether the roots of Nihonjinron lie in the Japanese psyche or in a Japanese reaction against Western hegemony, are key questions to scholars of Nihonjinron. Although there are many differences in the interpretation of the origins and character of Nihonjinron, most studies share two common assumptions. The first is that Nihonjinron exists as a distinct and recognisable body of work within Japan. The second common assumption is that the dominant theme of Nihonjinron, cultural uniqueness, is rooted either in Japanese history or in the peculiarities of Japan's relationship with the West.

My aim is not to survey the literature that compromises Nihonjinron, nor to examine the truth of Nihonjinron claims. Instead, I aim to question these two assumptions, in the context of a discussion of the origins and development of Nihonjinron in the post-war period. I shall argue that what is commonly defined as Nihonjinron is neither a coherent nor distinct body of literature within Japan. Any discussion of the significance and origins of Nihonjinron presumes that Nihonjinron exists as a recognisable and definable collection of texts. Challenging this presumption highlights the role that observers of Japan have played in shaping their own subject matter.

I will also show that where ideas of cultural uniqueness are present in Japanese writings they are not part of a Japanese obsession with their own culture, but part of a broader—and Western—preoccupation with cultural uniqueness. The category of Nihonjinron itself is a creation of previous Western preoccupations with the function and influence of culture. Previous studies of the theories of Japanese culture and uniqueness have suggested that the methods and concepts of Western anthropology were familiar to Japanese theorists and that they readily employed them in the study of their own society.[14] I will argue that, on the contrary, not only did Western thinking create, mould and colour Japanese perceptions of themselves, but the supposed Japanese obsession with their own uniqueness is but another facet of the Western imagination. Situating Nihonjinron more clearly in the international discourse on culture and cultural uniqueness demystifies Nihonjinron and exposes the formative role that Western thought has played in shaping ideas of Japanese culture, both outside and inside Japan.

The chapter is divided into three main parts. First, an examination of what Nihonjinron is; second, a discussion of some of the main theories that attempt to explain its origins and role in Japanese society; and third, an analysis of Nihonjinron, not as a peculiarly Japanese style of thought, but as a Japanese version of a Western interpretation of the post-war world.

What is Nihonjinron?

The nebulous nature of Nihonjinron is highlighted by the twin problems of defining and quantifying it. The many different definitions and estimates of the extent of Nihonjinron indicate that it is neither easily recognisable nor readily understood. The simplest answer to the question 'what is Nihonjinron?' is to define it as a body of literature, emanating from within Japan, that describes the character of the Japanese people and explains why they are different from other people or unique. The quality and range of subject matter covered by what is commonly accepted as Nihonjinron is extensive. Many of the books are very popular in style and content, little more than tabloid-style trash. Robert Smith claims that, far from being scholarly or literary discussions of the nature of Japanese identity, the quality of most Nihonjinron is very poor.[15] Some descriptions of Nihonjinron even include popular reading such as *Shonen Jump,* which stresses the Japanese values of friendship, effort and success (against all the odds), and is the most widely-read comic book magazine for teenagers in Japan.[16] Nihonjinron also includes newspaper articles, television and radio programmes, and adverts. The more academic texts cover subjects ranging from history, to anthropology, to linguistics, all of which purport to explain why the Japanese are different from other people. When the forms of Nihonjinron are assembled in a list, it becomes obvious that there are as many forms of Nihonjinron as there are forms of written or pictorial (and in some cases oral) communication.

The ideas most commonly associated with Nihonjinron are disparate, but are generally concerned with defining Japanese society and the Japanese personality. The ability of the Japanese language to express the Japanese character, the inability of non-Japanese to comprehend the essence of Japanese culture,[17] and the homogeneous nature of Japanese society are all recurring themes. Two concepts central to most Nihonjinron are 'groupism' and 'shame culture'.[18] Groupism is generally understood as the mechanism whereby the individual is responsible to, is nurtured by, and operates within the confines of, a group. At all times the interests of the group, whether it is a corporation, the nation, or a family, are paramount.[19] Shame culture is usually defined as the opposite to Western 'guilt culture'. In the West, individual behaviour is regulated by feelings of guilt, an emotion peculiarly suited to Western individualism. In Japan, however, it is shame that characterises behaviour. The two ideas are connected: since an individual's first loyalty is to his group, rather than to himself, the fear of shaming himself in their eyes, or of inflicting shame on his group members, regulates his actions.[20]

Given that Nihonjinron is found in such a variety of popular, academic and informal media, it is difficult to quantify accurately. When a phenomenon embraces so many forms it is difficult to separate it from the normal everyday discourse that characterises every modern technological and literate society. The yardstick used by most commentators to help them quantify Nihonjinron was provided by the Nomura Research Institute. A survey conducted by the Institute in 1978 estimated the publication of approximately 700 books between 1946 and 1978 on the theme of Japanese uniqueness. Of these, 58% were published after 1970, and 25% appeared between 1976 and 1978. Yoshino Kosaku believes that this figure underestimates the extent of Nihonjinron.[21] Befu Harumi and Manabe Kazufumi claim that by 1990 the number of published Nihonjinron had risen to 1,000. As proof of how extensive Nihonjinron is they point to the multiple reprinting and classic status of many of those texts. Doi Takeo's *Amae no Kozo* (1971), for example, has been reprinted more than 130 times. Peter Dale, author of probably the most famous book in English on Nihonjinron, *The Myth of Japanese Uniqueness,* argues that since the publication of his work in 1986 there has been a 'continuing boom in the genre'.[22]

In assessing the impact and extent of Nihonjinron other commentators have looked not at the number of texts (books, articles, comics), but at the growth in the popularity of apparently uniquely Japanese values. The Japanese government conducts a survey every five years of 5,400 people, monitoring their attitudes and beliefs on a number of different issues. Burks has noted that there is a tendency for the questions to concentrate on the differences between Japanese and non-Japanese: throughout the 1970s the surveys show evidence 'of a clear reassertion of traditional elements in national character'.[23] Similarly, Wilkinson also points to a broader 'internal search to redefine Japaneseness, a turning back to Japanese roots' that goes beyond the counted texts.[24] Not only have Japanese polls registered the growing popularity of apparently traditional Japanese values, but the 1983 poll showed the highest level of regard for family, filial piety and *ongaeshi* (repayment of kindness) since the 1950s.

The attempt to quantify and classify Nihonjinron runs into some practical difficulties. Nihonjinron as physically translated into books (academic or popular), or magazine and newspaper articles is almost impossible to count. One reason for this is that the definition of Nihonjinron changes depending on the authors who are analysing it. For instance, Befu

Harumi and Manabe Kazufumi include Japanese translations of texts written by non-Japanese authors. In 'The Myth of Japanese Uniqueness Revisited' Peter Dale claims that there has been a 'boom' in the genre, but does not indicate on what basis he makes this judgement.[25] In his earlier work, *The Myth of Japanese Uniqueness,* he quotes the Nomura survey as evidence of the number of texts belonging to the genre. This is the same source quoted by Yoshino Kosaku, and by Befu Harumi and Manabe Kazufumi.

The most interesting feature of the Nomura survey is its definition of Nihonjinron texts. It appears as though all texts that refer to the Japanese or the Japanese way of life have been included under the heading of 'Nihonjinron'. This means that the primary source of evidence for the portrayal of Nihonjinron as a distinct body of work within Japan possibly numbers texts which are not necessarily part of a discourse on Japanese uniqueness. If we also consider that some commentators include under the heading of Nihonjinron not only texts, but behaviour and attitudes, our definition of Nihonjinron expands to include almost anything in Japan that is about the Japanese. The amorphous nature of Nihonjinron raises the question of how valuable it is as a key to understanding Japanese society. Nihonjinron appears real only in the pages of the articles and books that seek to examine and define it. Moreover, as one survey indicates, it certainly seems more real to those who investigate it than to the Japanese themselves.[26] It seems that although many Japanese are aware of Nihonjinron their understanding of what Nihonjinron embraces is so broad that to argue most Japanese are interested in Nihonjinron is tantamount to observing that the Japanese are interested in Japan.

It is important to note the elusive nature of Nihonjinron because many of the explanations of the origin and role of Nihonjinron in Japanese society assume that it exists as quantifiable entity. There are a number of different theories about the origins and role of Nihonjinron in Japanese society. A brief comparison of some of the major theories allows us to see their common features and what distinguishes them from one another.

Nihonjinron as Personality

One explanation is that the introspective nature of Nihonjinron is an intrinsic feature of the Japanese personality and Japanese culture. It argues that the Japanese are predisposed to thinking themselves unique. A typical example of this type of explanation is Jared Taylor's *Shadows of the Rising Sun.* Taylor argues that the defining feature of Japanese culture is its self-obsession and the tendency to mystify its own cultural traits. Ishida Takeshi from the Institute of Social Sciences at the University of Tokyo has developed a similar theory, arguing that in Japan it is normal for the Japanese to maintain an introspective system of values and interests.[27] Zbigniew Brzezinski also argues that Japanese society is prone to emphasising its special and unique qualities. Brzezinski believes this is because Japan is a society trapped between two cultures—Western and Asian. Neither wholly one or the other, the Japanese are forever searching for an elusive identity that is pure Japanese:

> It is striking how often the Japanese will emphasise their Asianess, either when speaking of their Asianess, or speaking of their affinity to the Chinese or when recalling American discrimination against the Yellow race, yet just as often the Japanese will boast that they are really the only Western-type society in a sea of Asian backwardness....[But] fears are now voiced that national traditions may be obliterated altogether and must therefore be deliberately promoted.[28]

An interesting feature of explanations that locate the origins of Nihonjinron in the uniqueness of the Japanese is that they bear a striking resemblance to Nihonjinron themselves. A common Nihonjinron theme is that the eternal spirit of the Japanese has shaped the Japanese through all time. Similarly, these explanations of Nihonjinron presume that Nihonjinron has existed throughout Japan's history precisely because it too is a product of a timeless personality and elusive spirit, rather than of specific factors rooted at points in Japan's history. Parallel to this argument is the idea that Nihonjinron is not an exclusively post-war phenomenon. Roger Buckley identifies the 'stress on homogeneity at the national and societal level' as a persistent theme throughout Japan's history.[29] However attractive Buckley's argument may be to the authors of Nihonjinron, it ignores the very different forces and historical circumstances that have shaped Japan. As writers like Wilkinson have shown, even in the short time that Japan and the West have been in contact both have portrayed themselves in a variety of ways for a variety of reasons.[30] A variation of this argument is that Nihonjinron has existed as part of Japanese thinking throughout its history as a modern nation.

There are two major factors which suggests that this interpretation of Nihonjinron is inaccurate. The first is that pre-Second World War Japanese expressions of national identity or discussions of national character are comparable to similar discussions conducted by other nations as they entered the modern period.[31] In this sense the discussions or texts that are used as examples of early Nihonjinron are not the promotion of Japanese society as uniquely superior to all others but an attempt by

Japan's élite to form a sense of nationhood. The interesting feature of many of these discussions is that they were not preoccupied with a specifically Japanese form of nationhood, but were sympathetic to Western variations.[32] The second factor is that at certain times Japanese intellectuals, politicians and the public have admired and copied Western ideals. If the Japanese are inherently predisposed to celebrating their cultural uniqueness it is unlikely that they would openly admire the culture of others with any enthusiasm. Yet during the Meiji period European political ideals were consciously emulated. The earliest phases of political and industrial modernisation were all based on Western models of development.[33] From 1866 to 1878 the nine best-sellers in Japan were translations of Western works or books about the West. The most popular Western book during the Meiji period was *Self Help* by the Scottish moralist Samuel Smiles. This is a particularly interesting book—not only because it is Western—but because the ideas it promotes, especially the merits of individualism and the importance of hard work over status, are contrary to the ideals of group and respect commonly associated with traditional Japanese values.

Conspiracies, Manipulation and Control

A second group of theories seeking to explain Nihonjinron suggest that it was manufactured by the Japanese ruling élite. One strand of this theory argues that Nihonjinron plays a cohesive function in post-Second World War Japanese society. By emphasising the racial and cultural homogeneity within Japan, Nihonjinron serves to bind the nation together. This theory rests on the premise that there are competing groups with conflicting interests within Japan. In *Images of Japanese Society* Ross Mouer and Sugimoto Yoshio interpret many of the ideas central to Nihonjinron—that Japanese society is fundamentally different from any other, that it is one organised around groups and consensus rather than individualism and conflict—as tools for managing Japanese society.[34]

The idea that Nihonjinron is part of a process whereby control of the masses by Japan's élite is central to the stability of modern Japanese society is supported by Gavan McCormack and Sugimoto Yoshio. They argue that, while the emphasis on the uniqueness of Japaneseness is understandable as a reaction to years of Western chauvinism, it is not a spontaneous development within Japanese society. Rather, it is a 'project' invented and encouraged from above.[35] Others have speculated that the ideas associated with Nihonjinron are not only encouraged from above, but imposed from above in the form of legislation and censorship.[36] In a series of interviews with the radical journal *Ampo,* journalist Douglas Lummis describes a culture of self-censorship in the Japanese media. He argues that the majority of the Japanese media have been unwilling to report events that contradicted the ideals of Japanese society.[37] Similarly, Kawamura Nozomu has interpreted Japaneseness as the mechanism by which the Japanese ruling élite imposes certain values and patterns of behaviour on the Japanese people. In his later works Kawamura develops this argument. In *The Sociology and Society of Japan* he argues that there are aspects of Japanese society which are different from Western-style capitalism. However, the origins of these differences are not due to innate differences in the Japanese psyche or to the peculiar nature of Japanese feudalism, but come from Japanese capitalism itself.[38]

As Yoshino Kasaku argues, although this theory has various merits—the ideas central to Nihonjinron do indeed serve the interests of the ruling élite—it does not explain why different groups within Japanese society would accept them. Several commentators have noted that in the immediate post-war period there was often conflict in Japan. The threat of disruptive trade union activity, for example, was present until the early 1950s. Theories of Nihonjinron which explain its origins and role as a mechanism for social control fail to explain how Japan made the transition from a society characterised by dissent and chaos to the popular image of a Japan at peace with itself.

There is a second problem which these theories of Nihonjinron leave unresolved. That is, if the role of Nihonjinron is to facilitate and enforce social stability and public loyalty to Japan's élite then it seems to be a flawed strategy. Although the image of Japan as a nation of obedient, passive and overly polite citizens remains intact,[39] many have also noted that this stability is more myth than reality. In *Japan Beyond the End of History*, David Williams pinpoints a number of developments within Japan that undermine the image of a conflict-free society. He points to the recent property boom and collapse, the integration of women into the workforce, and the breakdown of consensus amongst the young as just a few of the more obvious sources of instability and tension within Japan.[40]

The journalist Nishijima Takeo claims that Japanese adherence to the values of group consensus and unquestioned obedience and respect towards traditions, elders and authority is strictly a generational phenomenon. According to Nishijima, the present generation and their parents—'60s children—find the values and behaviour insisted upon in Nihonjinron unacceptable. He characterises the children of the first baby boomers—teenagers of present day Japan—as almost entirely ignorant of their cultural heritage and of the style of behaviour that was expected of their grandparents:

They say exactly what they think, as if they knew nothing of the dual value structure traditional among Japanese that scrupulously discriminates between honest inner thoughts and the polite fictions needed to navigate society.[41]

While the popular image of Japan and the Japanese as 'among the best behaved people in the world'[42] persists, Anthony Head dismisses this image as a cliché and notes that the reality on the streets of Japan is very different. For example, in recent years there have been more deaths by guns in Japan than in Britain, yet many commentators insist that Japan is a conflict-free country despite the evidence.[43]

There is no room here to explore how far Japanese society matches the popular image of a society free from conflict. However, it is true that traditional work practices and traditional family structures are breaking down. If this is the case then we can tentatively make two suggestions about Nihonjinron. The first is that if its function is to ensure the loyalty of Japanese masses towards the élite then it is failing. Secondly, if it does have some impact, this impact appears to be differential among the generations and interest groups within Japan.

Japanese Identity

The last explanation of Nihonjinron to be considered here is not a single theory but a group of theories that share a common theme: namely, that Nihonjinron is the modern form of Japanese national identity. Although it takes a variety of forms, the idea that Nihonjinron is the result of a national search for meaning and sense of self in the post-war period is popular among many academic commentators.

One explanation that falls into this category identifies the forces shaping Nihonjinron as a reaction against Western ideological hegemony. This theory argues that a nation's identity is usually formed in reaction to the culture or identity of another nation. It is this foreign or alien Other that is responsible for the shape or character of the new identity in question. Tetsuo Najita and Harold Harootunian from the University of Chicago, for example, argue that it is precisely this process that is responsible for the moulding of Japanese identity throughout its history:

At one level the image of a monolithic West replaced an earlier interpretation of China as the 'other'. In the twentieth century and especially after World War One, Japan's conceptualisation of the West affirmed a theory of militant and articulate revolt against the 'other'. Twentieth century thinkers imagined a Japan destined to reach new levels of achievements realised by no single Western nation. Through this doubling of images, they shaped a theory of action aimed at maintaining a pure, indigenous cultural synthesis protected from outside elements that might disturb the perceived equilibrium.[44]

In *Language and Popular Culture in Japan,* Brian Moeran also identifies a reflexive process at the heart of Nihonjinron. He disagrees with Edward Said's view, that the relationship between Japan and the West is one of 'power, of domination, of varying degrees of complex hegemony'. Instead, in Nihonjinron he sees a Japanese reversal of old power relations between the West and the once subservient Orient. For Moeran, Nihonjinron is almost a Japanese joke: the last laugh of a nation which once bore the brunt of Western contempt for Orientals, but which now takes its place as one of the world's leading powers. Nihonjinron is merely the mechanism whereby the Japanese take the Western, Orientalist outlook and reverse it upon the West itself.[45] Befu Harumi presents a similar scenario in *Civilisation and Culture: Japan in Search of Identity.* He believes that as Western customs and practices were imposed on Japanese public life after the Second World War the Japanese were forced to respond to this erosion of their national culture by re-emphasising their uniqueness. In this way, Nihonjinron elevates Japanese practices and lifestyles into the fundamental building blocks of Japanese identity.[46]

In some ways, the explanation of Nihonjinron as a reaction to the dominant ideology of the West is echoed by Peter Dale, who characterises Nihonjinron as commercialised nationalism. Dale argues that, although the claims to cultural, linguistic and economic uniqueness are false, Nihonjinron is the primary form of Japanese identity. He believes that the formation of nationalism and a national identity has been subjected to different forces and dynamics from those operating in the formation of nationalism in Europe. In Europe, each nation was forged through combining and fusing different races and cultures. In Europe, nationalism is constructed. In Japan, by contrast, nationalism is natural. This is because of the 'homogeneity of race in Japan', and the early development of a single market, a single language and a single culture. Since these elements really existed in Japan, the task of the Japanese élite was not to invent or impose them on a hostile population (as was the role of European élites), but 'rather to discover what was there and bring it to consciousness'.[47] For Dale, Nihonjinron is Japanese identity, but its peculiar function is not merely to characterise the Japanese, it is to distinguish them from all other peoples. According to Dale, this is why the Japanese education system has a particularly strong emphasis on culture, why Japanese linguists argue that the Japanese language embodies the essence of the Japanese nation, and why there have been serious attempts by Japanese intellectuals to ground cultural differences in science. In this scenario, Japanese identity as it is expressed through Nihonjinron is generally the identity of difference, and specifically the identity of difference from the West. Dale believes the desire of the Japanese intelligentsia to emphasise difference and therefore uniqueness encourages competition among academics and authors to see who can describe the 'most unique' of Japan's unique qualities. In this climate all Japanese are consistently encouraged to believe not only that they are different from every other people, but that it is difference which has made Japan a great nation.

Tessa Morris-Suzuki also characterises Nihonjinron as a form of identity. This is not an identity formed in opposition to the West, but an identity created out of a need for certainty and belonging in a rapidly changing society:

> ...the introspective fascination with 'Japanese' culture is also, I think, an ironic result of the enormously rapid process of change which has trans-formed every aspect of the Japanese lifestyle, housing, clothes, transport, working habits, leisure, language—over the past hundred years. In the midst of such endless innovation there is something very attractive about the notion of an unchanging cultural essence, a still centre, which can reassure you that you are still who you always thought you were.[48]

Similarly, Yoshino Kosaku's analysis of Nihonjinron has lead him to call it a form of cultural nationalism. He defines cultural nationalism as a process which aims to 'regenerate the national community by creating, preserving or strengthening a people's cultural identity when it is felt to be lacking, inadequate or threatened'.[49] He notes the differential impact of Nihonjinron on various groups, and constantly asks the question: why should groups who have no interest in siding with the nation's élite accept the ideas of Nihonjinron? His answer is that different groups, to different degrees, assimilate the ideas of Nihonjinron. Some groups ignore them while others embrace them. Where they accept the ideas, this is because of factors external to Nihonjinron itself. Yoshino Kosaku concludes that in the majority of cases adherence to Nihonjinron is a pragmatic process. He acknowledges some truth in the claim that in Japan cultural identity is focused around the concept of difference, however, he argues that it is not the difference from the West that is emphasised but the difference in Japan. While Western identities stress that they are the norm, the expression of beliefs and values that can be applied universally, the Japanese stress 'their particularistic difference in order to differentiate themselves from the universal Chinese and Westerners'.[50] For Yoshino Kosaku , the central difference between Western and Japanese identity is that the first is universal and the second particularistic.

Yoshino Kosaku's emphasis on the usefulness of Nihonjinron as a major force in society is echoed in the last theory to be considered here: the view of Nihonjinron as a secular religion. Once again, many of the ideas central to this theory overlap with ideas already mentioned. However, the interpretation of Nihonjinron as a religious force in society adds several new elements to the idea of Nihonjinron as identity.

In Japan religion appears to be a contradictory force. The most Japanese of all religions is Shinto. Yet Shinto is not only legally prohibited as a state religion, but it is only one of three major religions in Japan. Another seeming contradiction is that while in recent years there has been a massive increase in the number of new religious movements in Japan, and while one in three Japanese homes are host to either a Buddhist or Shinto shrine, recent surveys indicate that as a nation the Japanese are among the least religious people in the industrialised world. In a 1979 survey conducted by the Japanese government, in answer to the question 'Do you have some kind of religious faith or attitude?', only 34% said yes. This means that nearly two thirds of all Japanese claim to have no religious faith or attitudes. This low level of religiosity is more clearly appreciated if it is contrasted to a country such as Britain where only 4% of the population claims to have no religious beliefs.[51] This picture of a relatively irreligious Japan is further confused by the fact that, although nearly two thirds of Japanese are atheists, an International Gallop Poll found that 74% of Japanese think a religious attitude is very important for their quality of life and for society as a whole. These factors have lead some people to conclude that in Japan religion assumes a different form and plays a different role from the one normally assumed in the West.

The American sociologist Robert Bellah defines religion as the popular attitude towards ultimate fate. Bellah describes many of the values and beliefs associated with Nihonjinron as part of a distinctly Japanese religious world-view. He also argues that particularism rather than universalism characterises the Japanese belief system. In the West, individuals are committed to universal ideals that are applicable to everyone. In Japan, individuals are committed to groups which may have different values and codes of conduct from any other group. As Bellah explains:

It is the particular system or collectivity of which one is a member which counts, whether it be family, town or Japan as a whole. Commitment to these tends to take precedence over universalistic commitments such as commitment to truth or justice.[52]

Other studies of religion in Japan have developed this theory. A survey conducted by the Japanese Agency for Cultural Affairs explains that the contradictory religious picture of Japan is due to the fact that in Japan religion is not defined by following the doctrines of a single religion, but by adhering to the traditions of Japan.[53] It is not a belief in the afterlife or a particular moral code that constitutes the religious framework within which people live their lives. Rather, in Japan, it is respect for the past, an understanding of the uniqueness of the Japanese way, and an appreciation of the subtleties of Japanese culture that make up the national religion.

Winston Davis, Professor of Religion at the University of New York, argues that 'Nihonjinron seeks to create a sense of national identity primarily by expanding on these values'.[54] By 'these values' Davis means ideas commonly associated with Japanese traditions. In this analysis, tradition, religion, and Nihonjinron are almost interchangeable. There is no sacred/secular demarcation because all these elements play the same role: providing the framework around which Japanese identity is structured. Shinto expert Helen Hardache also notes that what, in a Western environment, would commonly be understood as a system of religious beliefs and practices, in Japan appear to a be a part of secular life. It would be more accurate, she argues, to understand Shinto and the Japanese approval of religion as the expression, not of spirituality, but of Japanese identity.[55] Shinto is best understood as the embodiment of being Japanese. This is why in Japan there is no contradiction in being Shinto, marrying as a Christian, and being buried with Buddhist funeral rites. In the West religion is often compartmentalised into a section of an individual's life. In Japan there is no such distinction because Shinto is at one and the same time a religion and the expression of Japanese identity.

The theories that fall into this category share several features. The first is that to varying degrees they dismiss the thesis behind Nihonjinron—that the Japanese are unique—as false. Both Dale and Yoshino Kosaku explicitly reject many Nihonjinron claims. For instance, Dale aims to demystify the Nihonjinron tenets that Shinto is an integral part of the ancient Japanese character, and that the Japanese language is uniquely subtle and complex because it embodies the Japanese character. He argues that Shinto is not an ancient Japanese religion, but a body of ideas and practices which was cynically manufactured by statesmen in the Meiji period. He claims that some Shinto theologians like Hirata Atsutane went as far as to borrow ideas from such diverse sources as Hegel and the *Book of Genesis* in an attempt to construct an 'ancient Japanese cosmology'.[56] Yoshino Kosaku adopts a similar approach, challenging the central Nihonjinron claim that the Japanese are uni-racial and live in a culturally-pure society—an idea popularly summed up in the notion that 'you have to be born a Japanese to understand Japanese mentality'.[57] He rejects the claims of anthropologists such as Masuda Yoshio who maintain that, unlike the Europeans who have habitually mixed blood and culture, the Japanese have kept themselves pure; or of ethnologists such as Ishida Eiichiro who argue that the Japanese are peculiarly adept at moulding and integrating other cultures without polluting their own. Kosaku Yoshino not only argues that these theories are historical myths that deny concrete archaeological and historical records, but shows that they ignore the reality of modern Japanese society which is composed of a number of different groups.

The second element that these theories share is the recognition that Nihonjinron is not a fixed entity, but a phenomenon that has changed and evolved over time. In his follow-up to *The Myth of Japanese Uniqueness*, Dale illustrates the development of Nihonjinron ideas, and what he perceives as their growing strength and integration into mainstream Japanese thinking.[58] Eosin Kosaku clearly distinguishes between strands of Nihonjinron at different periods in modern Japan. He has noted that in the post-war period the same cultural traits have been interpreted differently. Writing about the role of Nihonjinron as a form of sacred identity or secular religion, Timothy Fitzgerald stresses that these ideas are not timeless. Ideas of cultural uniqueness and what he calls ritual order have grown and developed over time.[59]

The final factor these theories have in common is that they identify Nihonjinron as a body of relativist ideas. By stressing racial, social and cultural uniqueness, Nihonjinron attributes characteristics which are peculiar to the Japanese. The world-view painted by Nihonjinron is a relativist one because it implies that values and truths that are supposedly applicable to all peoples—democracy, freedom, truth—are not applicable to the Japanese. This observation is supported by the many Nihonjinron writings that emphasise the instrumental role played by a Japanese spirit or indefinable Japanese essence in history. However, the most interesting feature of the theories that identify the particularistic kernel in Nihonjinron writings is that they frequently compare the particularism of Japanese thought with the universal elements within Western thinking. As already noted, some writers have made the point that the stress on particularism and cultural uniqueness is a response to the universalism of the West. The implication is that in the West there is a tendency to produce universalistic thinking and that for some reason Japanese society generates a style of thinking that is relativist. Writers such as Peter Dale, Najita Tetsuo and Harold Harootunian may argue that Japan has generated a form of thinking that is particularistic in response the domination of the West, but they still emphasise that the relativism originates in the heart of Japan.

The Origins of Uniqueness

In the opening paragraph of her essay 'The Invention and Reinvention of "Japanese Culture"' Tessa Morris-Suzuki paraphrases Marx:

> A spectre is haunting Europe, indeed, the rest of the world: not, of course the spectre of Communism, but of that other big C—Culture.[60]

It is appropriate that Tessa Morris-Suzuki should begin her discussion of the nature of Japanese culture by establishing its place within a wider, global debate on the meaning and significance of culture. The celebration of cultural uniqueness is not unique to Japan. There are other countries which promote their culture and other nations which insist that their national language is more than just a tool for communication. In 1993, the French government issued an official booklet filled with French words that could substitute the English words sometimes used in official documents. In January 1996 the French also imposed a ban on the amount of time in which non-French music could be played on French radio.[61] French politicians insist that elements of French culture embody the very spirit of the French. Consequently, France is attempting to prevent the dilution of its identity by halting the intrusion of non-French culture.

France and Japan are not alone in their preoccupation with culture. Edward Said believes that the potential threat of a foreign culture and the need to defend domestic cultural practices is an important issue in international relations towards the end of the century.[62] The relationship between the developed and the developing worlds is often defined and regulated by cultural considerations.[63] Writing in *Foreign Policy*, William Lind argues that culture generally, and Western culture in particular, should provide the basis for a new foreign policy. The culture of a nation should be the standard by which the West accepts or rejects potential allies.[64] Samuel Huntington develops Lind's thesis in his essay 'The Clash of Civilisations', arguing that cultural divisions surpass economic or ideological divisions in the modern world.[65] Culture is as familiar in the wider academic world as it is in the field of international relations. Immanuel Wallerstein, for instance, has identified the domination of the concept of culture in the social sciences, noting that it has replaced many of the traditional methods of approaching problems and issues.[66]

Behind the preoccupation with culture lies the assumption that each culture is different.[67] Lind and Huntington select culture as the defining element in the relationships between nations because they believe that culture encompasses the essential differences and similarities between them. Groups who share your culture are your allies. Groups with different cultures are at best different and at worst potential enemies. When Lind warns that Africa, Asia, India and the Islamic world are not merely nations or regions, but different *cultures*, he is reminding his readers that alien cultures have different values and standards. Fear of the power of alien cultures and the celebration of one's own culture have become part of the discourse on power and domination: powerful cultures threaten weaker cultures; the latter must be protected.[68]

There is no room in this chapter to give a complete history of the idea of cultural uniqueness. However, even a brief overview is enough to establish a proposition which is crucial for a fuller understanding of Nihonjinron. That is, the concept did not originate in Japan. In *The Retreat of Scientific Racism*, Elazar Barkan claims that the term 'culture' was first used to refer to differences in societies by Edward Burnett Tylor, the founder of anthropology at Oxford University, in 1875. In *Culture*, Raymond Williams argues that the German philosopher, Joachim von Herder was the first to use 'the significant plural "cultures" in deliberate distinction from a singular "civilisation"'.[69] Both agree that the origins of the idea of cultural uniqueness are rooted in the West. Not only are the ideas of cultural uniqueness not unique to Japan, but the origins of cultural uniqueness lie outside Japan.[70]

It was in the period surrounding the Second World War that the idea of cultural difference assumed a form that is recognisable today. Before this time, although cultural differences were discussed and studied (especially in anthropology), Western values and Western civilisation were considered superior to those in any other societies.[71] It was only with the impact of the Second World War that the idea of a globe fragmented in a myriad of different cultures began to dominate other interpretations of the world. The origins of modern ideas of cultural uniqueness lie in the conditions created by the devastation and destruction of the Second World War. The Allies had won. Their military, technological and economic power had overthrown fascism and held the Soviet Union at bay.

Yet the upheavals and chaos unleashed by the Second World War prompted a profound rethinking of many pre-war ideas and certainties. One of those certainties was that Western civilisation was morally superior to the rest of the world. The American author Peter Schrag noted that 'Western confidence began to totter at Dachau and Hiroshima'.[72] Writing in 1952, the Harvard sociologist Pitirim Sorokin went so far as to describe the whole of the twentieth century as a 'period of possibly the greatest crisis in the whole of humanity'.[73] At the end of the war, the humanist Cyril Connolly believed that 'Morally and economically Europe has lost the war'.[74] For many, the Allied victory was overshadowed by the barbarity of the war itself, and by the pessimistic conclusion that: 'the savage mind and the mind of Western civilised man are essentially alike'.[75] Speaking on behalf of a generation appalled by two world wars, H. G. Wells sounded an apocalyptic note: 'Homo sapiens, as he has been pleased to call himself, is in his present form played out.'[76]

As a consequence of this collective disquiet, pre-war assumptions concerning the relationships between nations were also questioned and reshaped in the light of new doubts.[77] Western thinkers lost confidence in their right to judge and evaluate other societies from a standpoint of unquestioned superiority.[78] Elazar Barkan argues that a direct result of the Second World War was the discrediting of the idea of racial superiority.[79] Societies no longer interpreted the differences between them as racial, but as cultural. Societies that were non-Western were no longer lesser societies but cultures of a different character. The idea of culture and the importance of cultural difference was celebrated as a revolt against the previous notion of universal values and standards that held true for all societies. In *Culture and Poverty*, Charles Valentine welcomes the arrival of culture as a concept in the social sciences precisely because it overturns so many previous certainties:

> The idea of culture has been a most important weapon in the intellectual attack against racism, ethnocentrism, bigotry and cultural imperialism.[80]

The idea of cultural uniqueness as a way of understanding the differences between societies gained legitimacy in the aftermath of the Second World War. However, it was the systematisation of these ideas, through their adoption by the major international organisations of the day, which leant them real authority. In November 1945 the United Nations met to establish a special branch of its organisation devoted to science and culture: UNESCO. The aim of this branch was to prevent any future reemergence of Nazism. Underlying its formation was the belief that one of the factors leading to the Holocaust was the failure of different cultures to under-stand and appreciate each other. UNESCO's objective was to help create a world where there was no single or dominant civilisation but a myriad of fundamentally different cultures. The stated creed of UNESCO was one of:

> ...assuming to all, full and equal access to education, the free pursuit of objective truth and the free exchange of ideas and knowledge.[81]

In 1951, UNESCO commissioned the French anthropologist Claude Lévi-Strauss to write a keynote text, *Race and History*. For some, the work of Lévi-Strauss is synonymous with the promotion of ideas that support human universality. His belief that the task of anthropology was to 'extend humanism to the measure of humanity',[82] and his insistence that there are universal characteristics shared by all men seem to make him a strange choice for an international body newly dedicated to the promotion of cultural relativism. However, there are limits to the univer-salism described by Lévi-Strauss.[83] *Race and History* illustrates not only the limits of his universalism but the extent to which he believes in the innate differences between cultures. In this work he argued against the idea that there was a ranking hierarchy of cultures, or that primitive and undeveloped societies progressed and became more civilised. He inter-preted the fusing and mixing of cultures as a process that is fundamentally destructive.[84] There were no hierarchies of cultures because each culture was unique. Some cultures, especially Western, were stronger than others, but essentially they were fixed and unchanging.

The UNESCO declaration is significant because it represents two intertwining trends. First, it is the culmination of a long process within anthropology whereby a belief in the universality of man and society had been undermined. In her analysis of the developments within British anthropology between 1885 and 1945, *The Savage Within,* Henrika Kuklick illustrates the general trend to idealise non-Western cultures at the expense of Western society.[85] She argues that pre-eminent anthropol-ogists such as Bronislaw Malinowski, Sir Edward Evans-Pritchard, and Augustus Pitt-Rivers all attributed fixed and innate qualities to the different cultures they studied. This trend was not restricted to British anthropol-ogists. In America the school of thinking led by the anthropologist Franz Boas pursued similar themes.[86] In his work *Cultural Materialism,* Marvin Harris shows how, in the period leading up to the Second World War, the tendency to 'make personality the dominant factor or even to assign it equal weight' was a persistent theme in the study of cultures.[87]

When UNESCO commissioned Lévi-Strauss to write his key-note text neither they nor he were challenging established ideas within the field of anthropology and the study of cultures. In their insistence on differences between cultures and the illegitimacy of ranking them in hierarchies, they were following an already established tradition.

The second trend established by the UNESCO declaration was the broader use of these previously specialist ideas to understand and interpret contemporary societies and the relationships between them. Not surprisingly, when American academics set out to analyse Japanese society and Japan's conduct in the Second World War, they did so in the context of the ascendant ideology of their time: cultural relativism. Towards the end of the Second World War there were a number of initiatives by American academics to understand the strength of Japanese society. Of the many books and papers that were published at this time the most famous was Ruth Benedict's *The Chrysanthemum and the Sword*. As a follower of the Boas school of anthropology, Benedict's work contains most of the ideas popular at this time. With her opening words she powerfully asserts the inalienable difference of the Japanese:

> The Japanese were the most alien enemy the United States had ever fought in an all out struggle. In no other war with a major foe had it been necessary to take into account such exceedingly different habits of acting and thinking.[88]

She argued that motives and priority of motivations varied from culture to culture. The norms and patterns of accepted behaviour are different in each culture, as are the factors which restrain and compel individuals to conform. She was the first to characterise Japan as a shame culture, a society where individualism was constrained and unrecognisable in its Western form.[89] Her book reads like a Western Nihonjinron text, and is appreciated by some Japanese authors of Nihonjinron as a text that 'is still helpful for an understanding of the two contrasting aspects of Japanese culture'.[90]

Benedict is probably the most famous Western exponent of cultural uniqueness in Japan, but she was only one of many. The sociologist Robert Bellah, for instance, published another classic text, *Tokugawa Religion* (1957), which argued that there was a unique system of values in Japan. He linked the culturally unique features of pre-Meiji Japan with the unique form of spirituality found in Shinto.[91] From 1962 to 1963 the American Committee on the History of Society in Japan published a number of lectures as a culmination of several years work. The theme running through each lecture was that at the most fundamental level Japan and the Japanese were different from their Western counterparts. Joseph Kitagawa's lecture on 'Modernity, Culture and Religion', where the failure of the Japanese élites to introduce Western-style individualism is attributed to the resistance of the Japanese people, is a typical example of the established practice of attributing social change to the power of culture.[92]

The academics discussed in this section are representative of an intellectual trend in the post-war period. In 1964, UNESCO itself contributed to the discussion of Japanese culture as part of its *Records of Civilisation: Sources and Studies* series. It reiterates the by now undisputed truth that 'we cannot take any one culture and call it *the* culture',[93] and states its aim as to answer key questions:

> How can the Japanese people meet the challenge of the expanding West?
> How can they adapt and reorganise to preserve their own society and culture? What is worth preserving that is distinctly Japanese?[94]

In the same period in which Western academics and international institutions were consolidating their views on Japanese cultural uniqueness, Japanese writers were coming to terms with a number of profound upheavals in their own country. Every tradition, every major Japanese institution, and every ideal that had characterised what it was to be Japanese was either discredited, dismantled or suppressed by the American occupation. State Shinto, the organising principle of the imperial house, was made illegal. Not only was it banned from schools and all public occasions, but it was blamed for fueling the rise of ultra-nationalism. Japanese nationalism was discredited. The Emperor was forced to renounce his divinity in 1946. Military defeat and the American occupation meant that Japan was a country with no religion, no history, no leadership and no government.

If we consider conditions in Japan in the first fifteen years after the war and the new Western orthodoxy that it is a country's innate culture that makes it what it is, it is possible to understand the original form of Nihonjinron. In the first post-war decade Nihonjinron was an expression of Japanese demoralisation, defeat, and military and economic subordination to America. However, the most important feature of this demoralisation was that it was expressed in the language of the dominant power: the language of cultural uniqueness. Typical examples of Nihonjinron of this period are *The Japanese are Like That,* by the Japanese journalist Kawasaki Ichiro, and *Thought and Behaviour in Modern Japanese Politics,* by Maruyama Masao. From the first page, *The Japanese are Like That* is both an affirmation of the role of culture in shaping a nation's destiny, and a guilty acknowledgement that it was Japan's culture that played a key role in its behaviour in the Second World War:

> From time immemorial the Japanese have been a most thoroughly ruled people. Likewise, there has never been a popular struggle for liberty or individual rights, as in France, England or in the Americas.[95]

Thought and Behaviour in Modern Japanese Politics pursues a similar theme. Not only does Maruyama Masao affirm Benedict's observations of the peculiar social laws that dominate Japanese life, but he is quick to acknowledge the particularly virulent form of Japanese nationalism: ultra-nationalism.[96] When he compares nationalism in Japan with the nationalisms of Western nations he asks why the Japanese version is so extreme. Again, his interpretation of Japanese society is directly related to the interpretation of Japan's occupiers: there are no external laws around which universal values could be based, the Japanese are incapable of acting as morally responsible individuals because they act in groups, and without a strong authoritarian leader they are reduced to the twelve-year-old children General MacArthur once called them. The Japanese lack of individuality was perceived as a key difference between Nazi and Japanese war criminals. In the war tribunals that dealt with the Nazis, the Germans remained strong and uncowed by defeat. The source of their crimes was a personal desire for power and evil that remained intact even after their defeat at the hands of the Allies. The roots of Japanese war crimes lay not with the individual, but in the power each individual gathered from his membership of the group, in this instance the nation. Once the Japanese were deprived of this group support their strength failed them. As Maruyama notes in his observations of the war crimes trials at the end of the war; while the Nazi Göring maintained the audacity to 'roar with laughter' in the face of his captors, his Japanese military counterparts could only 'turn pale' and 'weep'.[97]

By contrast, Nihonjinron from the mid-1970s to the mid-1980s is far less defensive in its interpretation of the impact of Japanese uniqueness and the role of Japanese culture.[98] Most Nihonjinron analysts believe that this confidence is linked with the economic might of Japan in this same period.[99] The emergence of Japan as an economically dynamic power at the heart of the most vibrant area of the world, the Pacific Rim, has obviously contributed to the lack of cultural subservience so prevalent in the earlier works. However, as anyone reading the later Nihonjinron texts will notice, the emphasis on cultural uniqueness is the common thread running through all Nihonjinron.

Two recurring themes in Nihonjinron of this period illustrate the link between Japan's growing independence in the world and the use of cultural uniqueness as an expression of that new strength. The first theme is the liberation of Japanese culture from a sense of shame and a rejection of the idea that their culture made every Japanese guilty for the war. Whereas Benedict traced the origins of Japanese militarism to the apparently Japanese tendency to deny individualism and organise in groups,[100] some Japanese commentators began to interpret those same cultural qualities as a source of national pride. Groupism was reinvented as an integral part of an honourable Japanese tradition and a source of stability.[101] Aspects of Japanese history that were previously identified as the explanation for Japan's conduct in the war were now celebrated as part of a rich and noble past.[102] The second theme is an unfavourable criticism of the West. Most Nihonjinron are a combination of the two themes.

The transition from the interpretation of Japanese culture as a source of shame to a source of pride is clearly illustrated in the writings of the journalist Kawasaki Ichiro. In his 1955 work, *The Japanese are Like That,* he expressed admiration for the American occupation of Japan and humbly admitted that Japanese culture lacked many enviable qualities of the West. Fourteen years later he published *Japan Unmasked*, in which he defended Japanese politeness and scorned Western brashness. He accused the Japanese of being too gullible, of believing Westerners without reservation and of failing to appreciate their culture. Fifteen years after the end of the Allied occupation he noted that:

> …the Japanese are at last beginning to feel, in a vague way, that theirs, after all, is not a nation to be ashamed of, and attention is once again being focused on 'Japan' as the central value of the Japanese.[103]

In similar vein, in *Japan's Last War* Ienaga Saburo argues that before the war ended many Japanese were forced to live like animals; that it was partly the reality of war itself that dehumanised them. He also argues that not all Japanese supported Japanese militarism, citing thousands of labour disputes during the war as evidence of this.[104] He blames the Allies for their handling of the occupation and accuses them of willfully ignoring democratic and pacifist elements in Japanese society.[105] Exposing the severity with which the Allies ruled post-war Japan is a feature of other Nihonjinron, as writers counter accusations of Japanese brutality with examples of American harshness.[106] Similarly, in *Japanese Society Today* Tadashi Fukutake celebrates the economic success of Japan and manages simultaneously to denigrate Western industrialisation by warning his countrymen that unless they take measures to preserve their culture Japanese society will become as alienated and as fragmented as its Western counterparts.[107]

The last two books mentioned above are representative of the tendency to link Japanese strength and the celebration of cultural values. What is often forgotten is that during this time not only was the orthodox Western interpretation of Japanese society still one which emphasised cultural difference, but the reliance on culture as a method of explaining the growth of Japan is more common today than ever.[108] Popular books such as *The Japanese* by Jean-Francois Delassus, or *Japan Today* by Roger Buckley are typical of what amounts to little more than Western Nihonjinron. Delassus's work is merely a scrapbook of cultural stereotypes, his chapter headings alone (Crowds....Everywhere Crowds; A Feudal People in Modern Times; The Hara-Kiri Redemption; Vacation Camps for Adults; and Dangerous Despite Itself)[109] reveal how heavily his analysis of Japan relies on standard Nihonjinron assertions.

Conclusion

An analysis of Nihonjinron is a complex affair partly because Nihonjinron itself is so nebulous. The concept is open to different interpretations and many Nihonjinron claims are questioned by the Japanese themselves. One commentator has argued that there is growing proof that Westerners are learning Japanese despite their unfamiliarity with Japanese society. It seems as though the lure of the Yen is proving a great incentive to Westerners who would otherwise find the language too difficult.[110] Other features of Japanese culture are also frequently demystified. Myths about the nature of the Japanese worker, or the Japanese race, are not taboo, but are openly debated.[111]

An examination of Nihonjinron texts suggests that their reliance on culture as a method of explaining society, and their insistence on the uniqueness of the Japanese are really no different from either Western interpretations of Japan or the West's preoccupation with the strength of its own culture. The significance of Japanese writing on culture is not that it is unique, but that it is a part of a growing discourse on the nature of culture that has gathered momentum and legitimacy since the end of the Second World War. As the editor of a new reader on multiculturalism points out in his introduction, today there is only 'a motley crew' who would dare to argue against the idea of cultural uniqueness.[112]

It is the questions about Nihonjinron that are rarely asked which are the most interesting. In a world where Japan has rebuilt itself from the ruins of the Second World War, where Japanese products are found in most Western homes, and where world statesmen are forced to acknowledge Japan's leading role in international affairs, it is not surprising that the West should remain fascinated with Japan. What is not clear is why the West should be fascinated with what the Japanese think of themselves. This is perhaps especially surprising since the evidence suggests that not only are the Japanese not exclusively xenophobic or anti-Western, but that they are no more obsessed with themselves than any other nation. If what is commonly known as Nihonjinron is no more than national self-interest why is Nihonjinron itself so interesting to Westerners? There is no room here to explore this question in the detail it deserves. However, it does seem that the interest of the West has facilitated a discourse on Japanese theories of themselves that is more substantial than the theories it seeks to explore. A comparison of Nihonjinron texts with texts about Nihonjinron shows that, of the two, it is the latter that are the most coherent. The texts which are commonly associated with Nihonjinron, on the other hand, are a disparate collection of works ranging from children's books to scholarly works, and including much popular literature, attitude surveys, and television and radio programmes. It is the commentaries on Nihonjinron themselves that give it the semblance of a recognisable trend in Japanese society. To put it even more bluntly, the so-called Japanese obsession with their own uniqueness exists more clearly in the eyes of the West than in Japan itself.

More in-depth surveys of what actually comprises Nihonjinron suggests that most Japanese are familiar with only the most popular style of Nihonjinron (articles in magazines and newspapers), and even then they are not always aware that what they are reading is a definable body of literature.[113] The Nomura Research Institute's 1978 survey of the quantity of Nihonjinron, the basis on which most authors (including Peter Dale and Kosaku Yoshino) argue that Nihonjinron is extensive, is also ambiguous. Books were designated 'Nihonjinron' simply if they had the word 'Japanese' in the title or if they discussed 'obviously Japanese concepts'.[114] It is by no means established that discussion of culture is any more prevalent in Japan than the discussion of the importance of culture in any other country. What is clear is that the origins of this debate are not Japanese. Just as the very first modern debates on cultural uniqueness are European, so too the first—and the most influential—discussions on the cultural uniqueness of Japan are American.

NOTES

1. Endymion Wilkinson, *Japan versus the West*, Harmondsworth, Penguin, 1983, p125.

2. Ibid., p60.

3. Kawasaki Ichiro, *Japan Unmasked*, Tokyo, Charles E. Tuttle Company, 1969, p9.

4. Hugh Cortazzi, *The Japanese Achievement*, New York, St. Martin's Press, 1990, p279.

5. Edwin Hoyt, *The New Japanese*, London, Hale, 1991, p11.

6. *The Economist*, 6 March 1993.

7. Jared Taylor, *Shadows of the Rising Sun*, New York, Quill, 1983, p28.

8. Roy Miller, 'The Spirit of the Japanese Language', *The Journal of Japanese Studies*, Vol. 3, No. 2, 1977, p251.

9. Quoted in Ardath Burks, *Japan: A Post Industrial Power*, London, Westview Press, 1981, p204.

10. Yoshino Kosaku, *Cultural Nationalism in Contemporary Japan*, London, Routledge, 1992, p39.

11. Minami Hiroshi, 'The Introspective Boom: Whither the National Character', *Japan Interpreter*, Vol. 8, No. 2, 1973, p159.

12. Yoshino Kosaku, 'The Changing Discourse on Race, Ethnicity and Nationalism in Japan', *The ASEN Bulletin*, No. 8, Winter 1994-95, p11.

13. The two most influential English language texts on Nihonjinron, Peter Dale's *The Myth of Japanese Uniqueness*, and Yoshino Kosaku's *Cultural Nationalism in Contemporary Japan*, are concerned with investigating the claims of Nihonjinron and the origins of Nihonjinron respectively.

14. Tessa Morris-Suzuki, 'The Invention and Reinvention of "Japanese Culture"', *The Journal of Asian Studies*, Vol. 54, No. 3, August 1995, p768.

15. Robert Smith, *Japanese Society*, Cambridge, Cambridge University Press, 1985, p110.

16. A keynote article in *The East*, a popular English-language Japanese magazine, argues that the ideas behind *Manga* are adapted to expressing the peculiarities of Japanese culture: '*Ishin-Denshin* is a key phrase for those who wish to understand Japan. Initially a Zen Buddhist term, it refers to non-verbal communication. Japanese culture preserves and cherishes this "culture of tacit understanding", which not surprisingly is a prominent feature of Manga stories.' ('Japanese Culture Through the Lens of Manga', *The East*, Nov/Dec 1995, p52.)

17. A typical example of this type of Nihonjinron is Suzuki Takao's 'Language and Behaviour in Japan', *Japan Quarterly*, July/September, 1976, Vol. XXIII, No. 3. Suzuki argues that Japanese 'actually alters the linguistic definition of the self to accord to changed condition'. This is different from Western languages because Westerners only have one identity, themselves as individuals. In Japan, individuals have several identities (as expressed in their language) because they operate as part of a group.

18. Aoki Tamotsu argues that in the post-war period 'groupism' and 'shame culture' 'have been the perennial motifs of Nihonbunkaron'. See: Aoki Tamotsu,

'Anthropology and Japan: Attempts at writing Culture', *Japan Foundation Newsletter*, October 1994, p3.

19. See Robert Bellah, *Tokugawa Religion: The Values of Pre-Industrial Japan*, Boston, Beacon Press, 1957, p31, for a classic description of groupism in Japan.

20. See: Peter Dale, *The Myth of Japanese Uniqueness*, New York, St. Martin's Press, 1986, pp176-188, for a discussion of the idea of shame culture.

21. Yoshino, *Cultural Nationalism in Contemporary Japan*, p227.

22. Peter Dale, 'The Myth of Japanese Uniqueness Revisited', *Nissan Occasional Papers*, No. 9, 1988, p2.

23. Burks, op. cit., p207.

24. Wilkinson, op.cit., p88.

25. Dale, 'The Myth of Japanese Uniqueness Revisited', p2.

26. Befu Harumi and Manabe Kazufumi found that the majority of Japanese were interested in Nihonjinron and that many even thought it was on the increase. However, they also found that the majority understood Nihonjinron as a way of thinking about Japan's role in the world. More importantly, they noted that the very act of asking people to concentrate on the concept of difference between cultures creates the possibility for the question to be considered, where before it may not have been an issue. See: Befu Harumi, and Manabe Kazufumi, 'Empirical Status of Nihinjinron: How Real is The Myth?', in Adriana Boscaro, Franco Gatti, and Massimo Raveri (eds.), *Rethinking Japan*, Folkestone, Japan Library, 1990.

27. Ishida Takeshi, 'Development of Interest Groups and the Pattern of Modernisation in Japan', in *Papers on Modern Japan*, Canberra, Research School of Pacific Studies, 1965.

28. Zbigniew Brzezinski, *The Fragile Blossom: Crisis and Change in Japan*, London, Harper Tourch Books, 1972, p15.

29. Roger Buckley, *Japan Today*, Cambridge, Cambridge University Press, 1985, p97.

30. See Wilkinson, op.cit..

31. Yoshino Kosaku notes that a criticism of Nihonjinron literature is that it lacks the comparative perspective. He points to a parallel discussion in Germany and to Nietzsche's remark that: 'It is characteristic of the Germans that the question "what is German" never dies among them.' Yoshino, *Cultural Nationalism in Contemporary Japan*, p5.

32. See Wilkinson, op. cit. (chapter 2, 'The West as Seen by Japan'), for a description of Japan's changing view of itself in relation to the West.

33. See: Sidney Gifford, *Japan Among the Powers 1890-1990*, New Haven, Yale University Press, 1994, and David Williams, *Japan: Beyond The End Of History*, London, Routledge, 1994, for detailed accounts of the relationship between Japan and the West during the Meiji Period. Both authors illustrate the changing character of this relationship and show that for substantial periods the Japanese were keen to emulate popular aspects of Western culture as well as its political systems.

34. Ross Mouer and Sugimoto Yoshio, *Images of Japanese Society*, London, Keegan Paul International, 1986.

35. Gavan McCormack, and Sugimoto Yoshio (eds.), *The Japanese Trajectory*, Cambridge, Cambridge University Press, 1988. The interpretation of national identity and nationalism as myth or invention is part of a wider discussion beyond the confines of the origins of Nihonjinron. Benedict Anderson believes that common identities are not forcibly imposed from above, but are shared imaginations. See: Benedict Anderson, *Imagined Communities: Reflections on the Origin and Spread of Nationalism*, London, Verso, 1993. See also: Anthony Smith, *National Identity*, London, Penguin, 1991, for a detailed discussion of the mythic nature of nationalism.

36. See: Montse Watkins, 'Coming back to Japan', *Ampo*, Vol. 23, No.4, 1992, for a description of the way labour policy and law is used to influence ideas of race and culture in Japan.

37. An example of this self-censorship is the attitude of the media towards the illness of Emperor Hirohito. He recalls how he reported that in reality there was no public grief over this event but that some publications were unwilling to print his comments and so break 'Japan's great Taboo': 'There's a very great difference between the consciousness of the Japanese people as represented in the media and the consciousness of people that you really meet in the world. In the media, everybody is mourning, but people in my neighborhood don't seem to care at all.' (Douglas Lummis, 'Control and the Media', *Ampo*, Vol. 24. No. 3, 1993, p45.)

38. Kawamura Nozomu, *Sociology and Society of Japan*, London, Kegan Paul International, 1994, p148.

39. Edwin Reischauer, *The Japanese*, Tokyo, Charles E. Tuttle Company, 1988, pp225-233.

40. David Williams, *Japan Beyond the End Of History*, London, Routledge, 1994, p5.

41. Nishijima Takeo, 'How the Baby Boomers Stirred Up Society', *Japan Quarterly*, Vol. XLLL, No. 1, March 1995, p12.

42. Trevor Fishlock, 'They Still Dance to His Tune', *Daily Telegraph*, 7 July 1992.

43. Anthony Head, 'Japan and the Safe Society', *Japan Quarterly*, Vol. 42, No. 2, April-June 1995.

44. Najita Tetsuo, and H.D. Harootunian, 'Japanese Revolt Against the West: Political and Cultural Criticism in the Twentieth Century', in Peter Dumas (ed.), *Cambridge History of Japan*, Cambridge, Cambridge University Press, 1987, p711.

45. Brian Moeran, *Language and Popular Culture in Japan*, Manchester, Manchester University Press, 1989, p183.

46. H. Befu, 'Civilisation and Culture: Japan in Search of Identity', in T. Umesao, H. Befu, and J. Kreiner (eds.), *Japanese Civilisation in the Modern World*, 1984 (Special issue of *Senri Ethnological Studies*, No. 16).

47. Dale, *The Myth of Japanese Uniqueness*, p38.

48. Morris-Suzuki, op. cit., p772.

49. Yoshino, *Cultural Nationalism in Contemporary Japan*, p1.

50. Ibid., p11.

51. Winston Davis, *Japanese Religion and Society*, New York, State University of New York Press, 1992, p233.

52. Bellah, op. cit., p13.

53. Agency for Cultural Affairs, *Japanese Religion*, Tokyo, Kodansha International, 1972.

54. Op. cit., p38.

55. Helen Hardache, *Shinto and the State, 1868-1988*, Princeton, Princeton University Press, 1989, p134.

56. Dale, *The Myth of Japanese Uniqueness*, p48.

57. Yoshino, *Cultural Nationalism in Contemporary Japan*, p24.

58. Dale, 'The Myth of Japanese Uniqueness Revisited', p2.

59. Timothy Fitzgerald, 'Japanese Religion as Ritual Order', *Religion*, Vol. 23, No. 4, Oct 1993, pp316-322.

60. Morris-Suzuki, op. cit., p759.

61. Kirsty Lang, 'Compulsory French Pop Songs Make Radio Waves', *Sunday Times*, 7 January 1996.

62. Edward Said, *Culture and Imperialism*, London, Chatto & Windus, 1993, p352.

63. The links between non-governmental organisations (NGOs) in the developing world and governments in the West have raised the question of whose culture defines the relationship between the two. For instance, some NGOs in the developing world object to Western bodies imposing concepts of individual and human rights which, they argue, are alien to their culture. See: H. G. Steiner, *Diverse Partners: Non-Governmental Organisations and the Human Rights Movement*, Cambridge, Harvard Law School, 1991, p22.

64. William Lind, 'Defending Western Culture', *Foreign Policy*, Fall 1991, p44.

65. Samuel Huntington, 'The Clash of Civilisations', *Foreign Affairs*, Vol. 72, No. 1, 1993.

66. Immanuel Wallerststein, 'Culture as the Ideological Battleground of the Modern World System', *Theory, Culture and Society*, Vol. 7, 1990, pp31-55.

67. It is precisely the tendency to emphasis difference rather than similarity that Yamazaki Masakzu identifies as a fatal flaw in cultural theorising. See: Yamazaki Masakzu, *Individualism and the Japanese*, Tokyo, Japan Echo Inc., 1994, p7.

68. See: John Tomlinson, *Cultural Imperialism*, London, Pinter Publishers, 1991, for a history of the term 'cultural imperialism'.

69. Raymond Williams, *Culture*, London, Hogarth Press, 1990, p10.

70. Although Kurt Singer believes that the Japanese exhibit unique cultural traits, he notes that the very first identification of an innate relationship between national character and culture was the work of 'Herder and Hegel'. See: Kurt Singer, *Mirror, Sword and Jewel*, London, Croom Helm, 1973, p29.

71. See Frank Füredi, *Mythical Past, Elusive Future,* London, Pluto Press, 1992, chapter 5, for a discussion of the collapse of Western confidence in this period.

72. Peter Schrag, *The Vanishing American,* Englewood Cliffs, NJ, Prentice Hall, 1974, p18.

73. Pitirim Sorokin, *Social Philosophies in an Age of Crisis,* London, Hamilton, 1952, p6.

74. Quoted in Brian Appleyard, *The Pleasures of the Peace,* Harmondsworth, Penguin, 1989, p51.

75. Elazar Barkan, *Retreat of Scientific Racism,* Cambridge, Cambridge University Press, p33.

76. Quoted in Robin Fox, , *Search for Society,* New Brunswick, NJ, Rutgers University Press, 1989, p3.

77. In the essays collected in *Civilisation on Trial* (Oxford, Oxford University Press, 1957), the historian Arnold Toynbee provides a graphic and emotional example of the sense of loss and uncertainty felt by many intellectuals at this time.

78. Gabriel Kolko agues that despite the Allies' victory at the end of the war, in practice they were never able to rule the world as effectively or with as much confidence as they had before 1945. He points out that, at the height of American strength, America lost the Korean War. See: Gabriel Kolko, *Confronting the Third World,* London, Unwin Paperbacks, 1993, p5.

79. Barkan, op. cit., p1.

80. Charles Valentine, *Culture and Poverty,* Chicago, University of Chicago Press, 1968, p2.

81. Quoted in Alain Finkelkraut, *The Undoing of Thought,* London, Claridge Press, p53.

82. Claude Lévi-Strauss, *Structural Anthropology Volume 2,* Harmondsworth, Penguin, 1977, p32.

83. See: Kenan Malik, *The Meaning of Race,* London, Macmillan, 1996, chapter 5.

84. Claude Lévi-Strauss, *Race and History,* quoted in *Structural Anthropology Volume 2,* p356.

85. Henrika Kuklick, *The Savage Within,* Cambridge, Cambridge University Press, 1991.

86. See: Barkan, op. cit., chapter 2.

87. Marvin Harris, *Cultural Materialism,* New York, Vintage Books, 1980, p260.

88. Ruth Benedict, *The Chrysanthemum and the Sword,* London, Routledge & Kegan Paul, 1967, p1.

89. Ibid., p224.

90. Ishida Takeshi, *Japanese Society,* New York, Random House, 1971, p3.

91. Bellah, op. cit., p53.

92. Joseph Kitagawa, (ed.), *Religion in Japanese History,* Chicago, University of Chicago Press, 1966.

93. *Sources of Japanese Tradition* (compiled by Tsunoda Ryusaku, Wm. Theodore de Bary and Donald Keene), New York, Columbia University Press, 1964, p353.

94. Ibid., pV.

95. Kawasaki Ichiro, *The Japanese are Like That*, Tokyo, Charles E. Tuttle Company, 1955, p191.

96. Maruyama Masao, *Thought and Behaviour in Modern Japanese Politics*, London, Oxford University Press, 1963, p3.

97. Ibid., p12.

98. The recurring theme of Nihonjinron during this time is that Japan's culture is responsible for its economic success. 'Why has Japan "Succeeded"? Western Technology and the Japanese Ethos', by the Japanese economist Morishima Michio, is typical of this genre. Not only does he argue that Shintoism and Emperor worship have contributed to the modern Japanese success story but also that the Allied plans to rebuild Japan after the war were similar to plans that the Japanese intended to implement themselves. The implication is that Japan would have become the economic giant she is today without American intervention. (Morishima Michio, *Why Has Japan "Succeeded"? Western Technology and the Japanese Ethos*, Cambridge, Cambridge University Press, 1982, p159.)

99. Yoshino Kosaku describes Nihonjinron of this period as a form of economic nationalism, arising from the recognition that Japanese business methods were being emulated in the West and the strength of the Japanese economy. (Yoshino, *Cultural Nationalism in Contemporary Japan*, p163.)

100. See Benedict, op. cit., chapter 2.

101. See: '"En", the Starting Point of Groupism', *The East*, March 1984.

102. See: Inoue Mitsusada, *Introduction to Japanese History*, Tokyo, Kokusai Bunka Shinkokai, 1988.

103. Kawasaki, *Japan Unmasked*, p25.

104. Ienaga Saburo, *Japan's Last War*, Oxford, Blackwell, 1979, p209.105. Criticism of the Allies' conduct in the immediate post-war period is a feature of many texts that seek to defend Japanese values and cultural traditions. Kyoko Inoue argues that the Americans failed to take into account the differences of culture when they imposed a constitution on Japan. She also believes that the Japanese who were involved in the making of the constitution were unable to grasp the Western concepts of rights or the separation between church and state that the constitution demanded. See: Kyoko Inoue, *MacArthur's Japanese Constitution: A Linguistic and Cultural Study of its Making*, Chicago, University of Chicago Press, 1991.

105. Criticism of the Allies' conduct in the immediate post-war period is a feature of many texts that seek to defend Japanese values and cultural traditions. Inoue Kyoko argues that the Americans failed to take into account the differences of culture when they imposed a constitution on Japan. She also believes that the Japanese who were involved in the making of the constitution were unable to grasp the Western concepts of rights or the separation between church and state that the constitution demanded. See: Inoue Kyoko, *MacArthur's Japanese Constitution: A Linguistic and Cultural Study of its Making*, Chicago, University of Chicago Press, 1991.

106. By May 1946, 210,288 Japanese were purged from their jobs and positions. 920 were executed, and war crime trials continued until November 1948. 100,000 teachers were forced to resign, and in December 1945 all history and geography courses were suspended while official textbooks were revised to portray the Japanese as aggressors in the Second World War. See: Robert Smith, op. cit., p24.

107. Fukutake Tadashi, *Japanese Society Today*, Tokyo, University of Tokyo Press, 1974, p10.

108. Charles Hampden-Turner, and Fons Trompenaars, *The Seven Cultures of Capitalism*, London, Judy Piatkus Ltd., 1993.

109. Jean-Francois Delassus, *The Japanese*, New York, Hart Publishing Company, 1970.

110. 'The Internationalisation of the Japanese Language', *The East*, March/April 1995, p48.

111. See: Higuchi Kiyoyuki, 'Japan—The Terminus of Asia', *Japan Quarterly*, Vol. XXLV, No. 4, October/December 1977, for a discussion of the origins of the Japanese.

112. David Goldberg, (ed.), *Multiculturalism: A Critical Reader*, Oxford, Blackwell, 1994, p20.

113. Befu, and Manabe, op. cit..

114. Yoshino, *Cultural Nationalism in Contemporary Japan*, p227.

PART TWO:
MEDIA MEMORIES

FEAR AND LOATHING
IN THE BRITISH PRESS

Phil Hammond and Paul Stirner

his chapter examines the ways in which the Japanese are portrayed as culturally different in the British press.[1] We show that in many press reports the perception of cultural otherness is itself what constitutes the 'newsworthiness' of Japan. Investigating this further, we show that in content this portrayal of difference is generally hostile to Japan: applying double standards of judgement, and implying that the Japanese are untrustworthy and deceptive. Examining economics reporting—usually seen as more neutral, factual and objective than other areas of coverage—we suggest that not only is there a confusing picture presented, but that the implicitly hostile discussion of difference becomes apparent here too. We go on to argue that underlying the discussion of culture is a perception of racial difference. As we demonstrate in relation to the coverage of the 1995 Pacific War anniversaries, this is expressed today in terms of Britain's supposed moral superiority over Japan. However, such ideas of difference and superiority are not mere hangovers from the past. Rather, we suggest, the explanation of the trends identified is to be found in the West's uneasy relationship with Japan in the present.

Japanese Weirdness

Any regular reader of the British press will be familiar with trivial, often brief, stories of the 'strange but true' variety—such as the *Daily Express* story about the bridegroom from Yokohama who accidentally ran over and killed his new wife after their wedding reception (29 November 1994); or the item about the Osaka couple who dined out free for months by dropping a cockroach into their soup at restaurants and threatening to call the health inspectors (*Daily Express*, 6 December 1994). Although this genre of reporting sometimes refers to established stereotypes about the Japanese—for example, that they have bizarre sexual proclivities; as illustrated in a *Guardian* women's page item on 'Japanese men's penchant for worn, unwashed schoolgirl knickers' (12 December 1994)—many such stories could be about any country. However, in Japan's case, there is such a surfeit of these items that they are invariably remarked upon in commentaries on British reporting of Japan.[2] It is not just that weird things happen there. Japan is seen as a weird country.[3]

The fact that Japan is seen as weird means that the authors of these stories of strangeness often reflect on how the particular weird event or oddity is related to the peculiarity of the Japanese character. A *Guardian* story (taken from the *Baltimore Sun*), for example, made the startling revelation that there are swimming pools in Japan: '...it is time to head for the indoor beach park, with its predictable waves, clean, rubberised sand-grained flooring and perfect weather—rain or shine'. (16 June 1995)

The article explained how such a novel idea as a swimming pool could only be understood if placed in the proper context of Japan's unique culture:

> ...the concept is not that radical in Japan: attempts to improve on the environment have a long history. Japanese gardens are supposed to be cultivated and trimmed into perfection. Nature is not expected to happen naturally.

As if gardening were not enough to suggest Japan's strange, synthetic culture, the report went on to reveal the strict social regimentation reflected in rules supposedly unheard of in the West: 'tattoos, nudity, swimming clothed and picnics are not permitted.' With the exception of the first of these—presumably aimed at the flamboyantly-tattooed *Yakusa* gangsters—such rules would not be exceptional in Britain (where one can also find entire indoor resorts—Centreparks—and an abundance of trimmed gardens). In this example, it is only the supposed 'otherness' of Japan which makes the report newsworthy: there is simply no other rationale for treating the story as 'news'.

Even in cases where a story might be judged to have some news value, it can still be treated as a springboard for musings about the Japanese national character. A *Sunday Times* article on the exploits of a Japanese man, Sagawa Issei, convicted of murder and cannibalism, for example, concluded with the suggestion—conveniently confirmed by an anonymous 'expert'—that:

> The curiosity of the Japanese about Sagawa is rooted in their perception of his victim as less than a person. "It would be very different if his victim had been Japanese", one expert said. (27 November 1994)

Of course, a lurid tale of cannibalism is in a sense just a longer, Sunday broadsheet version of tabloid trivia. The point, however, is that regardless of the subject matter, journalists writing about Japan seem prone to adopting a 'weird' angle, and/or to generalising wildly about Japanese difference. Joanna Pitman, for instance, in a *Times* analysis page feature on Japanese advertising, found that: 'The creative juices in Japan's advertising industry clearly flow in radically different directions from those of our own, but then the industry itself is utterly different.' (10 February 1995)[4]

Put these two trends together—a tendency to focus on the more eccentric or exotic aspects of Japanese society, and a tendency to generalise about the 'national character'—and a distinctly odd picture of the country emerges.

In the *Independent*, for example, the *Yakusa* provided a paradigm for understanding Japan: 'Like most things in Japan, they are smart, discreet and highly organised.' (3 July 1995) The point was repeated in a *Guardian* article (taken from the *New York Times*) on the same topic: 'As with almost everyone in Japanese society, organised crime figures know their boundaries.' (7 September 1995)[5] Hugo Gurdon, writing in the *Telegraph* on the rise of Yamamoto Samu, whose best-selling book about his exploits molesting women on the Tokyo underground had made him a TV star, found an even more bizarre generalisation: that Japan is 'A nation addicted to frottage'. More seriously, he argued that: 'Astonishingly, groping is often a group activity, like everything else in Japan.' (27 November 1994)

The effect of these stories of weirdness is to underline time and again how different Japan is from the West. The perception of Japan as quintessentially different means that a genre of stories treats as 'news' any indication that Japanese people like Western culture. In July 1995, for example, a number of newspapers carried a story about how large numbers of Japanese visitors to Beatrix Potter tourist attractions were causing conservation problems. The story was based on a press release from the National Trust, but a spokesman from the Trust, Adrian Marklew, described the way the story was reported as 'awful, dreadful; that's the last thing we're saying' (interview with Jiji Press, 24 July 1995). What horrified Marklew was the anti-Japanese slant journalists gave to the story: 'Japanese asked to stay out of Beatrix Potter's garden', ran the *Times*' headline; while the *Telegraph* reported 'Lake District hit by Japanese flood' (24 July 1995). Peter Popham, in the *Independent*, explained the Japanese fascination for Beatrix Potter characters in terms of the enthusiasm of Japanese teenagers for cuteness, and for all things foreign:

> Peter Rabbit represents the outside world as it ought to be—cute, cuddly, naughty in a loveable way. Filling her bedroom with stuffed images of Peter, the Japanese schoolgirl may be expressing her yearning for a relationship with the outside world that poses no threat. (25 July 1995)

The implied fanaticism of Japanese enthusiasm for English culture— 'a monstrous regiment' of tourists according to Popham—is what is seen as requiring explanation. A few days earlier, the *Guardian* carried a similar story about Japanese fans of *Anne of Green Gables*, which reported: 'a cult obsession with the children's book...taken to extremes.' (18 July 1995)[6]

The news angle in these stories is the notion that, since the Japanese are so very different, any sign of an affinity for Western culture must, in itself, be worthy of remark.[7] A further element sometimes to be found in such reports, however, is the large amounts of money the Japanese are willing and able to spend on their enthusiasms. There would appear to be a certain resentment that the Japanese can afford to indulge their passion for 'our' culture. Thus, the *Guardian* told its readers of the Japanese man who paid £110,000 for a teddy bear at a London auction (6 December 1994); while the *Times* reported on the Japanese newlyweds who paid £20,000 for a trip to Britain in order to have their marriage blessed in a Welsh chapel (29 December 1994). A feature on 'The Japanese choice in art' in the *Daily Telegraph* informed us that: 'The world remembers Japan best for $82.5m for Van Gogh, $78.1m for Renoir and $51.3m for Picasso.' (3 July 1995) The main point of this article, though, was to try to explain the Japanese taste for 'what we frankly dismiss as "bad pictures"'—paintings by Utrillo, Buffet and Laurençin. The article asked:

> Are these painters tied together in a way which we don't understand, but which tugs powerfully at the Japanese imagination? Or is it (rather) that taste for the worst in the School of Paris 1910-1935 is the mistake of a new moneyed class in Japan—men who buy brand names, large signatures and simple, obvious images?

The Japanese, it would seem, are the *nouveaux riches* of the world, spending astronomical amounts of cash in appallingly bad taste. Professor Allan Solomon, writing a diary column for the *Times Higher Education Supplement*, summed up this view: 'Is money the new Japanese culture? This must be the most materialistic nation on earth.' (2 December 1994) As these comments suggest, an undercurrent of hostility often runs beneath the stories of strangeness and difference.

Double Standards

Just as articles concerning Japanese weirdness sometimes highlight as peculiarly Japanese things which are commonplace in the West (such as swimming pools or gardening), so too a double standard is often applied when criticising Japan. Frequent examples of this are to be found the press discussion of women's place in Japanese society, in which Japan is frequently taken to task for being sexist. The *Guardian* (28 November 1994) reported how:

> Women in Japan are being subjected to rather strange tests in their job interviews: they have been insulted, harangued about how women should not go out to work and forced to perform feats of strength...for

office jobs. Not surprisingly, this type of interview rarely results in appointment.

Similarly, Hugo Gurdon revealed that in Japan 'Women are not respected, but are seen as servants, men's objects, society's slaves' (*Sunday Telegraph*, 27 November 1994). He went on to paraphrase two Japanese feminists to the effect that: 'a cruel and indifferent political establishment...pays lip service to sexual equality and respect for women but...signals it is not taking the issue seriously.'

Commonly, articles are concerned with the ways in which Japanese women are rebelling against traditional gender roles. Yet such stories—for instance, that of the apprentice Geisha girls who revolted against their Spartan training regime[8]—ultimately serve merely to underline the point that Japan is still old-fashioned when it comes to sexual equality. 'Despite sexual inequality more blatant than in other advanced economies—and without even an organised movement in the sense that many Western women know—[Japanese women] are gracefully taking the centre stage of social and economic affairs', wrote Brian Deer in the *Sunday Times* (7 August 1994). Similarly, Kevin Rafferty reported that:

> Some old-timers cannot understand the modern hunger for equality. One wife in her seventies says: "I am the empress of my house, and my husband never dares enter the kitchen. Each month he handed me his paypacket and I gave him pocket money." (*Observer*, 6 August 1995)

This article also related how the behaviour of female bank employees had undergone 'quite radical changes':

> A decade ago they would bow on opening the door, bow again on approaching the guest, kneel and bow to serve the tea, bow again on moving away, bow at the door and finally bow from the other side of the closing door. These days they don't kneel and have cut the bows to three, on entering the room, serving the tea and departing.

'Such', commented Rafferty ironically, 'is the progress of Oomanribu (Women's Lib)'.

The topic of women's inequality in Japan seems to hold an endless fascination for British journalists. For Gwen Robinson, writing a *Times* Magazine feature on the nocturnal antics of young Japanese women (3 June 1995), the subject appeared to offer an opportunity to run the gamut of clichés to be found in British reporting of Japan. Young women concealing their night-time revelries from their parents showed that 'in Japan the challenge is to balance the competing demands of tradition and modernity'. Their activities at night clubs, meanwhile, demonstrated 'a positively infantile streak'.[9] The article quoted a Japanese academic, Iwao Sumiko, to confirm that crowds of young women going clubbing—a phenomenon readily observable in any British city on a Saturday evening—could only be understood in terms of Japanese 'groupism': '"They're still not really free from group pressure. They go in groups, and the costumes are almost a uniform."' Not content with cataloguing a tension between tradition and modernity, a childlike nature, and groupism, Robinson also recounted the familiar tale of Japanese sexual depravity:

> Tokyo has bars where businessmen don nappies and are spanked by other figures. Vending machines sell schoolgirls' used underwear. At live sex shows the audience are issued with Polaroid cameras to snap close-ups of women's genitalia.

Nightclubs with male strippers, however, evidently required further explanation:

> In Britain, male strippers are an old story. In modern Japan, often described as an "economic giant and a social pygmy", where female sex-uality is still subordinate to male need, something else is at work.

It is this contrast between enlightened Britain and benighted Japan that is really the point of such articles.

Hugo Gurdon, writing about Japan's low birth-rate, explained that: 'For Japanese women, marriage and child-rearing mean a lost career, less money, more housework, an unhelpful husband and absentee children.' (*Telegraph*, 2 December 1994) This picture can hardly be unfamiliar to the experience of British readers. Yet the effect of such articles is to suggest that Japan is inferior to the West in the matter of attitudes towards women. A *Guardian* article (taken from the *New York Times*) put the point more explicitly: 'Kayo Enomoto, a 23-year-old travel agent who spent a year in the United States, wonders how she will find an acceptable husband in Japan.' (10 July 1995) A passing *cause célèbre* for the British press in summer 1995 was the case of Helen Bamber, a dealer for a Japanese financial firm in the City of London, who took her former employer to court claiming unfair dismissal on the grounds of sex discrimination. 'Japanese sex bias forced me out, says City dealer' was the *Telegraph's* headline (3 August 1995); "'Japanese firm didn't promote me because I was not servile enough'" reported the *Mail* (4 August 1995). Whatever the merits of Bamber's case, it is not difficult to see why British newspapers should have relished reporting it a few days before the fiftieth anniversary of Hiroshima: it provided evidence of British moral superiority over the Japanese.

This story was followed up by Peter Popham in the *Independent* (12 April 1996), shortly after Helen Bamber had won her case, and £100,000 from her former employer. 'Is sexism an Asian value?', asked Popham rhetorically. The answer, of course, was 'yes'. With graphics of the Rising Sun and the Union Jack, the article contrasted two profiles of a Japanese woman and her British counterpart. Each ended with an assessment of the woman's prospects: 'Good' in the British case; 'None' for the Japanese. The argument was supported with statistics concerning the percentage of the female population of both countries either working or available for work: around 50% for Japan, but over 70% in Britain. Before jumping to conclusions, however, we might do well to recall that a 1995 United Nations survey on sexual equality placed Britain thirteenth in a table of 130 countries.[10] Japan was eighth. This does not mean Popham's argument is entirely without foundation: the UN survey did reveal that Britain ranked higher than Japan in terms of women's participation in politics and business (nineteenth and twenty-seventh places respectively). Yet this hardly seems a sound basis on which to suggest that sexism is an 'Asian value'; an alien concept which Japanese employers are importing into Britain.

Deceptive Appearances

The hostility toward Japan which leads to the application of a double standard of judgement is also expressed through another recurring theme in the coverage of Japan: that of deceptive appearances. The theme is present in many areas of reporting, and extends from the trivial to the more serious. The *Guardian*, for example, ran a feature on the British photographic artist Paul Graham, whose work was said to 'juxtapose the candy-coated surfaces of modern life [in Japan] and the realities they mask'. The significance of the article derived from its timing. Published on 18 August 1995, in the week leading up to the VJ-Day anniversary, it fed into a broader media debate (discussed in more detail below) about Japanese 'amnesia' regarding the Second World War. Accordingly, the front page of the section in which the article appeared informed us: 'Paul Graham's pictures examine how Japan conceals its past.'[11]

A key area in which the theme of deceptive appearances repeatedly surfaces is in the discussion of Japanese politics. This area of reporting is one where the double standard of judgement is also often applied. Hugo Gurdon, for instance, wrote in the *Telegraph* (7 December 1994) that:

> Tokyo asks to be listened to, but refuses to talk straight. Fearful of offending, it tries to be all things to all people—for example, telling western allies it believes in universal human rights but making sympathetic noises to dictators who say suppression is excusable in developing economies.

Gurdon's chosen example of foreign policy could stand equally well in an article on Washington, Paris or London. Similarly, two days earlier, Gurdon wrote that:

> Part of Japan's malaise is that it is not a real democracy. There is a crisis of legitimacy. When voters kick out one government they get the same policies back again under the next regime. (*Telegraph*, 5 December 1994)

Again, this would be just as plausible as a description of many Western countries.

The theme of a deceptive disjuncture between appearance and reality sometimes also contains the idea that Japan is superficially modern, but remains Asian underneath. This contrast between the traditional and the modern is often pointed up by the pictures which accompany newspaper articles about Japan. For example, the illustrations to a *Sunday Times* Culture Essay on Japan by Brian Deer (7 August 1994) were captioned:

> A nation of contrasts: Tokyo woe [for commuters]...and the remnants of a more tranquil way of life.

> Ancient and modern: old values survive alongside cutting-edge technology.

This points to a key organising idea in the reporting of Japanese politics: appearances are deceptive in Japan because beneath the veneer of Western -style modernity lies a society which is fundamentally Asian and traditional.[12] Discussing Japanese politics in the article, Deer commented that:

> In this culture...Western logic simply does not apply....Here, where "yes" and "no" can mean the same thing, or sometimes mean nothing at all, nobody takes it for granted that things are truly the way they appear. The political system is perhaps the best example of perceptual illusion.

Since most British newspapers give very little coverage to Japanese politics—and even less of any depth—the overall impression likely to be formed by any reader is that politics in Japan are unfathomable in any case. This is only reinforced, and British newspapers themselves excused for their poor coverage, by the repeated assertion that Japanese politics are 'not what they seem'. A similar discussion of deception impinges on the reporting of Japanese economics, to which we now turn.

Economics Coverage

Economics coverage tends to be more objective and neutral. This is especially true of more straightforward factual reporting; written with investors in mind, items on companies and industry trends have to try to give an unbiased opinion. The *Financial Times* provides the most comprehensive coverage, giving a full news page devoted to Asia-Pacific and World Trade stories, with further reports in the second section of the paper covering companies and markets. The paper reports the trading results of major Japanese companies, the movements of the Tokyo money and stock markets, with reports and analysis on the economic trends and performance. The other British broadsheets cover the Japanese economy less extensively. However, economic stories appear in the main pages of the broadsheets quite frequently.[13] Typically written by the paper's main Tokyo correspondent, rather than a specialist economics or business writer, issues covered during the period of our study included: trade barriers and the ongoing bilateral trade negotiations between Japan, the USA and the European Union; and recent company performance, with an emphasis on household names in the electronic and automobile sectors. The Tokyo correspondents also write occasional features on Japanese business practice.

The main business story of 1995, the parlous state of the Japanese economy, shows how commentators attempted to explain the underlying problems. In one week in July 1995, for example, the *Financial Times* reported 'further evidence of the weakness of Japan's economy'. There was 'an air of gloom surrounding the Tokyo stock market' (15/16 July 1995). Though the paper reported a continuing moderate economic recovery, many companies were struggling. Toyota warned that it might have to 'close plant in response to a decline in exports caused by the high Yen and the weak domestic demand due to economic stagnation' (19 July 1995). Sony was to move some functions abroad to trim costs in response to the Yen's rise. The strong Yen was also hitting the mining industry, and the *Financial Times* quoted a group of mining associations to the effect that: 'domestic mines and smelters are being turned into ruins.' (18 July 1995) The property market was also in trouble: Aoki faced massive debts because of 'property projects abandoned after the late 1980s economic bubble burst' (21 July 1995). Rather than stopping there, coverage noted that many economic indicators suggested underlying economic strength: a strong currency, a large current account surplus and low unemployment by contemporary Western standards.

This kind of reporting of Japan's current economic difficulties is broadly objective and presents views shared by Japanese economists, civil servants and industrialists. However, when reporting the underlying reasons for the performance of the Japanese economy, the coverage reflects more fundamental differences about understanding Japan and also a lack of clarity on economics itself. This introduces an element of confusion and contradiction into commentaries. For example, in a leader of 17 April 1995 the *Times* explained the apparent paradox between a strong underlying economy and economic problems, noting that:

> …the strong Yen has undermined domestic production and investment. But Japan's trade barriers have prevented the strong currency drawing in enough imports and producing a new trade equilibrium with which both Japanese industries and their foreign competitors could have lived. Instead, the interaction of free currency trading and Japan's regulatory protectionism has produced a doomsday machine.

The *Times* went on to argue that 'Japan must realise that a "strong" currency is not necessarily a symbol of a strong economy and certainly does not confer economic power'.

Here, the *Times* writer shows that the economic causes of Japan's problems are unclear. The strong Yen is the *result* of a highly productive economy (as Britain's successive devaluations have been the result of a weak economy). That the economy has not continued in its dynamism and has moved into the recessionary phase of the business cycle, at the same time shouldering US debt, is not caused by the high Yen. For years Japanese companies were able to invest in new technologies, making their products cheaper and more competitive, and an appreciating Yen was largely irrelevant to their trade both nationally and internationally. Once the economics point is clouded the writer's prejudices come into play: the lack of free trade becomes the problem for Japan, and a doomsday scenario is extrapolated.

Writing in the *Economist* (13 July 1996), Brian Beedham expressed his frustration with the baggage that many brought to the discussion of Japan:

The trouble with writing about Japan these days is that so many other people are doing it, too, and they could be writing about utterly different countries. On the one side beam the optimists who say that by around 2010 Japan will in its politics, its economics and its foreign policy be much the same sort of place as the democracies of Europe and America. On the other side glowers a band of conspiracy theorists who think that a fundamentally non-Western Japan is privately pursuing its own agenda, and some who even seem to believe that any apparent evidence to the contrary (such as the only-just-ended four years of near-zero economic growth) is an ingenious piece of Japanese theatre designed to deceive the onlooker.

Beedham expresses his view of the debate between those ('modernisation theorists') who argue that Japan is converging towards—if it has not actually arrived at—Western (European and American) economic and political models; and those ('revisionists') who argue that there is a distinctive and different economic and political system in Japan.[14] These differing and contrasting views, though rarely explicitly acknowledged, underpin much of the broader economic coverage.

For the modernisation theorists, the recession of the early 1990s is welcome evidence that Japan is experiencing similar economic problems to Western states. It is evidence that if the Japanese had an alternative way of managing the economy (a view many would in any case dispute) then this is no longer successful. Market forces, and increasing foreign competition, will force Japan to restructure the economy and reorganise the labour market (ending, for example, 'jobs for life'). Take, for instance, a report by James Cox for *The World at One* (BBC Radio 4, 21 August 1994). He commented:

> Japan, the industrial giant; Japan, the maker of the machines that make the world go round; Japan which, in Western demonology at any rate, copies other people's products and makes them better, faster and cheaper. This is the production line at Strapak, Japan's biggest exporter of packing machinery—but there's a problem. Strapak's biggest machine costs one million Yen; an exact copy made in Taiwan retails for 400,000 Yen. The Japanese are being trumped at their own game.

Putting to one side the slightly gloating tone in which Strapak's problem is discussed, the message is clear. The world has caught up with Japan, and the country no longer has any secret formulae to make products 'better, cheaper and faster'.

This proposition is central to the modernisation theorists' argument: Japan does not do things differently. Instead, it is the Japanese themselves who invent the idea that they are different. Writing in the *Financial Times* (12/13 August 1995), Bethan Hutton argued:

> The Japanese have an entrenched belief in their own uniqueness. This has been used to justify barriers against imported skis (Japanese snow is different), imported beef (Japanese stomachs are different), and imported ideas (Japanese brains are different). Most imported investment theories have met the same fate—because, of course, the Japanese stock market is different. But for once, even non-Japanese agree there could be some truth in the assertion.

Though willing to concede that the Japanese stock market might just be different, Bethan Hutton, like most *Financial Times* writers, takes a 'modernisation' position. She finished this piece by concluding that 'gradually the Japanese stock market is growing up to be not so very different from the rest'. The *Financial Times* and the *Economist* (polemically so) are on the modernisation side of the debate, reflecting their free market approach. It should also be noted that the tendency for most newspapers to downplay differences on the economics pages has been more developed since the slowdown of the Japanese economy: it is comforting, for commentators in a dour British economy, to believe that Japan is little better off.

By contrast, the revisionists proclaim that the Japanese economic system does have significant differences and that these continue to have an effect. The growth of revisionist thinking on Japan is immediately apparent from a visit to the business section of any bookshop. Often a whole shelf is devoted to books explaining Japanese business methods or extolling the Japanese approach to business and economic management. Academic revisionist writers have characterised the Japanese system as 'competitive communism' or 'communism with beauty spots'. Such ideas are reflected in the more thematic journalistic writing on Japanese economics which shades into a discussion of Japanese cultural difference.

As this suggests, even in reporting business and economics, media coverage of Japan is influenced by underlying assumptions about the nature of Japanese society and Japanese cultural difference. The *Times*, in an anonymous opinion page article (21 July 1995), for example, found that Japanese cultural difference accounted for both past economic success and present problems in the financial sector:

> It is what Polonius might have called comical-historical-tragical, the

tragedy of a virtuous race. The very qualities which have made the Japanese uniquely effective producers—long-headed, consensus seeking hard work—also seem to disqualify the Japanese in the hair-trigger and rather nasty world of financial speculation.

This *Times* piece also argued that Japan has difficulties in emulating and joining the West:

> They might find it very hard to be more like us, and many of them don't want to be. For the moment they can blame Matsushita [head of the Bank of Japan]; but, as they discover that it will take much more than a new banker to solve their problems, they may be tempted to return to the isolation which is the real Japanese tradition.

As with Hutton, this article also sees cultural difference as existing largely in the eyes of the Japanese themselves, but clearly assumes that Japan is fundamentally different.

Anatole Kaletsky in the *Times* (13 April 1995), uses the economic problems in Japan to gloat, indulge in his private fantasy and explain how the Japanese have still not shaken off their cultural legacy:

> Tomorrow, the Japanese Government will announce its fifth massive package in five years to stimulate the economy, support the Tokyo stock market and stabilise the Yen. If the package fails, then Japan will be facing a national disaster that will make the Kobe earthquake look like a minor hiccup for all its tragic human cost. Failure would open up the real possibility of the second most powerful nation on earth—and one whose history has been notable for sudden outbreaks of extremism, barbarism and chauvinist violence—experiencing a 1930s-style economic crash and a political breakdown exemplified by this week's election of two bawdy comedians to run the cities in Osaka and Tokyo.

Whilst routine reporting of the Japanese economy is usually objective,[15] uncertainty about underlying economic dynamics allows room for journalists to voice their own prejudices about the nature of the Japanese. Such coverage tends to reflect the wider academic debate between modernisation theorists and revisionists, though with a greater prominence given to the free-market, modernisation position. The best economics reporting shows that journalists can make coverage of Japan interesting, informative and objective. When these reporters start to pose questions about the nature of Japanese capitalism or its long term prospects they usually begin to suffer from explanation by difference, or from free-market dogma.[16]

Race and Culture

As we have seen, British journalists seem to spend much of their time laughing at the Japanese. Sometimes it is Japanese customs which are ridiculed, as in Hugo Gurdon's commentary on the etiquette of handkerchief use in Japan: 'never blow your nose on a handkerchief but snort, hawk horribly and spit in public or else sniff until you can blow your nose on a disposable tissue in private.' (*Sunday Telegraph*, 11 December 1994) In other articles, the humour is more barbed. In another story of Japanese big-spending, for instance, the *Daily Mail* (25 July 1995) told of Japanese visitors to London attempting to buy 'Svelte', a Christian Dior body cream, in bulk. The article began by poking fun at the Japanese because they are short, and sound funny when they speak English:

> It was a tough word to handle because it had an "l" in it. The Japanese woman, a little doll about the size of a doorstop, took her shot and the doorman at Harrods had to listen hard. He didn't think he was hearing much.
> "Svet", the woman said. After that it was like "Svat". The woman reached in a handbag and took out a piece she had cut from a Tokyo magazine. She reached up so it dangled in front of the doorman's eyes.
> "Ah, Svelte", he said...

While it would appear that laughing at the Japanese for being 'culturally different' is acceptable, the explicit mention of racial difference is generally taboo. A BBC Radio Newcastle presenter, Kevin Rowntree, for example, who referred to the Japanese as 'our little yellow friends', provoked outrage from his listeners and employers in what the *Newcastle Journal* described as a 'race row' (6 February 1995). However, as argued elsewhere in this volume, the discourse of cultural difference provides a way to voice the prejudices of racial thinking in a more acceptable fashion. As might be expected, therefore, there are moments when the implication of racial difference rises to the surface in discussions of 'culture', in subtle but discernible ways.

Martin Jacques, writing in the *Sunday Times*, for instance, thought that he could distinguish 'which cultural characteristics are genetic, and thereby enduring, and those which are essentially contingent and developmental' (13 November 1994). His argument was that the Westernised aspects of Japan were relatively superficial, while certain other features were 'cultural genes'. The latter category included some familiar ideas about Japanese society: 'In the relationship between group and individual, the emphasis on education, the place of the family and the nature of the political system, Japan differs markedly from the West.' Jacques's choice of a genetic metaphor to describe cultural difference is suggestive of the close relationship between ideas of cultural difference, and those of biological, racial difference. The notion of 'cultural genes' illustrates well the way in which cultural differences are seen as being just as fixed, innate and unchanging as natural or racial differences.

The theme of the superficiality of Japan's Westernisation was taken up by several writers in trying to explain the Japanese reaction to the Kobe earthquake in January 1995. The reporting of the disaster was poor enough to be remarked on at the time. A 'Quake Watch' column in *Private Eye* (27 January 1995), for instance, ridiculed the press' double standards:

> Foreigners' lives, as every news editor knows, are far less valuable than those of Britons....The tone was set by the Press Association news agency, which put out the following story within hours of the quake: "A teenage British model was thrown out of bed by the tremor which tore through Japan today and had to flee her apartment in her night-dress....The British embassy in Tokyo...said early indications were 'reassuring'." Not so reassuring for the thousands of dead Japanese, of course—but who cares about them?

Similarly, Brandon Robshaw, writing in the *Guardian*, found a 'festival of *schadenfreude*' in the British press (1 February 1995). This took many forms, from gloating over the projected economic repercussions for Kobe, through criticism of the slow official response to disaster relief, to glee over Japan's punctured pride in its technological sophistication. Robshaw also discovered double standards of judgement: 'Of course, Japan is not Utopia. Nowhere is, by definition. But Japan is certainly no further from Utopia than this country.' Comparing the coverage of Kobe with that of the earthquakes in Armenia and San Francisco in the 1980s, he found that: 'the disaster is being used as an opportunity to score points over them. It's almost as though an Asian country has no business being a First World country.'[17]

This was really the most salient point: Kobe provided the British press with an opportunity to emphasise Japanese difference, and the superficiality of its modernity. For John Casey (who professed to 'love Japan and the Japanese'), writing a comment piece in the *Evening Standard*, Japanese stoicism was a puzzle to be explained:

> Perhaps we are finding it harder to understand this aspect of the Japanese just because we are becoming hyper-emotional ourselves. But it is also true that the Japanese psyche is not easy for Westerners to comprehend....When you first arrive in Japan you feel at home—because it is so Westernised....Yet you soon feel that you are in an extraordinarily strange and foreign country. The strangeness is partly in the way Japanese have both assimilated, and not always quite understood, foreign culture.... The first thing to remember in Japan is that things are usually not what they seem. (18 January 1995)

In the *Financial Times*, William Dawkins found the explanation for the apparently stoical attitude of many Japanese in religion:

> It is no accident that Japan's main creed, Shintoism, is devoted to the worship and appeasement of natural phenomena. This keeps alive the traditions of an agricultural race, long accustomed to the feeling that their livelihoods, and even lives, are in the hands of the elements. (21-22 January 1995)

In effect, it is being suggested here that the world's most technologically-advanced society has to be understood in terms of the pantheism of ancient peasant communities. It was left to the *Independent's* Peter Popham, however, to draw out the implications of this argument:

> Just as the earthquake itself strips away Japan's Western veneer, revealing its Asian core and leaving it with the sort of massive death toll one would expect in a city of the Third World, so the prospect of a fatal quake exposes the unchanged, Asian contours of the Japanese soul. (18 January 1995)

This goes to the heart of the matter, spelling out the idea that, however modern and Western it might appear, Japan 'really' has an 'unchanging' Asian soul. Inherent 'cultural' difference thus shades into a suggestion of racial difference: it is Japan's 'Asian-ness' which is held to be key. Furthermore, this difference is implicitly seen as inferiority: a point underlined here by the Third World comparison in the *Telegraph* (28 November 1994), made by Hugo Gordon :

> Appearance offers no clue about the facts. In Japan, what you see is not what you get. The supremacy of presentation over reality is apparent everywhere and the Japanese don't try to hide it—they are proud of it.

But the consequences are not confined to trivia. They extend to the core of society. For instance, Japan has all the appearance of a democracy but few if any of the things which make it real, like responsible and representative government. Tokyo hates comparisons with repressive or backward countries, but they are unavoidable.

It might also be noted that the idea of Japanese difference as implacable because of being 'genetic' leads to the idea that Japan's exclusion from the Western club is a fault of Japan itself. As Jacques put it:

> Japan has always seen itself as the outsider at the Western teaparty, always challenging, always seeking acceptance....Japan regards the world as somebody else's, as the West's; consequently it does not take proper responsibility for its own actions, as exemplified by its mercantilist economic policies.' (*Sunday Times*, 13 November 1994)

These comments are also suggestive of the contemporary economic causes of Western hostility to Japan, a point brought to the fore by the way the article was packaged by the *Sunday Times*. The cover of the supplement in which Jacques's article appeared depicted a large Sumo squatting over a prostrate Anglo-Saxon wrestler; the latter in pain from the Sumo's armlock.[18] In the background, the stylised sun of the Japanese flag rose over Mount Fuji. The article, however, was more optimistically titled: 'Western culture defies the rising Eastern sun.' Though Japan might be triumphing over Western economies, the West was still culturally superior.

Re-fighting the War

The sentiment of hostility towards Japan, coupled with a desire to find some way to claim superiority in the face of increasingly obvious economic inferiority, found its keenest expression in the most prominent and long-running Japan story of even such an eventful year as 1995: the wartime fiftieth anniversaries. The two key anniversaries—of Hiroshima and VJ-Day—together threw into stark relief the features of Japan coverage explored above. Firstly, there was a long-running debate in the British press concerning Japan's supposed failure to apologise for the war. In the course of this discussion, many of the usual assumptions about Japanese difference were posed with greater sharpness. Secondly, the handling of the anniversary of the atomic bombing of Hiroshima helped to clarify what lay behind the apologies debate: a quest to assert British moral superiority.

The tabloid press undertook a crusade to extract an apology from Japan for the war. 'Japan must be made to apologise', proclaimed the *Daily Mail* (23 July 1995), for example. Yet the press did not initiate the campaign. In fact, the tone for the fiftieth anniversary year was set by the British government at the beginning of 1995, when it decided not to extend the same invitation to the Japanese for the Victory over Japan anniversary as it would to the German government for the Victory in Europe celebrations. The government had already attempted to push the issues of apology and recompense semi-officially itself, sending Sir Kit McMahon to Tokyo in 1994 in an effort to find supporters for Prime Minister John Major's proposed compensation fund. After this unsuccessful visit, the veterans themselves fronted the campaign for an apology, and three veterans groups from the Pacific war were invited to the government's VE/VJ press conference in January 1995.

The advantage of this approach was later unwittingly illustrated by a *Daily Express* headline: 'Say sorry to POWs, Major orders Japan.' (29 June 1995) In fact, of course, Major had done no such thing. The headline, though characteristically indicative of *Express* loyalties, served merely to point up the absurdity of the idea that a British Prime Minister could possibly be in a position to 'order' the Japanese government to do anything. Rather, having signalled the tone of the VJ-Day commemorations, and with an orchestrated programme of official events, the British government could leave the floor open to veterans and journalists to wage a campaign to assert Britain's moral superiority on their behalf. The press did not disappoint, as many papers went out of their way to espouse the cause of former prisoners of war. The *Daily Star*, for instance, in a story entitled 'An insult to heroes', juxtaposed a picture of a veteran with that of the Japanese Ambassador, with the caption:

> THIS man represents Japan. He will be an honoured guest at the VE-Day ceremonies. THIS man was tortured by the Japanese. He will not be invited to the VE-Day ceremonies. (22 January 1995)

It seemed that, as far as the *Star* was concerned, even to invite a Japanese representative to VE-Day, let alone VJ-Day, was tantamount to treachery. Though posed as criticism of the government, whose ceremonies they were, this was the sort of criticism which must have been highly acceptable, since it merely confirmed the differential tone already officially set for the two events.

This sort of reporting, though expressed more bluntly in the tabloids, actually pervaded all sections of the press. The story was considered such a big one, and had received such a long build up, that even a rumour of an apology was treated as newsworthy. 'Japan on verge of war apology', reported the *Guardian* (8 August 1995), hoping that such an apology might 'end fifty years of silence'. As noted in Chapter One, Japan had, in reality, pursued a 'diplomacy of contrition' for years prior to 1995, and Japanese politicians had apologised many times. The 'fifty years of silence' was no more than a convenient fiction. After such anticipation, real or imagined, when the apology did finally come, it made front-page news, even in 'serious' broadsheet newspapers such as the *Guardian* (12 August 1995). As might be expected, after such a long wait the apology was greeted with jubilation: 'Veterans welcome Japan's apology for prison camps', reported the *Express* (12 August 1995), describing the occasion as a 'Triumph after years of campaigning'.

This reaction was prompted by a letter from the Japanese premier, Murayama Tomiichi, to John Major. Yet it seemed the rejoicing had been premature. The 'triumph' was swiftly reinterpreted as a disappointment, as Murayama's letter was held to be merely a personal apology—despite the Foreign Office having said that 'It is usually assumed that such statements by one prime minister to another are on behalf of their country' (*Observer*, 13 August 1995). Other faults were found. According to the *Guardian* (14 August 1995), it had been an apology, but for the wrong thing: what was really required was 'an apology for going to war in the first place'.[19] As the doubts emerged about the significance of Murayama's letter, it was revealed that he had expressed no more—his 'profound remorse'—than his predecessor, Hosakawa, had in 1993. Although this made a mockery of the 'fifty years of silence' idea, nobody seemed to notice: such was the disappointment that nothing new had been said, both apologies were held to be worthless. It also emerged, incidentally, that the (non-) apology was two weeks old by the time it was released to the press. This was rather convenient timing: the British government had withheld news of the letter over the period of the Hiroshima and Nagasaki anniversaries, allowing the demands for apologies to rumble on while these more sensitive anniversaries passed.

From this point, the coverage of the apologies issue degenerated ever further into farce. The day after the jubilant front-page news of the long-anticipated apology, readers were informed: 'Sorry, that was not an apology.' (*Observer*, 13 August 1995) The following day, it was all back on again: 'Japanese premier insists he did apologise for suffering during war', reported the *Guardian*, while the *Independent* reassured: 'Japan: we really did apologise.' (14 August 1995) Yet the damage had already been done: 'VJ apology not enough say victims—Japanese told to admit atrocities', ran the *Express* report (14 August 1995). The next day, on 15 August, Murayama reiterated his apology, but it was doomed before he even uttered it. In a future-tense article on what Murayama was 'expected' to do, the *Guardian* seemed already to have pre-judged the outcome: 'Japanese PM fights shy of full apology.' (15 August 1995) Quite how the *Guardian* could know Murayama would 'fight shy of a full apology' in advance of hearing it remains a mystery, but the paper showed remarkable foresight in anticipating how the 'non-apology' would be received. On the following day, the *Daily Express*, under the headline 'He still won't go far enough', dismissed the reiterated apology as merely personal, despite reporting that the Japanese ambassador had stressed the statement had been made by the whole Japanese government and approved by the cabinet (16 August 1995). Some newspapers attempted to shed light on this confusion by seeking broader explanations. The *Sun* informed its readership that: 'There are 20 ways to say sorry in Japanese. We only want them to say one.' (14 August 1995) The paper even went to the trouble of specifying exactly which word was required. Yet, despite such helpful attempts at clarification, still a contradictory picture emerged. On the same day, the *Sun's* rival, the *Daily Mirror,* offered a contrary explanation for the communication breakdown: 'There is no such word as apology in the Japanese language.'

If the British press, for the most part unintentionally, struck a note of high comedy in relation to the apologies issue, coverage of the anniversary of Hiroshima was serious both in tone and in its implications. In browbeating the Japanese over their supposed failure to apologise, yet at the same time refusing to countenance the idea that the West might have anything to apologise for on the fiftieth anniversary of the bombing of Hiroshima, British politicians and journalists applied a familiar double standard.[20] Failure to apologise for Hiroshima in the present amounted to an assertion that it had been right in the past, and that similar action could be countenanced in the future. Most British journalists uncritically repeated the claim made by President Truman in 1945, that the world's first atomic bombs had been dropped on Japan in order to save lives.[21] In some cases, this was an unproblematic assertion. For the *Daily Express* (editorial, 7 August 1995), it was a simple question. Truman had made a 'brave decision', causing 'devastation in a just cause'. The *Express* also avoided any moral questioning by arguing that we should not forget 'Japan's own role in launching the nuclear age', as if Japan not only bore responsibility for its own destruction, but was implicated in the Cold War as well.

For others, deploring the destruction of Hiroshima was merely the prelude to justifying it by celebrating the fifty years of peace which it supposedly made possible. In the *Independent*, Simon Jenkins found a 'perverse reason to be grateful':

> Perhaps the peace of the world did require two cities to die. Perhaps Hiroshima did forestall a greater holocaust. (2 August 1995)

Such an argument was mere sophistry: the death of two cities (a polite way of saying the death of the people who lived in them) was justified by reference to a mythical 'greater holocaust' of the author's own imagining. However, among those beset by ethical scruples, Peregrine Hodson, writing in the *Times* (5 August 1995), exemplified the most common tactic for justifying the bomb: he relativised it. Hodson worried that 'the bombings of Hiroshima and Nagasaki were actions fraught with moral ambiguity'. Yet:

> ...certain events remain unquestionably evil: among them, the Final Solution, the Rape of Nanking, the inhuman torture of prisoners of war and the barbarous oppression of civilians in countries occupied by the Japanese Army.

The most that can be said of Hiroshima is that it had a certain 'ambiguity'; but the Rape of Nanking or the Japanese treatment of POWs can be described with confidence as 'unquestionably evil'. Similarly, Richard Lloyd Parry, in the *Independent on Sunday* (6 August 1995), reported: 'A-bomb destroyed a city founded on militarism.' The article was a serious attempt to question the exploitation of Japan's pacifist image by contemporary politicians, yet it was a strange way to mark the anniversary of the destruction of Hiroshima. For a British readership, the significance of Hiroshima could only be diminished by informing them, as Lloyd Parry did, that: 'Troops from here were active in the Rape of Nanking.'

Not only were British readers frequently reminded of Japan's wartime record, but the scale and importance of Japanese wartime atrocities were often grossly inflated. The comments of Peregrine Hodson, quoted above, implicitly put Japan's actions on a par with the Nazi Holocaust. The *Guardian* employed a similar approach when it asserted that: 'The ferocity of the Japanese army outstripped even that of Hitler's SS troops.' (8 August 1995) Such exaggerated treatment of Japan's war record, without any comparable questioning of the Allies' own wartime conduct, could only feed into the demand for apologies. 'We must never forget we are concerned with bestiality on a massive international scale', wrote the *Sun's* 'military advisor', Major-General Ken Perkins (14 August 1995):

'We are talking about apologising for one of the vilest chapters in the history of the world.' Indeed, it appeared that the more the Japanese apologised, the worse their crimes became. This was confirmed by the treatment of a personal reconciliation between a former prisoner of war, Jim Bradley, and his erstwhile prison guard, Abe Hiroshi. Bradley's visit to Japan in the summer of 1995 was filmed by Carlton Television for their *Big Story* programme (broadcast on 27 July 1995). The programme showed a moving and emotional meeting between the two men, in which Abe expressed his remorse and gratitude, and Bradley took his hand in forgiveness. Yet the *Daily Mirror* (27 July 1995), in a feature on the programme, described Bradley as only shaking hands 'reluctantly', while the narration of the programme itself continued, even after the scene of reconciliation, to use the shorthand description: 'The war criminal Abe Hiroshi.'[22]

A Japanese apology could never be sufficient, for the simple reason that apologising was not really the issue. The real issue was Western moral superiority. An apologetic attitude could only confirm the conviction that the Japanese were inferior. Today's concern to prove Britain's moral authority is the contemporary equivalent of the earlier determination, discussed in Chapter Two, to uphold 'white race authority'. The point was well-made by Ian Buruma, in a rare article questioning the campaign for apologies: 'It was the racial humiliation, the idea of a world turned upside down, more than the particular savagery, that prevents the veterans from reconciling with Japan.' (*Sunday Times,* 15 January 1995) Unfortunately in 1995 such an attitude was not confined to veterans of the Pacific War: the felt need to assert moral authority was shared by many British politicians and journalists.

Just as debates about Japanese cultural difference often take on racial undertones and provide an 'acceptable' way to discuss race in everyday reporting, so too the assertion of moral superiority in coverage of the wartime anniversaries sometimes acquired a racial dimension through an emphasis on 'cultural difference'. For the *Guardian's* Tokyo correspondent, Kevin Rafferty, for example, the Japanese were 'the people without guilt'. Rafferty explained that Japan was a shame culture, and as confirmation offered an anonymous quote from 'one Japanese': 'No, we don't feel guilt about the war—that is a Judeo-Christian concept.' (14 January 1995) The *Daily Mirror,* meanwhile, offered an alternative cultural explanation:

> ...much of Japanese culture is derived from the Busheido Code drawn up during the time of the Samurai warriors. For them to admit a mistake and say sorry was unthinkable. (14 August 1995)

While the *Mirror* reached back into history, the *Daily Mail* emphasised the contemporary relevance of Japanese 'culture', taking up the familiar themes of Japan's superficial modernity and deceptive appearances:

> Japan is a copycat society. Why is there no copying of Western ideas of shame and guilt? After all, from a business point [of view], it cannot help the Japanese to be remembered worldwide with a shudder as torturers who cut little bits off people. There is a cultural explanation for this. Japanese posturing as a modern liberal society may have gone far enough to deceive its postwar American occupiers, which was what it was designed for. But it should not deceive anyone in the West until Japan faces up to the evidence that our image of it as a country which goes in for systematic brutality has all too much truth to it. (23 July 1995)

The idea that Japan's past guilt tarnished the country in the present (*'goes in for systematic brutality'*) had been pursued by the *Mail* since January, when it had declared that Japan 'still has an awful lot to learn about basic human decency' (6 January 1995).

Perhaps the fullest synthesis of British prejudices, however, was that provided by the *Daily Telegraph's* Defence Editor, John Keegan, for whom the Japanese were 'the tribe that can't admit it was wrong':

> The real truth seems to centre on the fundamental belief that the Japanese hold about themselves, which is that they are different from all the rest of us—and not only different but superior. This is a belief common in tribal societies both small and large, and the Japanese are the largest surviving tribe in the world. It is one of their tribal customs not to admit that the tribe itself has done wrong, either in the present or the past. It would indeed be wrong to make such an admission: wrong for the tribe, wrong for the individual member. (15 June 1995)

By describing Japan as 'tribal', Keegan not only invokes the familiar idea that it must be understood as a 'group' society, but also suggests the back-wardness and inferiority of the Japanese. Keegan's real achievement, however, is to assert the superiority of the West while maintaining that it is the Japanese themselves who think they are 'different from the rest of us'. Clearly, what irritates Keegan is the idea that the Japanese will not admit their inferiority, but think they are 'superior'. In their approach to the fiftieth anniversaries of the Pacific War in 1995, British journalists expressed a similar fear of the Japanese to that which has struck at the heart of Anglo-American politicians and commentators ever since Japan's rise as an international power at the turn of the century.

Conclusion: Fear and Loathing

It is not difficult to detect the loathing for Japan in British press coverage of the country. The hostility lies just beneath the surface in discussions of cultural difference, or jokes about weirdness. When such contempt rises to the fore, however, as in the coverage of the fiftieth anniversary of VJ-Day, it is easy to lose sight of the fear which motivates this hostility. If the negative image of Japan which emerges from surveys of media coverage were confined simply to the issue of apologies for the Second World War, it might be understood as a mere historical curiosity; a hangover from the past which could be expected to disappear within a few more years. However, given that, as we have shown, the same basic assumptions underpin much of the reporting in all areas of coverage, such an explanation would be too facile—and too optimistic.

Instead, the roots of the hostility towards Japan should be sought in the present—a time when an economically powerful and politically ambitious Japan is increasingly seen by Western governments as their most dangerous rival around the world. If there was an unusual quality to the press coverage of Japan in 1995, it is that the wartime anniversaries provided a rare opportunity to recapture a 'feelgood factor'. Reflecting on the weekend of commemorations and ceremonies to mark Victory over Japan Day in August 1995, the *Guardian's* John Ezard was pleased to find: 'Now we have been given back a collective memory.' (19 August 1995) Young people were now aware of an earlier generation's sacrifice; there was something around which the whole nation could unite. For Phillippa Kennedy, writing in the *Daily Express* (23 August 1995), 'The whole weekend made you think that this is still a good country.'

A few months earlier, on the same day that the *Mail* was devoting three quarters of its editorial page to the 'enduring shame of modern Japan', the *Daily Star* ran a front-page story which illustrated how the past is used to bolster a comforting sense of British superiority in an uncertain present: 'Life in our Jap factory is like *Tenko*.' (6 January 1995)[25] The story detailed how workers at the Toyota car plant in Derby were suffering under 'a *Tenko*-style regime'. In fact, many of the conditions described—speed-ups, having to ask for a toilet break, or being telephoned at home by an employer when on sick leave—are increasingly common in British workplaces, and are far from being peculiarly Japanese. On the contrary, it is British employers who are responsible for some of the toughest working regimes. As a contemporaneous feature on 'The new slavery' in *Scotland on Sunday* revealed: 'Already tethered to their desks and computers for more hours than anyone else in Europe, British workers have now over-taken the Japanese in the amount of hours they give to their employers.' (8 January 1995) The paper reported that 16% of British employees work more than 48 hours a week—the highest proportion of any European country. With an average working week of 39.9 hours, Japan fell below the European average of 40.4 hours, while Britain had an above average 43.7 hour working week. Presumably, this lengthening of the working week is one of the reasons why Britain attracts Japanese investors. But it is evidently more comforting to imagine that deteriorating working condi-tions are the '*Tenko*-style' imposition of Japan, and to remind ourselves who won the war.

NOTES

1. This chapter is based on the results of the *Images of Japan* project undertaken by the London International Research Exchange. The project monitored British press coverage of Japan in November-December 1994, and July-August 1995; with a few exceptions, our examples are all drawn from these periods. Some examples from television and radio coverage are also used to illustrate particular points. Some material included in this chapter and in the Introduction first appeared, in a modified form, in Phil Hammond, 'Forever Enemy Aliens', *Living Marxism*, No.77, March 1995.

2. See, for example, Douglas Anthony, *Reporting Japan: British Media Attitudes Towards a Nation and a People*, Cardiff, University of Wales (Japanese Studies Centre), undated, but c.1991; and Bryan Appleyard, 'A smell-free never-never land', *Independent*, 13 April 1994. The trend is not, of course, confined to the British media. Rosemary Breger, for example, describes the 'exotic imagery' evoked in the German press (Rosemary Breger, 'The discourse on Japan in the German press', in Roger Goodman and Kirsten Refsing (eds.), *Ideology and Practice in Modern Japan*, London, Routledge, 1992). Similarly, in a survey of *Le Monde's* Japan coverage, Reinhard Drifte felt it worthy of remark that the paper refrained from the usual 'eccentric Japan' stories (Reinhard Drifte, 'Japan Through the Eyes of *Le Monde*', *Insight Japan*, December 1994, p16).

3. So much so, indeed, that one former *Times* correspondent has made an entire book out of such tales of strangeness: Joe Joseph, *The Japanese: Strange but not Strangers*, London, Viking, 1993.

4. The evidence Pitman presented did not really seem to warrant this claim: the 'utter difference' in the industry was simply that in Japan two big advertising companies dominate the market; the 'radically different' creative thinking just meant that Japanese ads are often obscure and prefer to work through ambience and mood rather than straightforward product branding.

5. BBC TV News found a metaphor for Japanese society on the other side of the legal divide. In an 'exclusive' report on human rights in Japanese prisons the BBC's correspondent reported that: 'They're regimented, but they are at least safe. Unlike many prisons in the West, violence among inmates is rare. In that sense Japan's prisons reflect society as a whole: fewer rights than in the West, but more security.' (BBC News 9pm, 11 September 1995)

6. Ironically, the Japanese enthusiasm for British culture seemed only to be matched, in 1995, by British xenophobia: the *Daily Telegraph* reported that, unlike the previous summer, as the fiftieth anniversary of VJ-Day approached the National Trust was having difficulty finding British volunteers to join Japanese participants in conservation work (29 July 1995).

7. Other examples included a *Guardian* report about enthusiasm for the Brontës in Japan: 'the sisters are so popular that signposts in Haworth carry Japanese directions' (7 December 1994); and the *Independent's* report that 'The Japanese are more devoted to [Thomas] Hardy than we are' (12 April 1995). Another story, about the popularity of the British children's character Paddington Bear among Japanese television viewers, quoted the managing director of a TV distribution company who thought Anglo-American animation possessed a 'magic' which 'transcends language and race'. The chairman of the company who had made the deal over distribution of Paddington Bear had a similar faith in the superiority of Western cultural products.

He felt the character's popularity was due to 'a reaction against the kind of Manga cartoons they have in Japan. There is a shortage of good wholesome programming'. Yet a spokesperson for the BBC felt that the Corporation's impending export of another children's favourite, Noddy, would be successful because of shared racial characteristics: 'The Japanese like him [Noddy] because of the way his eyes slant down. They think he looks a bit Japanese.' (*Guardian*, 6 May 1994)

8. See, for example, *Observer*, 4 December 1994; and *Times*, 3 December 1994.

9. Robinson herself acknowledged that 'The idiom of the child is one of the most overworked code words in the lexicon of Japan-watchers, according to the American historian and essayist John Dower', but she pressed on regardless.

10. Reported in the *Guardian*, 18 August 1995.

11. This was evidently a presentation which reflected Graham's own views. The article took the form of an interview, in which he said: 'many young Japanese are unaware of what their history *is* exactly, so successful has the wrapping been.The central problem is that Japan cannot face the past squarely for fear of risking faith in the present. That is the key to their apparent amnesia.' (*Guardian*, 18 August 1995)

12. This is a long-standing feature of the Western view of Japan. As indicated in the introduction, it can be found in Second World War propaganda, and, as discussed in chapter two, the idea can be traced back even further, to the modernisation of Japanese society in the latter part of the nineteenth century. Though it has taken on a different emphasis and significance in different periods, the persistence of the traditional/modern contrast expresses the Western conviction that Japan, as a non-white power, cannot be part of the club of élite nations: though it 'looks' modern and Western, it is 'really' traditional and Asian.

13. For example, 19 stories in the *Daily Telegraph*, and 15 stories in the Guardian in a four week period at the end of 1994.

14. See chapter one for a further discussion of these two schools of thought.

15. Rosemary Breger found that, contrary to her expectations, conservative German newspapers monitored between 1980-85 tended to present a more positive image of Japan than the liberal press. The explanation, she suggests, is that the conservative papers tended to carry more business and economic coverage which, in the context of the 'learn-from-Japan boom', was more favourably disposed towards Japan. See Breger, op. cit., p181.

16. The longer term trend which will colour the view of Japan, not covered in the period of our research, will be the shifts in international relations between Western support for China or for Japan.

17. The same kind of gloating resurfaced in relation to a hijacking incident in June 1995. A *Guardian* report (22 June 1995) on the hijacking, for example, was titled: 'World's "safest" country gets that sinking feeling.' Tokyo correspondent Kevin Rafferty reported people asking 'questions echoed by many...Japanese who have prided themselves on not being like other countries, but more "civilised" and civil to each other'. Kobe, the Aum cult's sarin gas attack, and the hijacking, he suggested, 'combine to teach Japan the painful lesson that all the riches in the world will not buy safety...'. Rafferty then went on to discuss how Japan now faced economic problems as well.

18. The theme of this illustration is quite a common one. An *Independent* article on Japan, for example, used a cartoon of a diminutive John Bull and Uncle Sam, clinging to each other and quaking in trepidation at the approach of a large Sumo wrestler (13 April 1994). Such images are reminiscent of earlier depictions of Japan as a threat, discussed in chapter two, in which a giant Buddha substituted for today's burly Sumo.

19. Ironically, just a few months earlier the *Guardian* had itself reported the Japanese Foreign Ministry's official apology for Pearl Harbour (22 November 1994).

20. Perhaps the most forceful expression of this was that of the Archdeacon of York, who, on the anniversary of Hiroshima, echoed the racial double standards of wartime propaganda when he commented on GMTV: 'In Germany we were fighting the Nazis. In Japan we were fighting an entire nation conditioned by militarism.' (GMTV, 6 August 1995)

21. There were, however, exceptions to the general trend: some comment articles questioned the received history of Hiroshima, while others were critical of the crusade for apologies and accompanying Japan-bashing. See: Gar Alperovitz, 'Hiroshima: Truman's deceit', *Sunday Times*, 30 July 1995; Sarmlia Bose, 'Enough guilt for everyone', *Spectator*, 19 August 1995; Ian Buruma, 'Why we find it so hard to forgive Japan', *Sunday Times*, 15 January 1995; John Casey, 'Now the dust has settled...Hiroshima *was* a war crime', *Telegraph*, 27 July 1995; Noam Chomsky, 'Guilt of war belongs to all', *Observer*, 30 July 1995; Ian Katz, 'Let's call it slap-a-Jap week', *Spectator*, 5 August 1995; Scott Lucas and Richard Hope, 'Still hated after all these years', *Guardian*, 19 August 1995; Peter Popham, 'Why the Bomb did not win the War', *Independent*, 7 August 1995; Richard Tames and Richard Woolfenden, 'Suffering and recovery', *Times Education Supplement*, 18 August 1995; and Ed Vulliamy, 'US refuses to face Hiroshima facts', *Observer*, 5 February 1995. The BBC also made a documentary about Hiroshima (*Hiroshima: The Decision to Drop the Bomb*, 6 August 1995), which questioned the official justification for the bomb enough to provoke an outraged response from the Conservative Party's Media Monitoring Unit (see: *Times* Letters, 4 August 1995; and Julian Lewis, 'The bomb and bias at the BBC', *Express*, 8 August 1995).

22. The *Mirror* also ran two other features on the story, the initial 27 July article having been on the day of the programme's screening. In the first of these later pieces the caption to a picture of the handshake read: 'Hand of peace: Jim Bradley cannot bring himself to hate Abe Hiroshi, the camp commandant.' (11 August 1995) This was when Murayama's apology was eagerly expected. Yet in the second article, after the fiasco over whether Murayama's words really had been an apology, the *Mirror's* reading of the reconciliation changed. The caption now read: 'Forgiving: British POW Jim Bradley's handshake last month with ex-camp commandant Abe Hiroshi—but it's not enough.' (14 August 1995)

23. *Tenko* was the title of a BBC drama series about life in a Japanese prisoner of war camp for women.

5 THE IMAGE MAKERS: BRITISH JOURNALISTS ON JAPAN

Tessa Mayes and Megan Rowling[1]

...one tends to look at the question of British perceptions of Japan through the prism of, first, the *Economist* and the *Financial Times* and, second, the BBC and the other broadsheet newspapers, and then the tabloid papers. From this one is apt to conclude that there remains a wide divide between the perceptions at the high policy level and the lingering stereotypes and apathies at the popular level. (Minister Numata Sadaaki, 'Projecting Japan Abroad: A Practitioner's View', lecture presented to The Japan Society, 21 March, 1995)

erceptions of Japan among Britons vary according to the education and experience of the individual. The view held by a young business executive dealing with exports to the Japanese market will differ from that of a war veteran who fought the Japanese in Burma, or that of a child brought up on a diet of Japanese computer games and *anime* (cartoons). As Minister Numata pointed out in the lecture quoted above, varying perceptions of Japan are reflected in the British press too. Clearly, a newspaper with an international business readership, such as the *Financial Times*, will exhibit a more sophisticated attitude towards Japan than will a tabloid such as the *Sun*. The question raised by his remarks, however, is whether the images of Japan to be found in the national press are really just a reflection of British opinion on Japan. In this chapter we work from the slightly different premise that the relationship between newspapers' and readers' perceptions of Japan is symbiotic: newspapers inform readers' perceptions as well as reflect them. In a society such as Britain, where there are few sources of information on Japan, it can be argued that material on Japan in the national press exerts a significant influence on public perceptions of the country. Therefore, those who write and edit that material play an important role in shaping the way in which Britons perceive Japan. An analysis of images of Japan in the British press would not be complete without presenting the views of journalists who create them—the image makers.

This chapter looks at the work of foreign correspondents based in Tokyo who cover Japan for the British national press and London-based foreign and financial editors. Based on interviews with a selection of journalists, it aims to provide insight into their situation and attitudes towards their work.[2] The previous chapter argues that the British press has a tendency to portray the Japanese as culturally different, often relying on this angle for the 'newsworthiness' of a story. Here, we aim to build on those conclusions by presenting the results of interviews in which we questioned Tokyo-based reporters and London-based editors about coverage of Japan. First we look at how journalists identify the problems affecting coverage and show that their opinions differ. We then go on to examine their perceptions of the practical difficulties of reporting on Japan, and argue that these are less restrictive than is commonly believed. More negative for coverage, as we aim to show, is the influence of domestic news agendas which rate Japan as 'newsworthy' only when a disaster or sensational event occurs, or when a story highlights the supposed strangeness of Japan as compared with the West. This chapter demonstrates how some journalists attribute this to editorial ignorance about Japan, and others to the nature of the Japanese who, they argue, regard themselves as unique and incomprehensible to Westerners. We point out, however, that not all journalists believe that Japan is so radically different and look at economics reporting which is often said to treat Japan more objectively than other types of coverage. Finally, we present the negative and positive views of journalists on the outlook for future coverage, and argue that the industry must develop more useful ways of approaching Japan if reporting is to improve.

Problems Affecting Coverage—Practical or Editorial?

Criticism of coverage of Japan is often levelled at the correspondents themselves. In a study entitled *Reporting Japan: British Media Attitudes Towards a Nation and a People* (1991), Douglas Anthony, Professor of Japanese Studies at the University of Wales, points out the incredible fact that 'resident correspondents have, in most cases, little or no systematic study of Japan in their educational backgrounds, little command of Japanese, little time, little opportunity to travel outside central Tokyo, little help, etc.'[3] He comments that these practical difficulties 'when allied to more general factors within the news industry, may produce both an inadequate quantity of reporting on Japan, and at the same time, a disappointing standard of reporting'.[4] Our research suggests, however, that although practical difficulties are often cited as the main reason for unsatisfactory coverage, UK domestic editorial and cultural agendas outweigh practical difficulties as a negative influence on what we read about Japan. After all, foreign reporters everywhere face practical problems, and most expect to overcome them. An obstacle not easily surmounted, however, is an editor's view of what readers want and expect of coverage on a particular country. This chapter argues that the tendency to report Japan in terms of its difference from the West, discussed in the previous chapter, can be largely attributed to editorial perceptions of what journalism on Japan should be. There are, of course, some reporters who share the views of their editors. But the interviews we conducted highlighted a considerable rift between reporters and editors over how Japan should be portrayed in the national press.

It could, in fact, be argued that the technical difficulties referred to by Professor Anthony now exert less influence on the work of Tokyo-based correspondents. All journalists working for British quality newspapers in Japan today are able to speak some Japanese, and the majority have studied or worked in Japan before arriving at their present job. Ironically, the increase in correspondents who have significant experience of Japan may be attributed to cutbacks made by the British press in Japan. Over the last four years, the recession in the newspaper industry has forced the British broadsheets (excluding the *Financial Times*) to downgrade the status of their journalists in Japan from 'correspondent' to 'super-stringer'. Super-stringers are paid a retainer as well as fees for articles used, but they are not fully-fledged members of a newspaper's staff, unlike correspondents. They do not receive additional living expenses and often need to supplement their income with other work. Without the traditional expatriate package, the job now seems to attract journalists who specialise in Japan, rather than foreign reporters who are merely curious about the place.

The journalists working as super-stringers for British newspapers in Japan in 1995-96 all stressed to us that their professional motivation was a genuine and on-going interest in the country and its people. Richard Lloyd Parry, super-stringer for the *Independent* in Tokyo, explained: 'The correspondents who I mix with out here...are here because they want to be here, because they love Japan, know the country and have a sophisticated understanding.' This would seem to be confirmed by the fact that some correspondents have published books about Japan: Lloyd Parry himself, for example, wrote a travel guide on Japan; Peregrine Hodson, super-stringer for the *Times*, wrote on his experiences as a banker in Tokyo; and the *Guardian's* super-stringer, Kevin Rafferty, wrote a behind-the-scenes analysis of Japan's great corporations.[5] Writing a book does not in itself prove that a journalist has a sophisticated understanding of Japan, but it indicates that the author has an on going interest in the country and a desire to communicate what he or she knows to the general public. For some journalists, the pages of a book offer the freedom to set down in print views and information on Japan which they cannot adequately express in their journalism. In the preface to his book, Kevin Rafferty makes a point of recording his frustration with the British press' handling of Japan:

> To my regret and continuing puzzlement, British coverage of East Asia and particularly Japan remains meagre....The emphasis on the crash-bang-wallop and the weird creates gaps in our understanding of the Japanese, which is surely stupid for a country, the UK, that still has pretensions of being an international trading and financial player.[6]

He goes on to suggest that the root of the problem lies with the attitudes of news desks and editors at home, rather than with reporters in Japan, though his view is not universally supported within the newspaper industry. When questioned about factors which have a negative influence on reporting, editors tended to focus on the practical difficulties which affect news gathering in Japan. While acknowledging these, correspondents talked more about how their work was affected by the attitudes and expectations of editors and readers at home.

One view shared by reporters and editors, however, was that the cost of visiting Japan prohibits tourism by the British public and restricts educational initiatives, resulting in a readership with a low level of knowledge and interest in the country. Nigel Wade, Foreign Editor of the *Daily Telegraph*, observed: 'I think that a lot more bridges would be built if it wasn't for the fact that, as a spin-off from Japanese trade policies, the Yen is so strong, and so there isn't a lot of casual tourism.' Lloyd Parry echoed: 'The factor behind people becoming more educated about Japan is the expense.' The implication is that Japan itself is to blame for a lack of knowledge among foreigners concerning its customs and language: if only it were cheaper, Japan would be more accessible, there would be a wider demand for information on the country and journalistic standards would improve. Unfortunately, the argument that better journalism is concomitant with wider public knowledge of a country often comes unstuck in reality. Many Britons are familiar with France, Germany or Spain, for example, but that does not prevent the jingoism of some British reporting on European countries, particularly at times such as the 'mad-cow' disease (BSE) crisis and the European football championship held in the UK in 1996. Even the broadsheets described the BSE crisis using conflict-style language, and the tabloids treated a Euro '96 semi-final match between England and Germany as a replay of the Second World War.[7] On the basis of such evidence, it seems unlikely that a resolution of practical problems facing journalists in Japan and increased familiarity among readers would lead to more balanced reporting of that country either.

Practical Problems

It is still important, however, to present an examination of the practical problems as perceived by journalists, since every journalist we inter-viewed referred to them as negative factors affecting coverage, albeit to varying degrees. Editors, in particular, were eager to identify financial or geographical constraints as the main barriers to reporting. Almost every editor we spoke to stressed the high cost of sending staff to Japan or of maintaining an office there. They argued that coverage is limited due to a combination of the strong Yen and the inability of British newspapers to cover costs as budgets are being squeezed. Not all Tokyo-based journalists, however, entirely agreed with this explanation. While admitting that it may be too costly for British papers to maintain full-scale news operations in Tokyo, a few reporters argued that editors do not make the most of their staff in Japan. The advice that Kevin Rafferty had for industry decision-makers in London was: 'if you've got somebody here, and I think you should have somebody here, then you should use them properly.' The additional expense incurred by doing so, he argued, would be small compared to the expense of maintaining somebody anyway. He suggested that editors should demand a wider range of material on Japan and allow reporters to explore alternatives to the traditional Tokyo-based approach to coverage.

Other journalists in Japan shared Rafferty's view, and mentioned that tight finances made it difficult to take trips out of the capital. Lloyd Parry observed:

> So many Japan correspondents are actually just Tokyo correspondents, because travelling in Japan is expensive....I like to get out of Tokyo as much as possible. It does give people a more accurate picture. But it's very limited, budgets just don't allow it.

He also made the point that, because government and corporate power is so centralised in Tokyo, there is little motivation for journalists to travel in search of stories. This is a view shared by Robert Guest, super-stringer for the *Daily Telegraph* in Tokyo, who explained: 'It's very definitely the case that power is concentrated in Tokyo; all the different ministries, all the government offices, all the company headquarters are all in a very small area, so most of the stories can be covered best from Tokyo.' The Japanese government is now going ahead with plans to shift government ministries to a satellite town about an hour's train ride from the capital. Yet, if and when this happens, it is unlikely to widen the horizons of British reporting. On the contrary, journalists may find it more difficult to attend official briefings outside Tokyo regularly for reasons of time and expense. There can be little hope for a wider reporting base unless the scale of British news operations in Japan is increased, and that seems unlikely given the financial constraints afflicting the British newspaper industry in the 1990s.

The chart below sets out the practical circumstances of British newspapers' operations in Japan in 1995-96. The national broadsheets are served by four staff correspondents (all from the *Financial Times*) and four super-stringers, whereas the tabloid press rely on stringers, freelancers and international agency coverage. All journalists employed by the broadsheets are based in Tokyo and work from offices provided by the newspapers. They are predominantly male.

National Dailies: Coverage of Japan for the Foreign News pages

Newspaper	Reporters (plus other major sources of news)
Financial Times	4 staff correspondents
Times	1 super-stringer
Daily Telegraph	1 super-stringer
Guardian	1 super-stringer
Independent	1 super-stringer
Daily Mail	2 freelancers plus agencies (Reuters, AFP, UPI)
Mirror	Stringers plus agencies (Reuters, AP)
Express	4 stringers (mainly use 1) plus agencies
Today	1 freelancer
Sun	Occasional use of agencies and freelancers
Daily Star	Agencies (Reuters, AFP)

Source: 'Images of Japan', London International Research Exchange, 1996

Most reporters in Japan gather their information from international news agencies, the Japanese media, briefings for foreign journalists and interviews. The Foreign Correspondents' Club in central Tokyo offers library facilities and translation/interpreting services to journalists, holds press briefings and helps reporters secure interviews. However, it is important to understand that foreign journalists' access to first-hand information is compromised by the system of reporting clubs which control the flow of news in Japan. In practice, a reporters' club consists of a group of representatives from the Japanese media who are assigned to cover a certain politician, government ministry, or company or industry. The club may be a physical place where reporters from rival media organisations work alongside each other in a designated room or building, for example at the Ministry of Finance. Otherwise, it is just a way of collectively describing those journalists covering a particular subject. Whatever form the clubs take, they have a monopoly on news and information. Until recently, non-Japanese reporters were denied membership, and even now there are only a handful of foreign journalists among their ranks.

Tokyo-based reporters have long argued that the Japanese system discriminates against foreign journalists. Apart from the exclusivity of the press clubs, some complain that officials give one view at briefings for the foreign press and another for domestic consumption. Lloyd Parry described how, in the case of the Second World War fiftieth anniversaries in 1995, the incumbent Prime Minister, Murayama Tomiichi, used one set of words when apologising for war atrocities committed by Japan at a press conference for foreign journalists and then altered them at an official memorial ceremony later. At the press conference, Murayama said: 'I apologise for Japan's actions.' Yet at the ceremony, in front of the Emperor, he said: 'We express deep, profound remorse', when referring to the same wartime events. Lloyd Parry explained that Murayama could not use the collective noun and the all-important word 'apologise' together because that would imply that the apology came from the government. At the time, Japan had a coalition government consisting of two main parties, the majority right-wing Liberal Democrat Party (LDP), and the minority left-wing Socialist Democratic Party (SDP), of which Murayama was a member. Murayama's party had long advocated an international apology by the government, but the LDP did not agree. Since the words 'deep remorse' in Japanese do not amount to a formal apology, they could be used with the collective 'we' at an official ceremony without offending LDP officials. What Murayama had said in the first person at the press conference could then be formally dismissed as a personal opinion.

It is perhaps not surprising that confusion reigned at the time about whether Japan had actually apologised to the world or not. Lloyd Parry wrote a leader in the *Independent* explaining his view of the domestic political factors influencing the issue,[8] but the overall tone of the British press was one of disdain at Japan's apparent equivocation and inability to behave like a responsible nation. The newspapers went into great detail about the different words used when apologising in Japanese, and how what had been said did not amount to a formal apology by the Japanese government. Of course, reporters are entitled to complain if one thing is being said to the national media and a different view given to the foreign press. But Kishimoto Kunihiko, a London-based reporter for the Japanese news agency Jiji Press, believes that this is not always the case in Japan. He argued that when foreign reporters condemn Japanese officials for misleading them, it is sometimes a misunderstanding on the journalists' part. In his view, the Japanese government did not deliberately confuse foreign reporters on the war apology issue because it never intended to give a formal apology in 1995. The government line, he explained, is that the official responsibilities of Japan towards victims of its wartime atrocities ended with the San Francisco Treaty in 1951, when a formal apology was made and compensation paid. The legal position, he added, prevents political parties from officially reiterating Japan's sorrow and shame, because to do so would effectively annul the treaty and lay Japan open to further claims for compensation.

Yet such ambiguities are not peculiar to Japan. In nearly all countries, including Britain, it is common practice to disclose certain information to the national press, ignoring or giving a slightly different spin to the foreign press. In the UK, there is no shortage of cases where foreign reporters are either not invited to briefings, or given a briefing at a later date when the so-called news is no longer news. A journalist working for a Japanese media organisation cited the London Stock Exchange as one British institution guilty of such behaviour, for example. Britain also boasts its own reporting club in the form of the 'lobby', or group of parliamentary reporters, which works in a remarkably similar way to those in Japan. It too is exclusive and largely closed to foreign journalists. In an ideal world, foreign correspondents would share equal access to news sources with domestic journalists. But it is an immutable fact that politicians and business people all over the world are more interested in gaining coverage in their own national press than in the foreign press. This can make life difficult for foreign journalists, but it is not only reporters in Japan who feel they are discriminated against in this way.

Another practical barrier to reporting brought up by journalists is language. Few correspondents speak fluent Japanese, although most are capable of daily conversation at least. Of the Tokyo-based journalists we interviewed, three had studied Japanese at college to varying levels and the others had acquired a functional command through less formal study or simply by living in Japan. Not being fluent is obviously a handicap when it comes to press conferences held in Japanese, interviews and understanding the local media. Reading Japanese also poses a problem because it requires mastery of a complicated set of characters which can take years of study. So those who are not fluent in spoken and written Japanese have to rely on English-language newspapers,[9] international agencies and the bi-lingual news broadcasts of NHK, the national broadcasting channel. The *Financial Times* employs two bi-lingual Japanese correspondents, and some journalists, such as Rafferty, employ bi-lingual Japanese assistants to help them overcome this problem. Others can not afford to. The obvious solution to the language barrier, as all reporters agreed, is for British journalists to have a better command of the language, and, as Japanese becomes more widely studied at British universities, the situation may improve.

Japan's geographical distance from the UK is also perceived as a problem. The time difference between Britain and Japan was cited by a small number of journalists as a hindrance to reporting: Japan is eight hours ahead of Britain in summer, and nine in winter. As Tokyo-based reporters start their day, their colleagues in London are going to bed and the newspaper is on the presses. At the end of their day, their London counterparts are arriving at the office. 'It can put you off researching your own stories', lamented one journalist, 'because by the evening [in Japan], when you've phoned the desk [in London], there are completely different news priorities at the start of their day and all your work could be wasted'. No reporter wants to spend a whole day researching and writing a story only to find that it is not required. As a result, reporters tend to phone London-based editors at the end of the working day in Japan, get their brief, and write in the evening. This means that it is often too late for them conduct primary research on stories, as most government and company press officers and officials have finished for the day. They might have to rely largely on secondary reports in the Japanese media for information, which can limit the scope and originality of an article.

Geographical distance also seems to give news from Japan as low priority in the minds of editors. For Japan-based reporters wanting to get their stories in print, this is frustrating. How do you convince a London-based editor of the value of a story from half-way across the world? David Richardson, Foreign Editor of the *Express* explained his priorities: 'We've got a small space for foreign news, so you are inclined to concentrate on Europe and the United States for traditional reasons.' Yet Edward Pilkington, a *Guardian* news reporter sent to Japan in 1995 to cover the Second World War anniversaries, argued that the balance of expansive reporting on Western countries compared with relatively little on Japan is 'skew-whiff', considering the increasing importance of Japan along with the growth of the 'Asian Tiger' countries. It is easy to reduce journalism to the maxim that, in general, a story about events nearer to home is more newsworthy. Yet, while Washington and Europe are geographically closer to Britain, and British readers are more familiar with these areas, Japan is a world leader in finance and technology. Why does it not then gain the amount and quality of coverage it would seem to deserve? As the views outlined above show, the practical difficulties involved in covering Japan undoubtedly restrict journalists. Taken alone, however, they do not fully explain the shortcomings of the coverage.

Japan's 'Newsworthiness': Disasters and Sensations in 1995

The situation becomes somewhat clearer when we look at the content of reporting on Japan. Nineteen ninety-five, for example, saw a marked increase in coverage. The Kobe earthquake (January), the sarin gas attacks on the Tokyo subway by the Aum Shinri-kyo religious cult (April) and the Second World War fiftieth anniversaries (August) gave an unusual spin to stories about Japan. 'Japan's a sexy place again', remarked one Tokyo correspondent, relieved at the temporary upsurge in demand for his work. Yet, while some journalists viewed the events of 1995 as justifiably 'big news stories', others said the coverage has followed a general trend towards sensationalism in foreign news reporting. Readers are offered more features on a country only when dramatic events or catastrophes take place. In Japan's case in 1995, the spotlight shone on its inadequacy to predict, prevent, cope with and apologise for disasters, including the Second World War. This fostered the impression that Japan is a primitive and amoral society, despite its outward pretensions to Western sophistication and its advanced technology.

In particular, the fiftieth anniversaries of World War Two prompted a deluge of coverage on Japan. Stories about British soldiers' experiences at the hands of their Japanese captors and the failure of Japan to apologise for its war atrocities topped the news agenda. Although Japan featured prominently on news and features pages throughout the month of August, most of the journalists we interviewed felt that the overall impact of the coverage was negative. Despite general agreement that the issues had to be covered—to answer enduring questions about apologies, to satisfy older readers, or simply to sell newspapers—several journalists argued that the legacy of Britain's wartime relations with her former enemy would continue to produce adverse perceptions of Japan among the British public. Lloyd Parry thought that the incessant demand by some newspapers that Japan should apologise for war atrocities focused too much on old wounds. 'A lot of that is, I think, racist....They want to have some kind of grudge against Japan for very complicated psychological reasons', he explained, adding that spiteful commentary stems from Britain's inability to come to terms with Japan's post-war economic success. Pilkington said that coverage of the war issue, though not racist, was 'distorted to the extent to which the press talked about it to the detriment of other very important issues, such as the [atom] bomb itself'.

Raymond Whitaker, the *Independent's* Asia Editor, however, made the point that journalists no longer portray the Japanese using the racist language of fifty years ago: 'The way we in the media seek to cover Japan today is very different.' Indeed, describing the Japanese in old-fashioned racist language is now considered by journalists an unacceptable and unhelpful way to view the Japanese. However, while picking out different non-white and non-Western physical traits of the Japanese might be a thing of the past, the question of wartime apologies showed how some newspapers were keen to promote the notion that the Japanese are incapable of remorse. Various explanations for this were aired, including the idea that the Japanese feel shame but not guilt for wrong-doing, so do not experience a natural compulsion to apologise. In other words, the message was that there is still a difference between Western and Asian people: 'they' differ from 'us' in their morals and culture. Although the anniversaries have passed, the question remains of whether the image of Japan as Britain's former enemy will ever change. Norman Luck, Special Projects Editor for the *Daily Express*, believes that future generations of Japanese will continue to pay the price for what their ancestors did during World War Two, just as the Germans have done. Others, like Guest, think that, as the war becomes a distant memory, old-fashioned prejudices will die out: 'Over the next twenty years, the World War Two stuff should die down....I think reporting will probably change with the generations', he observed.

Beyond 1995: The Quirky and the Strange

In fact, the vast amount of coverage on Japan in 1995 was unusual. As might be expected, 1996 saw coverage drop back to pre-1995 levels. Business sections had more stories on Japan than usual—because of financial and commodities market trading scandals involving Daiwa Bank and Sumitomo Corporation respectively—but these incidents may be regarded as the financial equivalents of the Aum Shinri-kyo gas attacks or the Kobe earthquake, and did not precipitate a general increase in coverage. Reporters believe that the outlook for an overall improvement in coverage depends on how editors continue to perceive the 'newsworthiness' of the country. Many feel that editors do not currently accord Japan the importance it deserves. One journalist talked of his surprise that, in January 1996, when Hashimoto Ryutaro was elected Prime Minister of Japan, his article was cut from six hundred to three hundred and fifty words, but the resignation of the Greek Prime Minister Papandreous later in the month was allotted two stories. He commented:

> Greece is interesting, it's part of the European Union, but I would have thought that Japan is of more interest and value to the UK. That's obviously not how it's perceived.

If this is the way broadsheet newspapers treat major political news from Japan, then it is no surprise to find that the tabloids have no room for it at all. Richardson commented: 'Even though Japan influences all our lives, not a lot comes out of Japan that would interest us....Internal Japanese politics are very difficult to fit into a tabloid newspaper.'

Richardson explained that he only uses his stringer in Japan for a 'Brits in the shit' story, referring to incidents where Britons are caught up in some kind of trouble or disaster, such as the Kobe earthquake. For other news, the *Express* uses agencies, but strongly favours quirky anecdotes above straight news. Richardson mentioned a story that had been reported on the wires the day we interviewed him: a schoolteacher had slashed her wrists in front of a class of eleven year olds because they would not be quiet. He described that incident as 'a classic example' of a *Express* story on Japan, but added that good stories from Japan are rare: 'If the best story is from Japan it will get in. But, invariably, the best story is not from Japan.' Mark Dowdney, foreign editor, explains that 'part of the definition of news is to report something different which is why you get those kind of reports on something that readers haven't seen before, especially in tabloids'. He adds: 'It's not for any sinister reason but it's the way we define news. It's true for any other country not just Japan.' It is not really surprising that a tabloid newspaper regards 'funny anecdotes' from Japan as news; much more shocking is the way that broadsheet editors make similar requests for quirky or even trivial stories. Peter Popham, an *Independent* feature writer who lived in Japan for eleven years, covered Emperor Hirohito's funeral in 1989 for the *Evening Standard*. He asked whether the paper would require a broad explanation of the reaction within Japan, or a detailed description of the characteristics of a Japanese state funeral. 'I was missing the only thing that mattered to the *Evening Standard*—Prince Philip', he remembered wryly, 'Did he bow? and How deep did he bow?'. Another journalist described how his first assignment for a national daily was to follow up a story about a gorilla in a Japanese zoo being shown porn movies 'to get him to perform'. Admittedly, quirky stories seem to have a place in most newspapers, but there is a preponderance of such articles on Japan in the British press. Coupled with a shortage of straight news on important political and economic issues, it implies that editors have little interest in portraying Japan as the culturally-diverse and internationally influential country it really is.

Editorial Ignorance

One view expressed by reporters was that many editors do not know enough about Japan to be able to evaluate it objectively. The majority of reporters were quick to admit that their editors have only a superficial knowledge of Japan. Lloyd Parry suggested that it is perhaps due to ignorance that some editors seem to delight in stories which depict the Japanese in stereotypes:

> It seems that with Japan more than any other country, people feel that they have to judge rather than just describe and analyse....People are prepared to talk about the Japanese in a way that they would never do about the French or the Americans or the Scottish, and that all needs to be recognised. And the reason that it's not recognised is that editors are usually as much in the dark about Japan as everyone else is.

One journalist told of the problems experienced by a colleague covering the Aum Shinri-kyo gas attacks in 1995. Asked to draw out what the attacks revealed about 'the Japanese character',

> He reluctantly produced the requisite 1,100 words and filed it, and they called him back saying: "This is fine but it's 1,100 words long and you haven't mentioned kamikaze and our readers expect—you know it's Japan—they expect kamikaze to be in there somewhere!" So, he said "Do it yourself", and they did.

Journalism that portrays a nation's people in stereotypes—the Japanese, for example, as a race of samurai, salary-men or geisha girls—is not unique to Japan, argued Guest. To him, it is an example of bad journalism and a result of the insatiable appetite in British newspapers for wacky stories. He observed: 'If one relies on reports from Western journalists about Africa, it sounds like it's non-stop chaos—catching AIDS and being chopped up with machetes.'

The flip side of what some journalists view as the editor's ignorance is that they are ostensibly free to write what they choose. Peregrine Hodson of the *Times* quipped that he was not under the Murdoch thumb as some might think. His Foreign Editor sent him to Tokyo with the mission simply to do a good job and report anything irregular. At the *Independent,* the only editorial guidance given to Lloyd Parry was to avoid articles which smirked at the Japanese. However, captivating the interest of editors with pieces on Japan in the first place is not always easy. As Rafferty points out in his book *Inside Japan's Powerhouses*, suggestions for features on Japan get short shrift from many editors across Fleet Street: 'Other departments of newspapers—education, health, law, women's affairs...sport—are firmly in the hands of editors with a domestic agenda and perhaps an occasional glimpse at Europe.'[10] When interviewed, he talked about how his idea for a weekly column on Japan was not approved by the *Guardian*, even though a 'Letters from Tokyo' column in the *Independent* by correspondent Terry McCarthy had been well-received by readers and diplomats alike. The fact is that, even if journalists are not required to write-to-order, some of their ideas are simply ignored. This makes their lack of a detailed brief seem more like an editorial cold-shoulder than freedom for the reporter to write what he/she chooses.

Cultural Difference and Japanese Uniqueness

Journalistic disregard for Japan is perhaps also a reflection of the fact that it is not a country that can be easily explained in reader-friendly sound-bites. Rather than going into the sort of background detail which would help the reader to understand a story, editors tend to favour articles which point out superficially how different Japan is from the West. As the previous chapter showed, the common approach of the British press today is to highlight 'cultural difference' between Britain and Japan. This translates into a simplistic 'us' and 'them' attitude which can seem implicitly hostile. The main justification for this would seem to be that, while Japan is a prosperous, developed nation, it retains unique traditions and customs which do not fit Western perceptions of a modern society. It is these aspects which reporters tend to focus on in their work. Hugo Gurdon, former Tokyo correspondent for the *Daily Telegraph*, believes that, in doing so, the British press is inclined towards what he calls 'zoo journalism'. When reporting on Japan, a country with a very different culture from that of Britain, he explained, 'we look at Japanese people as curiosities, we report Japanese culture or the Japanese way of doing things as curiosities in a fairly disrespectful way'.

Whitaker agreed that British journalists 'have a tendency to put the Japanese under the microscope as a very curious example'. When asked why, he was quick to explain that it was because 'the Japanese themselves very much like to be considered unique and mysterious'. Here he was referring to the theory of Japanese cultural uniqueness, or Nihonjinron, discussed in chapter three. Some Western journalists do believe it is the Japanese themselves who are responsible for ideas of their own cultural uniqueness. Whitaker remarked that, although defining the Japanese as a race apart is a logical 'non-starter', nonetheless 'it is something the Japanese have promoted in many ways, which has been seized upon by their enemies quite often'. Similarly, Gurdon talked about Japanese friends of his who had agreed with the common stereotype of the Japanese as 'workaholics who live in rabbit hutches', and argued: 'I would say...that the notion of a collective psyche is not simply a Western invention, it does seem to be perpetuated by the Japanese I encountered.' The logical extension of this argument is that if journalists fail to clarify what Japan is about, then the Japanese are equally at fault and foreigners can even consider their generalisations about Japan justified.

Gurdon may argue that journalists portray the Japanese in a certain way because that is how the Japanese describe themselves. Indeed, it can not be denied that some Japanese will confirm superficial Western ideas about Japan when asked for their opinion. Yet one only has to compare Japan with other societies to see that the notion of group culture, for example, is not universally applicable to the Japanese, nor even unique to Japan. A visit there will reveal plenty of individuals; likewise, a glance at British society reveals numerous examples of group behaviour. The reason why some Japanese go along with popular foreign ideas about their country is, according to one Japanese journalist, that they have become so used to hearing platitudes that it is easier to repeat than to repudiate them. As a result, it can be difficult for Western journalists to get beyond generalisations, especially if they have little experience of the country and can not speak its language well. Joe Joseph, ex-Tokyo correspondent for the *Times*, writes in his book *The Japanese: Strange but not Strangers*:

> Part of the problem is that we have been taught to expect the Japanese to be inscrutable. They go a long way to match the cliché and few of us try hard to melt our misconceptions.[11]

The logical solution would surely be to try harder.

As editor of the *Economist*, ex-Tokyo correspondent and author of three books on Japan, Bill Emmott goes to considerable lengths in his work to deconstruct some of the 'ingrained and unhelpful' myths believed about Japan in the West. In his book *The Sun also Sets*, in addition to shedding light on simple misunderstandings of the Japanese he also grapples with more 'sophisticated myths' such as the idea that Japan is dependent on exports. Citing figures, he shows that Japan's share of exports as a percentage of GNP is in fact large only compared to the United States. In this way, Emmott neatly exposes how the majority of the Western world fails to comprehend Japan. Foreigners should not be fooled by Nihonjinron, he explains, which 'is often used in business, trade and other negotiations to try to put opponents on the defensive'.[12] A little resourcefulness exposes Nihonjinron as a collection of myths, but some journalists are taken in. Others are not, but find it hard to deconstruct deeply rooted popular misconceptions within the confines of a short article.

Going beyond orthodox notions of Japaneseness can seem a daunting task, and one which some journalists regard as virtually impossible. Several journalists we interviewed echoed the common complaint that Japan is impenetrable in every respect. 'Japan is a country where the government and industry work together as a corporatist state. It's very hard to penetrate both in terms of understanding attitudes and penetrating in the sense of selling Scotch whisky or Jaguar cars or whatever else', said Wade. Joseph also holds the view that, try as they might, foreigners will never understand Japan. In his book, he writes of the difference between recent arrivals in Japan and long-term foreign residents: '...the recent arrivals look as if they've been in a state of bewilderment for the past two days. Long-term foreign residents have been bewildered for years.'[13] Yet a minority of journalists, such as Pilkington, do not share his fatalism. Pilkington had been warned by friends before going that Japan was a closed society and the Japanese difficult to comprehend, but said that his visit was an eye-opener:

> I found it a very open society. People were talking about issues of concern to them and in fact it was not so dissimilar to Britain or any other country in the West. The fact that this gulf of understanding exists is a worry.

It is a worry shared by other journalists who have first-hand experience of Japan. Some have felt strongly enough to express their concern in longer texts on Japan, but rarely in newspaper journalism. Jonathan Rauch, an American journalist, argues in his book *The Outnation: A Search for the Soul of Japan,* that although every society differs from the next, there is no evidence to support the assertion that Japan is outstandingly different when compared with other countries. Rauch went to Japan expecting to find difference 'with a capital D' as he puts it. However, he notes with some relief in his book that:

> ...nowhere could I find enough differentness [sic] to convince myself that the place is *especially* different....Japan is, alas and thank God, just another ordinary different place, peopled with all the familiar types....The Japanese are precisely as mysterious and unique as my aunt in Hackensack.[14]

Yet if, as is often the case with journalism on Japan, the 'ordinary' differences that Rauch refers to remain unexplained, they tend to assume a greater significance than they deserve and come to be seen as defining characteristics of the country. Often journalists argue that it is in the nature of the press to dwell on the differences rather than the similarities

between societies, and this may well be so. Indeed, journalism that highlights difference can be positive when it awakens curiosity in the reader
and attempts to satisfy that curiosity in a balanced way. But, when a journalist fails to give adequate explanation of difference, he or she is in danger of
strengthening rather than dispelling prejudice. Hodson observed that,
'As journalists, we want to get rid of prejudices and give analysis and
interpretation....What we're trying for is the truth'. His view is encouraging,
and there is little doubt that it is shared by colleagues. However, as the
analysis in the previous chapter indicates, it is questionable whether
Tokyo-based journalists are succeeding in their attempts to explain Japan
to the reader at home.

Economic coverage

At this point, it is useful to examine the views of financial journalists,
because economics reporting is one area which journalists generally
believe does shed light on Japan. On the financial pages, it often seems that
Japan is more widely covered and rarely ignored—as acknowledged by
Numata. There are in-depth reports on the Japanese economy and articles
exploring Japanese industry, business, banking and technology. Journalists
who cover Japan's economic and financial affairs say it is easier not to slip
into 'zoo journalism' because they are dealing mainly with statistics rather
than opinion and impressions. They believe that economics reporting is
less likely to be infused with a tone of moral superiority than other types
of coverage, citing Japan's exemplary model of low inflation and high
employment, and industrial management techniques which have been
widely copied in the West. Bethan Hutton, a freelance reporter who has
covered Japan for the *Financial Times*, explained that, as a business newspaper with an international readership, it aims to give a balanced view of
Japan: 'What the *FT* is about is providing information....It tries to be
objective about things.' She added that the greater column inches
devoted to Japan in the *Financial Times* mean that any articles on the
more 'eccentric' elements of Japanese society provide fuller explanation
than in other broadsheets. As a result, she believes coverage of Japan in
the newspaper is 'pretty good'.

Alex Brummer, Finance Editor of the *Guardian* thinks that Japan
'doesn't do too badly' on the business pages of his newspaper, although
he admitted it receives less attention than the United States and Europe.
In the same way that editors often regard Japan's political system as
completely different from Western-style democracy, Brummer supports
the view that Japan's economy and the way it is managed are unique.
Interestingly, he regards this as a barrier to coverage:

> Institutionally it's so different that it makes it difficult to bring [its economy] into line [with other countries]....Its views are very difficult to get at sometimes so we have to rely on secondary reports and other bits of information.

However, Emmott said that he has 'made a personal career' out of arguing against the perception that Japan's economy is completely different from those of other G7 nations: 'I'm of the view that Japan is at a different end of the spectrum from capitalist economies such as the United States, which is a much more free-market, individualistic economy, but relatively close to Japan on that spectrum are economies such as France, Germany and Italy.' He added:

> One of the problems in a lot of the writing about Japan is that it tends to compare Japan only with the United States and with Britain...[but] if you look at it in a genuinely international context you see Japan as being actually quite comprehensible if you know France, Germany or Italy. There are differences between the countries...but they don't put Japan as the extreme outlier.

In the past, Japan's astounding economic success instilled fear into competing British companies, argued Emmott. 'The easiest way to deal with that fear was to compartmentalise Japan as a set of aliens following a different set of rules rather than a set of people that had lessons for the way we ran our own economies', he explained. 'It's always easier when you're afraid of somebody to say that their success isn't because they do what you do better than you, but rather because they do something different.' Now, he believes, all that may be changing. Japan's recent economic problems have dented the view that it is an economic powerhouse. In addition, increased investment by Japanese companies in Britain, and more widespread experience of working with the Japanese are widening Britons' knowledge and understanding of Japan. As politicians are quick to boast, the UK is the beneficiary of 40% of Japanese investment into Europe and there are now just over 51,000 Japanese living in Britain.[15] It might be expected that this would lead to better coverage of Japan in the broadsheets, but Emmott is not sure that reporting on Japan outside the business press will necessarily improve as a result. He commented: 'The broadsheets are generally whittling away at their international coverage, and so I am not convinced that increased knowledge about Japan will result in increased depth and breadth in reporting in British newspapers.'

Future Prospects

It seems that there can be little hope for change unless editors perceive a greater demand for material on Japan among their readers. So far, they do not appear to have responded to the influx of Japanese investment in Britain and the growing number of Britons working for Japanese companies by significantly increasing coverage. Nineteen ninety-six saw a rash of cases where British employees took some of Japan's largest corporations to industrial tribunals with complaints ranging from sexual harassment to racial discrimination.[16] The common element of all these cases was deep cultural ignorance and misunderstanding on both sides. Of course, it would be wrong to suggest that poor employer/employee relations in Japanese companies in Britain are the fault of inadequate reporting on Japan in the British press. However, the recent increase in employment disputes argues in favour of the need for a greater cultural understanding, to which the British press could surely contribute. Lloyd Parry believes that editors underestimate their readers' desire to learn about Japan:

> The editors believe that their readers have got expectations and prejudices about Japan which must be met for them to feel comfortable and approving of the articles they're reading....They justify it in terms of the readers, but what it comes down to is a view they have of their own readers.

The scope and content of current newspaper coverage on Japan seems to indicate that editors take a fairly dim view of their readers' intellectual curiosity. In a society where alternative sources of information about Japan are scarce, this has set up a vicious circle. The average reader appears to know little about Japan, so editors conclude that interest is negligible and coverage of Japan is given a low priority. The state of ignorance is perpetuated.

Few journalists, however, would disagree with the proposition that their job is to inform as well as to entertain. There was a feeling among the Tokyo-based journalists we interviewed that the time has come to get on with informing the British public about Japan. Hodson argued: 'There is no hope if you don't believe you can educate people....As a responsible journalist, I should inform people so that they can get rid of their prejudices.' Hodson's aim was shared by colleagues, but whether it is attainable remains to be seen. Opinion on this matter is divided. Rafferty appreciates that fellow journalists in Japan are 'interested, conscientious and capable of writing stories which would reflect better what goes on', but does not believe that coverage will necessarily improve as a result. For him, the problem lies back in the UK: 'I don't see people on the desks...or at editor level in London who say..."we must explain Japan, we must explain it properly, that means we must give it space and grow the stories"...I don't see that happening.'

Other journalists, however, were cautiously optimistic that reporting will improve. Some argued that more imagination is needed. 'People should get off their bums and write something new', exclaimed one reporter. There are a number of factors journalists pointed to which they believe will alter the limited nature of British reporting: Japan's global influence in political as well as economic affairs is growing, a larger number of foreign reporters are learning Japanese and developing more sophisticated views of Japan, Hong Kong will cease to be the focus of press bureaux in the East in 1997 when attention will shift to Tokyo, and a new generation of journalists will tend to write about today's Japan rather than focusing on the war. Lloyd Parry voiced the view that reporters and editors have a duty to readers:

> What's necessary is a recognition that Japan is a very complicated place, and it can be written about in a way which is entertaining and interesting but reflects the complexity....Japan is going to become more and more important. It's not going to become less important to British people. So newspapers will not be doing their job and not serving their readers if they fail to reflect that complexity.

His view is shared by Whitaker, who predicted: 'It is simply for economic reasons, if for no other reason, that it is incumbent upon us to understand Japan and know what is happening there, and slowly that will make our coverage more diverse and sympathetic.'

If coverage is to improve, however, it is not simply a question of more pages being devoted to Japan. As this chapter has attempted to show, reporting on the country must also begin to develop more useful ways of approaching Japanese society if contemporary trends are to be properly explained. A superficial portrayal of the differences between Japanese and British culture merely offers a picture of Japan as an outsider, a country developing in isolation, rather than one heavily influencing, and influenced by, Western ideas and world economic and technological developments. Japan is often criticised for not being open to British journalists: it is said to be too far away, too expensive and, above all, a closed society incomprehensible to outsiders. Yet, as we have argued, it is British journalism that requires a shift in perceptions. Editors must commission wider and more detailed coverage of Japan; reporters must seek to deconstruct accepted Western images of the country and give context to the differences they describe in their work. If this does not happen, Japan will continue to be the great unknown.

NOTES

1. This chapter is a revised and expanded version of 'Why Japan is still inscrutable' by Tessa Mayes and Megan Rowling, *British Journalism Review*, Vol. 7, No. 2, 1996. We are grateful to Maija Pesola and Jane Watkins for their help with conducting interviews for both pieces.

2. The interviews were carried out between August 1995 and March 1997. A total of fifteen journalists were interviewed from the following newspapers: *Financial Times, Economist, Daily Telegraph, Times, Guardian, Independent, Express and Mirror*. The Sun declined to give an interview as did the *Daily Mail* (saying that it had no foreign editor when contacted). All job titles refer to the interviewee's position at the time of interview.

3. Douglas Anthony, *Reporting Japan: British Media Attitudes Towards a Nation and a People*, Cardiff, University of Wales (Japanese Studies Centre), undated, but c.1991, p18.

4. Ibid.

5. Richard Lloyd Parry, *Japan*, London, Cadogan, 1995; Peregrine Hodson, *A Circle Round the Sun: A Foreigner in Japan*, London, William Heinemann, 1992; Kevin Rafferty, *Inside Japan's Powerhouses: The Culture, Mystique and Future of Japan's Greatest Corporations*, London, Weidenfield and Nicolson, 1995.

6. Rafferty, op. cit., pxiv.

7. The imposition of a world-wide ban on British beef exports by the European Union, following the British government's announcement in March 1996 of a possible link between BSE in cattle and CJD in humans, resulted in an atmosphere of political tension which was widely referred to in the media as 'the beef war with Europe'. The emergency Cabinet meeting convened by Prime Minister John Major to deal with the crisis was dubbed 'the war cabinet', even by the national broadsheets. In June, tabloid coverage of the Euro '96 football competition revelled in facetious puns and headlines invoking national stereotypes, and, in Germany's case, World War Two. The *Daily Mirror* even dubbed the day of the England vs. Germany semi-final 'Wembley D-Day'.

8. *Independent*, 12 August 1995.

9. The three daily English-language newspapers are: *Japan Times, Asahi Evening News,* and the *Daily Yomiuri*. International news agencies offering comprehensive English-language coverage of Japan include Reuters, Agence France Presse, Associated Press and United Press International.

10. Rafferty, op. cit., pxiv.

11. Joe Joseph, *The Japanese: Strange but not Strangers*, London, Viking, 1993, p10. It is interesting to note that although Joseph makes this point, he does very little in his own book to try to melt any misconceptions his readers may have about Japan. In fact, Richard Lloyd Parry branded his work: 'an arrogant and misleading book, which puts a neat new spin on many of the old questions about Japan without troubling itself for much in the way of answers.' (book review in the *Sunday Times*, 28 March 1993) Lloyd Parry noted that, although entertaining, the book contains huge amounts of 'quirky trivia' which he regards as a 'staple of Western prejudice' towards Japan.

12. Bill Emmott, *The Sun Also Sets: Why Japan Will not be Number One*, London, Simon and Schuster, 1989, p25.

13. Joseph, op. cit., p19.

14. Joseph Rauch, *The Outnation: A Search for the Soul of Japan*, Little, Brown and Company, 1992, p54 and p157.

15. According to figures supplied by the Embassy of Japan in London, October 1995.

16. Two cases in particular attracted the attention of the British media: Helen Bamber, a dealer in the City of London, won £100,000 from her former employer Fuji International for sexual discrimination, and Cliff Wakeman, a manager at the Japanese information company Quick Corp., sought compensation for unfair dismissal and racial discrimination along with two other former colleagues. Both cases provoked media commentary on management practice at Japanese companies which was generally negative in tone.

6 ORTHODOXY & DISSENT: THE AMERICAN NEWS MEDIA & THE DECISION TO USE THE ATOMIC BOMB AGAINST JAPAN, 1945–1995

Uday Mohan and Leo Maley III[1]

I n American popular memory, as well as in the orthodox version of history favoured by most of the American media, dropping the atomic bomb on Hiroshima and Nagasaki was the sole alternative to a bloody invasion of the Japanese mainland. This historical myth has persisted for fifty years, and the media have helped to solidify it. For the most part, in 1945 and in the five decades since, the American media have failed to question the belief that the bomb was necessary to end the war. This journalistic failure belies the fact that the media have had long-standing reasons—concerning the American media's own past coverage and a growing body of scholarly evidence—to challenge the myth of the bomb's necessity.

A representative example of the American media's serious misunderstanding of the end of the Second World War comes from ABC television's prestigious news show, *Nightline*. In August 1985, on the occasion of the fortieth anniversary of the atomic bombing of Hiroshima, *Nightline* devoted a special programme to examining, in host Ted Koppel's words, 'what it was that they [Truman and his advisers] tried to avoid' by dropping the atomic bomb—that is, the invasion of Japan—an event the show chose to 'recreate'. Yet as historians have argued for some time, the invasion might well never have taken place, even without the bomb. These historians have shown what *Nightline* failed to make clear: Truman faced reasonable choices other than bomb or invasion.[2] As the *Nightline* invasion unfolded on American television screens, Koppel and other well-known ABC newsmen reported on the hypothetical assault on Japan, a scenario that appears to live in American popular memory as inevitable reality rather than counterfactual history. Supplying background information about the 'invasion' he was 'covering', one reporter commented: 'Women and children are both trained to use sharpened bamboo spears to kill invading American soldiers if they move inland....Japan is hoping to make the American invasion of Kyushu so costly that the US will agree to a negotiated end to the war.' Another reporter—closer to the 'action'—attempted to conjure up the bloody drama of 1945, adding: 'I have never witnessed such horrible scenes of death. Hundreds of our Marines have been cut down, seconds after they left the landing craft along Stutz and Zephyr beaches.'

For many Americans, it is these 'scenes' of an invasion that fully justify the use of the atomic bomb against Japan. This view of history—a simple if brutal choice between bomb or invasion—has been vigorously reinforced by the media. As Koppel stated:

When President Truman and others who participated in the decision to drop an atomic bomb on Hiroshima said later that hundreds of thousands, perhaps even millions of lives, were spared, it was the invasion they were talking about.[3]

This *Nightline* episode, emblematic of widespread media legitimation of the use of the atomic bomb, should not obscure a very important (and generally forgotten) historical fact: the news media have occasionally offered striking challenges to the myth that the atomic bomb averted an invasion and saved lives. Whether engaging in straightforward war coverage or directly criticising the use of the bomb, the media have provided limited but also highly suggestive evidence to support the view that the atomic bombings of Hiroshima and Nagasaki were unnecessary. Additionally, this alternative understanding of the bomb decision has often found a surprisingly hospitable home in conservative media outlets. A consideration of the exceptions to and conflicts within the general media consensus about Hiroshima shows that significant possibilities have always existed in the media for a more critical understanding of Hiroshima. A resurrection of this critical understanding will help to throw into sharp relief the decisions the American media have made in recent years when they addressed the question of the atomic bombing of Japan.

The Media in 1945

Historians continue to engage in a tug-of-war over the bomb decision. In recent years the battle has become particularly fierce, perhaps because orthodox historians have begun to fear they may be superseded entirely in the historiographic debate, if not also in the public arena. Scholars who discuss Truman's options for ending the war emphasise a variety of points, but the following issues have become critical: the marked deterioration in Japan's military situation; the importance of Japanese peace feelers; and the consequences of Russian entry into the war, especially if combined with changes in Allied surrender terms (to offer assurances that the Japanese would be allowed to keep their Emperor). As considerable information has become available, and as arguments have been put forth, criticised, and reconsidered, a growing number of historians have come to believe that the bomb was not necessary—and that Truman and his advisers knew the bomb was not necessary.[4] Martin Sherwin's formulation, made almost a decade ago, is suggestive: 'The choice in the summer of 1945 was not between a conventional invasion or a nuclear war. It was a choice between various forms of diplomacy and warfare.'[5] Significantly, ignorant of the development and pending use of the atomic bomb in the spring and summer of 1945, the media themselves dealt with the issues that now occupy scholars, but largely put them aside once Truman announced that the bomb had been used, and the war ended shortly thereafter.

In the months prior to the dropping of the atomic bomb, the American media engaged in extensive debate about the best means for bringing the war with Japan to an end. Throughout the spring and summer of 1945 the media commented frequently on the growing evidence that Japan was a prostrate nation that might well be on the verge of surrender. The press speculated at length about the likely impact on Japan of Russian entry into the Pacific War and the clarification of Allied surrender terms. A few examples show the sort of questions pre-bomb media coverage raises for post-bomb conventional wisdom that the atomic bomb was necessary to end the war.[6] A *Newsweek* headline from 16 April 1945 is telling:

> Lost Battles, Slap From Moscow Shake Props of Jap Ruling Clique: Shift in Tokyo Government Smoothes Way for Peace Feelers, Cuts Power of Army Group.

Even at this early date—nearly four months before the atomic bombing of Hiroshima, and over six months before the first scheduled landing of American troops on the southern-most Japanese home island of Kyushu—*Newsweek* noted that the Russian denunciation of the Russian-Japanese neutrality pact spelled 'pure disaster' for Japan.[7] A month later, *Newsweek* mentioned reports of 'at least one peace feeler' from Japan, confirming its earlier picture of Japan's hopelessness.[8] The possibility of Russian entry and Japanese desire to seek an end to the war were linked propositions on other occasions as well. A 30 July *Newsweek* headline read: 'Heavy Allied Blows, Fear of Reds Make Jap Leaders Seek Way Out.' The article noted that Japan, fearing Russian entry and hoping to negotiate an end to the war before the Russians came in, had sent the Soviets a peace feeler.[9]

The media also considered the critical issue of Allied demands for 'unconditional surrender' in some depth, especially on the editorial pages. Some of the most forceful and sophisticated arguments for clarifying surrender terms can be found in the *Washington Post*. In the three-month period leading up to the bomb's use—May to July 1945—the *Post* published several editorials urging conditional surrender, a political not a military solution to the war. A mid-June editorial was typical:

> ...the same two words [unconditional surrender] remain a great stumbling block to any [US] propaganda effort and the perpetual trump card

of the Japanese die-hards for their game of national suicide. Let us amend them; let us give Japan conditions, harsh conditions certainly, and conditions that will render her diplomatically and militarily impotent for generations. But also let us somehow assure those Japanese who are ready to plead for peace that, even on our terms, life and peace will be better than war and annihilation.[10]

On 13 July, the newspaper again editorialised:

...the main question...is whether we should make known not merely to Japan but also to ourselves, and particularly to the men who are bearing the greatest pain and burden of the battles, precisely what are our purposes in continuing them....If these purposes are clear in the minds of our statesmen, they are nevertheless masked under the purely rhetorical and meaningless phrase, "unconditional surrender"[11]

Similar sentiments were expressed in other publications. *Time*, for instance, noted on 16 July 1945, that the exact meaning of the demand for 'unconditional surrender' had not yet been clarified. 'Or, if it has', the magazine noted, 'it is still a deep secret':

US military policy is clear: blow upon blow until all resistance is crushed. But the application of shrewd statesmanship might save the final enforcement of that policy—and countless US lives.[12]

Publishers and top editors of major magazines and newspapers, such as the *Washington Post*, often enjoyed special access to American leaders during the Second World War. Not surprisingly then, Henry Luce, the owner of *Time*, *Life*, and *Fortune*, had privileged access to the views of certain high-ranking military leaders and government officials, many of whom believed by the late spring and early summer of 1945 that Japan was near defeat. In May and June 1945 Luce embarked on a personal fact-finding trip to the Pacific theatre. He returned to the USA convinced that the only obstacle to Japan's surrender was the vagueness of American demands for 'unconditional surrender', specifically the failure to assure Japan's military and political leadership that the Japanese would be allowed to keep their Emperor following surrender.

Luce was so certain that a change in surrender terms could end the war that upon his return from the Pacific he flew to Washington where he shared his views with Secretary of the Navy James Forrestal, Undersecretary of State Joseph Grew, select members of Congress, and (rather unfruitfully) with President Truman.[13] Shortly before the atomic bombing of Hiroshima, *Time* asserted optimistically that unconditional surrender had been downgraded in the Allied communiqué from Potsdam, and further informed its readers that the Japanese war was heading towards a conditional end. It added:

> Japanese officialdom was thinking of peace, discussing the possibilities, and seeing to it that this state of mind was made known to Washington, Moscow, London.[14]

A few days before the atomic bomb was dropped on Hiroshima, *United States News* (later *US News & World Report*) announced that 'Japan definitely and desperately is trying at this time to get out of the war'. Moreover, readers were assured, American 'officials are convinced that Japan's present attempt to end the war is real and is not a subterfuge'.[15]

However, despite this growing conviction that Japan could soon surrender with the help of judicious statesmanship and Russian entry, in the weeks and months immediately following the use of the atomic bomb most of the media failed to question or challenge the official justification constructed by President Truman and others. In this familiar narrative, Truman and his advisers faced a stark choice: bomb or invasion. No reasonable alternatives existed. A large majority of the American public in 1945 supported the atomic bombing of Hiroshima and Nagasaki: an August 1945 Gallup poll showed 85% of the American public approving of the recent use of atomic bombs on Japanese cities.[16] A second poll, published in the December 1945 issue of *Fortune*, a leading business magazine, is even more revealing. It showed 53.5% of the American public believing we 'should have used the two bombs on cities, just as we did'. An additional 22.7% believed that we 'should have quickly used many more of them [atomic bombs] before Japan had a chance to surrender'.[17] It appears that most reporters, columnists, and editors were just as uncritical of the popular justifications for the atomic destruction of two cities. One 1945 study concluded that only 1.7% of 595 newspaper editorials surveyed opposed using the atomic bomb.[18]

Important sections of the liberal and left-leaning press supported the atomic bombing of Japan. According to historian Paul F. Boller Jr.:

> To say that the *Nation*, the *New Republic*, and *PM* supported the bombing of Hiroshima and Nagasaki is to understate the matter. All three publications took for granted, from the beginning, the necessity and desirability of the bombings.[19]

To give but two examples, John P. Lewis, managing editor of the liberal New York newspaper *PM* wrote on 9 August 1945: 'While we are dropping atomic bombs, why not drop a few on Tokyo, where there's a chance to run up our batting average on the royal family—and clear the bases for democracy after the war.'[20] Ten days later, Max Lerner claimed in the same newspaper that: 'The few people who thought up, made, and dropped the atomic bomb did more to bring Japan to its knees than the American fleet and...the massive Russian armies.'[21]

Notwithstanding the vengeful mood and widespread public and media support for the use of the atomic bomb, some Americans, including leading military figures, went public with their belief that the atomic bombs had not been necessary to end the war. Major General Claire Chennault's opinion was summarised in a *New York Times* article on 15 August: 'Russia's entry into the Japanese war was the decisive factor in speeding its end and would have been so even if no atomic bombs had been dropped....' On 21 September, Major General Curtis LeMay said in the *New York Herald Tribune* that the atomic bomb 'had nothing to do with the end of the war', and that the war would have ended within two weeks without either the atomic bombings or Russian entry against Japan. Fleet Admiral Chester Nimitz added on 22 September in the *New York Times* that Japan had been defeated before the atomic bombings and Russia's entry into the war.[22] Such statements did not attract the interest one might have expected, given the character of the media's pre-bomb reporting. However, during the immediate post-war period, a few prominent media figures were outspoken in their criticism of the use made of the atomic bomb.[23]

One early critic was David Lawrence, the mainstream conservative editor of *United States News*. Within days of the atomic bombing of Hiroshima, Lawrence editorialised that:

> ...we had already been winning the war against Japan. Our highest officials have known for some time that Russia was planning to enter the war in the Far East....The surrender of Japan has been for weeks inevitable.[24]

Lawrence also promptly termed 'sheer exaggeration' Winston Churchill's claim that the atomic bomb had saved 1,000,000 American lives.[25] A few weeks later he added:

> Spokesmen of the Army Air Forces say it wasn't necessary anyway and that the war had been won already. Competent testimony exists to prove that Japan was seeking to surrender many weeks before the atomic bomb came.[26]

A hard-hitting news story by the *Chicago Tribune's* Washington bureau chief, Walter Trohan, published on 19 August 1945, reported that the Japanese had made several peace bids beginning in early 1945, and that these bids were along the lines of the eventual surrender terms the Japanese accepted. Moreover, Trohan added that General Douglas MacArthur had strongly urged negotiation on the peace bids.[27] At the end of August, Felix Morley, editor of the conservative *Human Events*, asked 'If December 7, 1941, is "a day that will live in infamy"', what will impartial history say of August 6, 1945?'. Noting that 'On the day of the destruction of Hiroshima the floodgates of official publicity were swung wide', the former *Washington Post* editor deplored the 'rivers of racy material prepared in our various agencies of Public Enlightenment poured out to the press and radio commentators whose well-understood duty it is to "condition" public opinion'.[28]

Significant voices in the religious press—then a far more important media forum than it is today—joined in questioning the morality of and necessity for the atomic bombings. For instance, *Christian Century*, the influential Protestant weekly, maintained in a 29 August editorial, 'America's Atomic Atrocity', that 'the facts are clearly on one side of this issue':

> The atomic bomb was used at a time when Japan's navy was sunk, her airforce virtually destroyed, her homeland surrounded, her supplies cut off, and our forces poised for the final stroke. Recognition of her imminent defeat could be read between the lines of every Japanese communiqué.[29]

Much of the Catholic press at the time was also critical.[30]

Continuing Dissent and Official Reaction

This initial criticism of the bomb—which combined ethical concerns and serious doubts about military necessity—continued into 1946. In June of that year Norman Cousins and Thomas Finletter (subsequently Secretary of the Air Force) jointly argued in the *Saturday Review of Literature* that the tight time frame after the bomb was successfully tested in New Mexico precluded a non-lethal demonstration of the bomb to the Japanese 'if the purpose was to knock Japan out before Russia came in...'.[31] A month later, liberal radio commentator Raymond Swing declared in an ABC broadcast that the Japanese had been 'looking for an opportunity to surrender, and the testimony of various Japanese leaders indicates that some other excuses would have been found at an early date even if the atomic bomb had not been dropped'.[32] At the end of August, the *New Yorker* published John Hersey's 'Hiroshima', an essay which did much to humanise the victims of the atomic bomb in the eyes of many Americans.[33] On 9 September, just days after Hersey's article captivated a national audience, Admiral William F. Halsey was quoted as saying that:

> The first atomic bomb was an unnecessary experiment....It was a mistake to ever drop it....It killed a lot of Japs, but the Japs had put out a lot of peace feelers through Russia long before.[34]

Norman Cousins used Halsey's comments to denounce immediately the 'crime of Hiroshima and Nagasaki'. He asked pointedly:

> ...now that we have learned from a Navy spokesman that Japan was ready to quit even before Hiroshima, what happens to the argument that numberless thousands of American lives were saved?[35]

These and other challenges to the official narrative, while expressive of a distinct minority of media and public opinion, were significant enough to disturb policy élites.

Some response was called for to bolster public support for the past use, and future development, of nuclear weapons. Henry Stimson, who had been Secretary of War under Presidents Roosevelt and Truman, responded with a seemingly authoritative essay, 'The Decision to Use the Atomic Bomb', published in the February 1947 issue of *Harper's*.[36] Stimson's article was written at the suggestion of Harvard University President James Conant, and ghost-written by the young McGeorge Bundy, with assistance from Harvey Bundy (his father), General Leslie Groves, Conant, and others. It reiterated the official line, this time in a format and a forum intended to put to rest once and for all criticism of the use of the bomb.[37] Stimson assured his readers that:

> ...this deliberate, premeditated destruction was our least abhorrent choice. The destruction of Hiroshima and Nagasaki put an end to the Japanese war. It stopped the fire raids, and the strangling blockade; it ended the ghastly spectre of a clash of great land armies.[38]

Stimson claimed that, had the bomb not been used:

> ...the major fighting would not end until the latter part of 1946, at the earliest. I was informed that such operations might be expected to cost over a million casualties, to American forces alone.[39]

Historians have found no documentary basis for this claim about casualty estimates, a claim that has done much to stifle questions over the last fifty years about the necessity and morality of the decision to use the atomic bomb.[40] As historian Gar Alperovitz notes, 'Perhaps the most enduring single obfuscation created'—or at least given authoritative reinforcement—by Stimson's essay is the belief that the atomic bomb saved vast numbers of American lives.'[41]

Stimson's well-publicised article was considered highly newsworthy. It was reprinted in a number of newspapers including the *Washington Post*, the *St. Louis Post-Dispatch*, and the *Omaha World Herald*, and received considerable radio airtime. The *New York Times*, to give but one example, treated Stimson's essay as front-page news, reprinted a substantial excerpt, and proclaimed in a lead editorial that: 'There can be no doubt that the President and Mr. Stimson are right when they maintain that the bomb caused the Japanese to surrender.'[42] Off the record, a number of political insiders privately expressed their dismay with Stimson's apologia.[43] But after publication of the Stimson article, criticism of Hiroshima in the late 1940s and 1950s was largely confined to the occasional dissent—by a few insiders in their memoirs, talks, and occasional articles, and by a few mainly right-wing or religious commentators. Not until the 1960s did scholarship begin to seriously challenge the myths constructed in 1945 and so ably reinforced in early 1947.

Henry Luce, however, did raise critical questions about the atomic bombing of Japan in the late 1940s. Consider the following quote from a 1948 speech given by Luce: 'If, instead of our doctrine of "unconditional surrender", we had all along made our conditions clear, I have little doubt that the war with Japan would have ended soon without the bomb explosion which so jarred the Christian conscience.'[44] Such sharply worded criticism, however, never made it into print in Luce's magazines. Hanson Baldwin was another media figure with high-level political and military contacts. Military editor of the *New York Times* and a graduate of the United States Naval Academy, Baldwin criticised the bomb decision in no uncertain terms. He argued in a 1950 *Atlantic Monthly* article that:

> We dropped the bomb at a time when Japan already was negotiating for an end of the war but before those negotiations could come to fruition. We demanded unconditional surrender, then dropped the bomb and accepted conditional surrender—a sequence which indicates pretty clearly that the Japanese would have surrendered even if the bomb had not been dropped, had the Potsdam Declaration included our promise to continue the Emperor upon his throne.[45]

While Luce, Lawrence, Trohan, Cousins, Baldwin and other individuals in the mainstream, conservative, and religious media criticised Truman's decision based on their access to military and civilian leaders and their pre-bomb understanding of Japan's precarious military and political situation, most journalists accepted without question, let alone criticism, President Truman's explanation for the use of the bomb.

In the 1950s, criticism of the use of the atomic bomb was largely relegated to leading right-wing publications such as *The Freeman*, *Human Events*, and *National Review*.[46] Right-wing commentators generally combined a moral and geopolitical critique. For the most part they believed that the war could have ended earlier had President Truman agreed to modify unconditional surrender terms. If the war had ended before August, the Soviet Union would not have entered the war with Japan. The Americans and not the Red Army would have taken the surrender in Manchuria. Thus, a number of conservatives argued, the 'Reds' would not have overrun China in 1949 and the Korean War could have been averted. Forrest Davis, for example, wrote in *The Freeman*:

> In the interval between May 29 and July 26, when the door finally was opened to Japan's surrender, the order was issued to drop A-bombs on Hiroshima and Nagasaki; a deed which, given the supposed willingness of Japan to capitulate, comes little short of being a high crime and one that may return unmercifully to plague us.[47]

Similarly, in a May 1958 article in William F. Buckley's *National Review*, a leading voice in the conservative movement, Harry Elmer Barnes contended that the atomic bomb was unnecessary; that by the summer of 1945 the Japanese were already defeated and making bids for peace. He considered the costly landings at Iwo Jima and Okinawa also to have been 'needless', and made quite clear his view that the intended target of the bomb was Russia:

> Perhaps the most striking fact established by research since the end of the war is that the main purpose in using the atomic bombs on Japan was not military at all, but diplomatic, and that the real target was not Japan but Russia.[48]

Barnes stated further that 'Stalin took this view, and many date the origins of the Cold War from the time he received news of the bombing shortly after the Potsdam Conference'. If this is true, Barnes reasoned, 'the tens of thousands of Japanese who were roasted at Hiroshima and Nagasaki were sacrificed not to end the war or save American and Japanese lives but to strengthen American diplomacy *vis a vis* Russia'. *National Review's* editors were clearly pleased with Barnes' essay. They featured it on the magazine's cover as the lead essay and made reprints available.[49] Six weeks earlier, the magazine itself had criticised President Truman's failure to account adequately for his atomic bomb decision. An editorial asked if using the atomic bomb on Japanese cities had been '*really* necessary?': 'Might a mere demonstration of the bomb, followed by an ultimatum, have turned the trick?' 'If there is a satisfactory answer to that question', the editors continued, 'the people of Hiroshima *and* the people of the United States have a right to hear it.'[50]

Such striking criticism by political conservatives of the atomic bombing of Japanese cities runs directly counter to the ahistorical belief, commonly expressed in the American media today, that criticism of the atomic bombing of Hiroshima and Nagasaki grew out of 1960s New-Left historical revisionism and anti-war sentiment. For instance, Cal Thomas, a nationally syndicated columnist and host of a television news show pontificated about Hiroshima 'revisionism' during the fiftieth anniversary of the atomic bombings:

> Those "heroes" and "heroines" of the '60s never saw a cause worth fighting for or a war worth winning. They have now delivered the final insult.
>
> As the [fiftieth] anniversary of the end of World War II approaches, they are reaching back a generation and demeaning their parents' sacrifice, patriotism and decisiveness, saying there was no need and no excuse for dropping atomic bombs on Hiroshima and Nagasaki.[51]

Others made similar assertions. *Washington Post* reporter Ken Ringle noted during the summer of 1995 that:

> Some Vietnam-era historians have been insisting since the 1960s that the United States dropped the first atomic bombs on Japan for reasons other than speeding the end of the Second World War and saving American lives.

Ringle attributed such 'revisionist' history to 'generational second-guessing'.[52] Meanwhile, Jonathan Yardley, the *Post's* regular book reviewer, derided the 'ragtag collection of academics and left-wing ideologues' who:

> …believe that Japan was on the verge of surrender well before the bomb,

that the decision to attack Hiroshima was motivated by extraneous political considerations both domestic and global, and that the mission of the
Enola Gay is an ineradicable moral stain upon the American people.[53]

Thomas, Ringle, Yardley, and many other contemporary media pundits
have been quick to play the 'culture war' card when discussing atomic
bomb scholarship. Engaging in nothing more than propaganda, these
commentators have failed to advance historical understanding of a divisive
national issue. In marked contrast to this current effort to fix the 1960s as
the period when the challenge to the image of the Good War began, so
tarring the liberal-left with historical perversion, a 1959 essay *defending*
the use of the atomic bomb in the *National Review* began by noting
matter-of-factly that 'The indefensibility of the atomic bombing of
Hiroshima is becoming part of the national conservative creed...'.[54]

Countermemory and Critical Scholarship

Although for some years it was the conservative media which were most
apt to criticise Truman's decision to use the atomic bomb, critical memories of Hiroshima never entirely disappeared from the mainstream media.
In 1960 *US News & World Report* published a series of interviews with
World War Two insiders regarding the atomic bomb decision. Of the five
men interviewed—former Secretary of State James Byrnes, former
Atomic Energy Commission head Lewis Strauss, former Under-Secretary
of the Navy Ralph Bard, and atomic scientists Leo Szilard and Edward
Teller—only James Byrnes unequivocally supported use of the bomb,
though he emphatically agreed that the United States wanted to finish the
war 'before the Russians came in'.[55] The interviews were striking not
only because of the willingness of most of the interviewees to question
the decision, but also because a determined interviewer sometimes
pushed hard to explore some of the alternatives to the use of the bomb.
At about the same time, Walter Lippmann, the highly respected
and influential commentator, added his voice to the list of those who considered the bombings unjustified. Responding to a question posed by
a CBS television interviewer about the decision to use the atomic bomb,
Lippmann said:

> Japan was ready for surrender before we dropped the bombs. And in my
> view, we should have negotiated a surrender before we dropped them.
> One of the things I look back on with the greatest regret, as an American,
> is that we were the ones that first dropped atomic bombs.[56]

Following Lippmann's response, Howard K. Smith, the CBS interviewer, immediately changed the subject.

In a 1963 *Newsweek* profile, Dwight D. Eisenhower, distinguished general and former president, recalled that he had opposed using the atomic bomb on Japan during a July 1945 meeting with Secretary of War Stimson:

> ...I told him I was against it on two counts. First, the Japanese were ready to surrender and it wasn't necessary to hit them with that awful thing. Second, I hated to see our country be the first to use such a weapon.[57]

Reprising his critique of the use of the bomb made twenty years earlier, Walter Trohan, in an August 1965 front-page *Chicago Tribune* story, criticised the failure of the American government to 'accept repeated Japanese peace overtures for more than a year before' Japan's eventual surrender.[58] A 1965 NBC documentary, *The Decision to Drop the Bomb*, included interviews with Ralph Bard and former Assistant Secretary of War John McCloy. Both officials raised alternatives to dropping the atomic bomb on an inhabited city. The documentary also mentioned that Truman had known about Japanese peace feelers and divisions in the Japanese leadership about continuing the war. The show also noted Manhattan Project scientist Leo Szilard's opposition to the use of the bomb, Secretary of State James Byrnes's anti-Soviet strategizing, and the Potsdam proclamation's lack of clarity about surrender terms. Even if the documentary ultimately underplayed the reasonableness of alternatives to the bomb, it began to move public knowledge away from a simple bomb versus invasion dichotomy.

Nineteen sixty-five also saw the publication of Gar Alperovitz's path-breaking study *Atomic Diplomacy*.[59] Using newly available sources, Alperovitz essentially began the scholarly questioning of Truman's decision that continues to this day. On 16 July, *Life* magazine published a highly positive review of Alperovitz's book by Ralph Lapp, a former Manhattan Project scientist. According to this high-profile review, Alperovitz's 'contention, brilliantly presented, is that the A-bomb hit Hiroshima but the real "political" target was Moscow.' 'I have no doubt', Lapp added, 'that thoughts of Stalin figured prominently in the decision on Hiroshima'.[60] Scholarship critical of the widely-held belief that it was necessary to use atomic bombs on Japanese cities has steadily accumulated since the 1960s when many formerly secret government documents and private papers began to be opened to historians, a process that is still ongoing. Ironically, as scholars accumulated evidence challenging the official narrative—a narrative that, as we have seen, one could legitimately challenge in earlier decades—the media became less hospitable to such questioning. This occurred especially as American politics grew more conservative after the challenge from the left waned in the 1970s, and as officials and commentators of the Second World War era who had refused the conventional wisdom about Truman's decision passed away. Criticism of the atomic bombings in the media from the 1970s onward largely became the purview of specialists—a few scholars published occasional op-eds or articles in the mainstream media over the years—but non-specialists, including most members of the media, almost never took on a critical role in the historical debate.

Increasingly, conservatives began to distance themselves from 'revisionism'. Nevertheless, David Lawrence continued to recall his early criticism of the Hiroshima bombing. Lawrence reprinted his initial August 1945 anti-bomb editorial several times in the years prior to his death in 1973, even as he remained a staunch anti-communist and Nixon supporter.[61] However, from the mid-1960s on, questioning of the necessity for the atomic bombing of Hiroshima and Nagasaki and criticism of American 'atomic diplomacy' was increasingly relegated to alternative and left-wing publications, such as *Liberation*, and occasional articles in a few specialist magazines, such as the *Bulletin of Atomic Scientists*.[62] In 1975 *US News & World Report* again (and for the last time) reprinted David Lawrence's 1945 editorial critique, as well as portions of the magazine's 1960 interviews questioning the use of the bomb.[63] Also, in 1975, a few scholars who had written about aspects of the bomb were published in the mainstream media—Robert J. Lifton and Richard Rhodes had essays in *Atlantic Monthly* and Barton Bernstein was published in the *New York Times Magazine*.[64] Apart from these instances, little critical analysis of the bomb decision appeared in the media in the 1970s.

By the 1980s the media had clearly begun to privilege the memories of Second World War veterans, and the findings of critical scholarship were rarely mentioned. Despite the release of important archival information from the 1960s onwards, the 'memory' that 'the atomic bomb saved my life' increasingly predominated in the media. In August 1985 *National Review* devoted its cover and lead article to a 'what if' story comprising fictional newspaper clippings. In this fanciful account the United States, motivated by humanitarian sentiment, demonstrates the atomic bomb on Tokyo Bay instead of using it on Japanese cities. Neither the Russians nor the Japanese are the least bit impressed. The United States launches a costly and indecisive invasion of Japan, the Soviet Union takes over Western Europe and all of Korea, President Truman is impeached, and

'President Byrnes' signs the 'Vladivostok peace treaty' returning US bases to the Japanese Soviet Socialist Republic. Numerous other calamities befall the non-Soviet world, resulting in such tragedies as a 1946 British withdrawal from India and South Asia.[65] Presumably the 'lesson' of this *National Review* piece—a lesson never explicitly stated—is 'don't second guess history'. Nowhere in this nor in subsequent 1985 issues did *National Review* acknowledge that it had, in effect, second guessed its own earlier willingness to criticise the Hiroshima decision.[66]

Demonstrating a similar capacity for amnesia, in 1985 *Human Events* offered a traditional defence of the Hiroshima and Nagasaki bombings, ignoring Felix Morley's impassioned 1945 editorial challenge to the legitimacy of the atomic bombings.[67] *US News & World Report* also reported the fortieth anniversary of Hiroshima with the official narrative in full sway. In a fifteen page series of stories, 'The Legacies of World War Two', the magazine focused largely on the social, economic, and technological roads travelled since the end of the war. The piece ended with a brief account of the *Enola Gay* mission and pilot Paul Tibbets' untroubled justification of the Hiroshima bombing. The section was titled 'A-Bomb He Dropped "Saved Lives."'[68]

Nineteen eighty-five saw the most intensive anniversary coverage to that date. The *Chicago Tribune, New York Times, Washington Post,* and *Los Angeles Times,* for example, published more than one hundred items over the course of the summer on topics including commemoration, radiation, bomb survivors, veterans and nuclear culture, and carried bomb-related book reviews. *Time* and *Newsweek* ran special sections totalling more than forty pages.[69] *Life* devoted an entire issue to the Second World War, including a section entitled 'Top Secret: A Great Invasion the A-Bomb Cancelled.'[70] As noted above, ABC's *Nightline* 'recreated' the invasion of Japan that never took place. Apart from a one-page essay in *Time* that the magazine ran three weeks after its special issue on the bomb,[71] and a single news story in the *New York Times,*[72] the media barely mentioned the serious nature of the historical controversy. Opinion pieces in the four above-mentioned newspapers only marginally improved the picture. Twenty-six columns, op-eds, and editorials mentioned Hiroshima.[73] Of the fifteen pieces that took a position on Truman's decision, eleven supported the use of the bomb. Not a single editor or columnist took issue with the atomic bomb decision. All four of the critical pieces—one in each newspaper—were authored by historians. The *Washington Post,* despite its active wartime role in supporting diplomatic means to bring about Japanese surrender, contributed the most to the imbalance, publishing six opinion pieces that supported the bomb decision, and only one that criticised it.[74]

Orthodoxy and Dissent in the 1990s

In late 1991, just before the fiftieth anniversary of the bombing of Pearl Harbour, the media got yet another opportunity to debate Truman's decision. During Pearl Harbour Commemoration Week, President George Bush bluntly stated that Truman's decision 'was right because it spared the lives of millions of American citizens...'.[75] Bush's statement was widely reported and generally applauded in the media. In the days following the president's comment, of around 130 print and television stories and opinion pieces mentioning Hiroshima, only three acknowledged, and in the briefest of phrases, alternatives to Bush's view. These dissenting statements were so brief and half-hearted as to have no noticeable impact on public debate.[76]

Given the depth and consistency of the media's one-sided approach to the question of the bomb's necessity, perhaps the furore over the *Enola Gay* (addressed in the following chapter) should have been expected. The Smithsonian Institution's plans to mount an exhibit that did not fit conventional wisdom about the end of the Second World War attracted extensive negative media coverage in 1994 and 1995. For the most part, the media were generally eager to criticise Smithsonian curators for being 'revisionists'. By going along with the claim that revisionism was beyond the pale, the media rewrote not only the history of the end of the War, but also the history of media and scholarly challenges to historical orthodoxy. Heated debate over the *Enola Gay* exhibit continued into the summer of 1995. Then, in July and August, the fiftieth anniversaries of the first testing and use of nuclear weapons received massive media attention. Many popular magazines published essays about the decision to use the atomic bomb. In late July, for instance, *Newsweek* and *US News & World Report* ran a photo of the Hiroshima mushroom cloud on their covers. Inside both magazines were long articles explaining the development of the atomic bomb, the decision to use it (with *US News* holding much more easily—and without any critical engagement at all—to the conventional explanation), and the legacy of their use. Newspapers, large and small, published thousands of atomic bomb-related articles in July and August,[77] and documentaries about the bomb decision were shown on American television. Historians with various perspectives debated the merit of actions taken fifty years ago on major network news programmes, as well as on some important television talk shows.

The fallout over the Smithsonian controversy indicated the extent and persistence of the gap between scholarship and media discussion of Hiroshima. Although this gap has increased since the 1960s, during the fiftieth anniversary of Hiroshima the media finally began to engage with critical scholarship in various ways, and a few more media outlets than in previous years acknowledged the legitimacy of alternative viewpoints. During the summer of 1995, significant discussions of the decision to drop the bomb were published in the *Atlantic*, *Newsweek*, *New Yorker*, the *Washington Post*, and the editorial pages of several newspapers. Television documentaries on the decision appeared on ABC, Showtime, Arts & Entertainment, the Learning Channel, the History Channel, and PBS. Programmes on other subjects, such as documentaries on Truman and Oppenheimer, also discussed the decision. Several prominent television news and talk shows—*Larry King Live*, the *Charlie Rose Show*, and the *MacNeil/Lehrer NewsHour*—aired debates on the bomb decision.[78] Most surprisingly, historical discussions of the Hiroshima decision even crept into morning and evening news shows on all the major networks.

However, clear limits were still often set on what could be said and how the issue could be presented to readers. Much of the critical re-examination of the atomic bomb decision was relegated to opinion pieces and a few feature articles. The historical debate itself seldom became the subject of news coverage, and almost never part of a related news story. Moreover, while more media outlets than in the past engaged the historical debate, most either downplayed or belittled critical scholarship while reasserting the conventional view of the bomb decision. Several commentators not only defended the decision, but set their defence in the larger context of a battle for American thought and culture. The *Boston Globe* provided a typical example of these tendencies in a news story on 'WW II revisionism'. After consulting and quoting three defenders of the bomb and only one critic, the reporter commented:

> Most revisionists apply retroactively the America-as-world-menace premise of the 1960s. A divine wind of scholarship, propelled by 20-20 hindsight, has transformed Hiroshima and Nagasaki into two more tools in Uncle Sam's bag of dirty tricks....Among the argument's ironies is what World War II did to enhance 1960s ideals, like anti-imperialism.[79]

The article was clearly intended to staunch rather than advance public debate.

The occasional presence of a handful of American historians on TV, radio, and in the print media challenging the conventional notion that President Truman had no reasonable alternative to dropping atomic bombs on Japan brought many journalists and commentators into battle. Mike Royko, a syndicated columnist for the *Chicago Tribune*, apparently willing to listen to critical historians three and a half years earlier, now derided them. In December 1991, after stating that he could not fault Truman's decision to use the atomic bomb on Japanese cities, Royko noted neutrally that some historians had suggested that Japanese surrender might have been accomplished by dropping the bomb on a deserted mountain-top as a demonstration of atomic power. In the summer of 1995, however, Royko belittled historians in a column entitled '"You had to be there", WWII veteran says about egghead revisionists'.[80] The relatively greater willingness of the media to air criticisms of the use of the bomb also drew condemnation and exaggerated judgements from some historians. For example, Donald Kagan, a Professor of History at Yale University, observed that the revisionist school 'now represents...a conventional wisdom universally parroted by educators, pundits, and the popular media'. This fantastic claim can perhaps best be understood as a sign that orthodox historians are feeling embattled about the Hiroshima question for the first time.[81]

Television Coverage in 1995

Television provided some of the most compelling examples of media willingness to accept the legitimacy of a historical debate (even in some cases to push the 'revisionist' interpretation), as well as of media desire to forestall a shift to a fuller understanding of Hiroshima. Several television news and interview shows acknowledged the existence of two legitimate sides to the Hiroshima debate. Rupert Murdoch's Fox network, for example, invited Gar Alperovitz and Thomas Allen to discuss their opposing views about Truman's decision during the morning news. The anchor maintained an even-handedness throughout the Alperovitz/Allen exchange, noting that both sides brought a great deal of evidence to a 'very interesting debate'.[82]

On the same day, CBS *Evening News* investigated the cases for and against the bomb. Beginning with the brief recollection of a Hiroshima survivor, pictures of atomic devastation, and Robert Lifton criticising the use of the bomb, reporter Anthony Mason added:

In reviewing declassified documents many historians are now concluding it wasn't simply a choice between the bomb or an invasion; that there were other alternatives. The President chose not to use them. In General Eisenhower's words, 'Dropping the bomb was completely unnecessary. Japan was already defeated'.

This introduction was followed by Gar Alperovitz presenting supporting evidence, with Mason adding that US intelligence had indicated that the war would be over by the time of the planned invasion, that Truman understood Russian entry into the Pacific War would finish off the Japanese, and that Truman also knew about Japanese peace feelers. Mason concluded by leaving the audience with several provocative questions:

> Was this demonstration of American strength meant for Tokyo or Moscow? Was this the necessary final blow of World War Two, or the opening strike of the Cold War?[83]

The case for the bomb was presented by reporter Wyatt Andrews. He noted that fifty years ago there had been little debate about the use of the bomb, and that Truman had given a straightforward reason for its use—it saved lives. Andrews backed up Truman's rationale for using the bomb largely by recalling Japanese brutality and fanaticism (showing pictures of emaciated American Prisoners of War and of Japanese military units undergoing training), and by having American veterans recount the inhumanity of the Japanese and proclaim their faith that the bomb saved their lives. Historian Robert Maddox also invoked Japanese savagery, and the Bataan Death March.[84]

A few days later, Charles Osgood, the anchor on CBS *Sunday Morning* and a long-time fixture in American broadcasting, opened a bomb-decision segment by noting that there is 'no definitive answer to the painful question' of whether the bomb had been necessary to end the war. Osgood was followed by Peter Kuznick, a professor of History at American University, commenting on how veterans have been falsely led to believe that the bomb saved their lives. A reporter then added:

> Working with recently declassified documents, historians have begun to paint a different picture. Many have concluded that Japan was on the verge of surrendering anyway, and that in any event, Truman was acting on more complex motives.

At this point, historian Martin Sherwin added that the bomb was meant as a warning to the Soviets.[85]

CBS, however, reverted to strict orthodoxy for its news division's production of a Second World War special, *CBS Reports: Victory in the Pacific*. This two-hour special featured Gulf War media celebrity General Norman Schwarzkopf and was anchored by Dan Rather. Mainly an account of the bloody battles in the Pacific, the narrative led up to a brief and misleading report on the atomic bombings. Rather provided only one piece of historical information about the bomb decision: some scientists wanted a demonstration, and this was considered and rejected.

The report then indicated that the bomb was dropped, and showed some atomic bomb victims. Rather, however, undercut these images, saying: 'But there is no sign of surrender from Tokyo.' The report went on to note that a second bomb was used and the Japanese surrendered six days later. This last statement served as a narrative cue for images of a happy America, with victory celebrations, reunions, and veterans being welcomed home. With the narrative of the war completed, the report switched to a brief consideration of the use of the bomb. As Rather strolled through downtown Hiroshima with Schwarzkopf, he commented:

> General...you still hear a lot of talk here, especially in Hiroshima, somehow America owes Japan an apology for dropping the bomb. Many Americans see that as an effort to set history on its ear.

The general replied:

> Yes, and you have to remember, there are a lot of World War Two veterans out there who are convinced that if we hadn't dropped the bomb, the invasion of Japan would have caused a lot more deaths, on both sides.

This was followed by a veteran, who voiced the following thoughts, partly over the image of the flag-raising at Iwo Jima:

> I'm glad that we did drop that atom bomb on 'em, just to pay back [for] Pearl Harbour. And I want those little people over there to remember that.[86]

The report finally concluded at Pearl Harbour, with Rather and Schwarzkopf conversing as they walked through the Punchbowl National Cemetery. Rather:

> General, we should note, for many, if not most, Americans who lived through those times, there'll always be the belief that the Japanese brought down nuclear doomsday upon themselves, by their actions going back three and a half years to Pearl Harbour, and before. And many if not most Japanese prefer to see themselves as the victims, choosing to forget what happened before Hiroshima.

Schwarzkopf:

> Did Hiroshima even the score for Pearl Harbour? I think the larger question is how many Japanese would have died if America hadn't dropped the

bomb and had to invade. There's strong evidence the answer is many more than the number killed at Hiroshima and Nagasaki. To say nothing of the many additional American lives that would have been lost.

Finally, Rather concluded with this stirring flourish: 'The tragedy of *these* times would be to allow remembrance of this war and its causes to slip quietly away, borne by the tides of time and history as vast as the blue Pacific itself.'[87]

ABC *News* took an entirely different tack for their special dealing with the bomb. They aired what will probably stand for some time as *the* 'revisionist' account produced by the American media.[88] Grappling with most of the key issues and some of the evidence emphasised by historians critical of the bomb decision, Peter Jennings narrated an interpretation of the decision that pushed against conventional wisdom harder and more compellingly than any other television treatment of the issue. For the special, ABC consulted with the major historians of the bomb decision and came up with a detailed look at the atomic bomb decision, and the way the orthodox history of the decision was consolidated. Jennings noted, for example, that Stimson's *Harper's* article came about because in 1946 'atomic decision-makers would feel obliged to rewrite history'. He added that:

> The most enduring single fiction to grow out of the *Harper's* article was the notion most of us have long believed: that one million American lives were saved by the bomb. There is no documentary evidence as to where the number came from.

Jennings provided further information about American confiscation of films and photographs of the atomic bombings, and White House vetting of the script of MGM's *The Beginning or the End*—the first film to deal with the bomb decision. The programme pointed to James Byrnes as the man who ultimately convinced Truman to use the bomb instead of trying other alternatives, noting, for example, that Byrnes removed explicit assurances concerning the Japanese Emperor from the text of the Potsdam Proclamation. The special noted, too, that Truman accepted conditional surrender from the Japanese, but called it 'unconditional'.

These and other critical historical findings and interpretations added up to a powerful intervention in the public debate about the atomic bombings. A few reviews—those in the *New York Times* and *Chicago Tribune*, for example—found the programme worthwhile and persuasive. However, many others in the media were predictably upset: Jennings and company elicited cries of outrage from the *Washington Post*, the *Washington Times*, and the *Wall Street Journal*, among others. In one news article, a congressman, a university professor, an Air Force historian, and the national commander of the American Legion denounced the special. The professor, Robert Maddox, called it 'the worst piece of garbage I've seen'.[89]

These critics might well have been mollified a few days later when ABC News made an abrupt about turn on the bomb decision. In doing so, ABC forcefully reinforced what CBS had also demonstrated: that one news programme's break with long-standing myths guaranteed nothing for how other programmes within the same network would deal with that myth. On the fiftieth anniversary of VJ Day, an ABC prime-time evening news special segment on Japan's surrender omitted entirely the context for the surrender supplied a few weeks earlier by the Jennings report. Instead, ABC emphasised Japan's refusal to surrender, and continuing American resolve for a full-scale land invasion. Even after the two atomic bombs had been dropped and Russia had entered the war against Japan, according to the broadcast, US 'preparations for an invasion of Japan had to continue, as did production of still more atomic bombs'. Further contradicting the Jennings report, ABC News added erroneously that Japan agreed to surrender unconditionally.[90]

The Print Media in 1995

Just as television selectively opened up to critical views on Hiroshima, so did the print media.[91] Questions about the bomb's necessity found their way into a few newspapers and magazines, including some smaller city newspapers. New York's *Times Union*, for example, published a 1,500-word news item on reasons for shifts in opinion about the bomb decision. The reporter explained these shifts by pointing to new archival information, but also to the 1960s as a seedbed of revisionism. The reporter further undercut critical scholarship on the bomb by allowing a supporter of the bomb decision to frame the reporting of the historical controversy. Still, the article was a step forward from outright vilification of critical historians or neglect of the scholarly debate.[92]

Many newspapers and magazines remained aloof from new information about Truman's decision. *US News*, sharply underplaying former editor David Lawrence's opposition to Hiroshima, continued to revise its earlier stance on the bomb: insistence on the necessity of the bomb's use replaced Lawrence's repeated questioning.[93] According to the magazine, Japanese militarists indicated—in messages the United States intercepted—

only the desire to fight on; and Truman's advisers told him that the bomb would probably save tens of thousands of American and Japanese lives. 'The atomic bomb', as the magazine put it, 'was a hair-of-the-dog remedy—a last swig of slaughter to end the slaughter'.[94] The only historian mentioned in the article was David McCullough, a scholar whose treatment of the bomb decision has attracted severe criticism despite his having garnered the Pulitzer Prize for his biography of Truman.[95] Noting that Dwight Macdonald's left-wing *Politics* had harshly criticised the use of the bomb in 1945, the magazine added: 'The post-war guilt trip of the left had begun.' This insight would certainly have puzzled Baldwin, Eisenhower, Lawrence, Lippmann, Luce, Morley, Trohan, and many others.[96]

Not all publications distorted and de-emphasised an historical understanding of the bomb decision. Writing in *Atlantic Monthly*, Thomas Powers, author of *Heisenberg's War*, did touch on the issues of peace feelers and unconditional surrender, though he ultimately came down on Truman's side. For Powers, the bomb simply crossed the line that had previously been traversed by the conventional bombings of Dresden and Tokyo. The horror of the atomic bomb, moreover, probably ensured that nuclear weapons were not used during the next fifty years.[97] Also taking the reader back to the events of 1945, the *New Yorker* published an excerpt from John Hersey's classic *Hiroshima*, a commentary on the nuclear jubilee, and a thoughtful essay of more than twenty pages on the bomb decision.[98] *Newsweek* and the *Washington Post* provided particularly ambitious, but ultimately frustrating and peculiar examinations of the atomic bomb decision. Both dismissed the work of critical historians as being tainted by 'perfect hindsight' (in *Newsweek's* words), and both promised to deliver what really preoccupied Truman and his advisors 'at the time' (as both news organisations put it). To this end, the two publications, using the same special researcher (Lucy Shackelford), devoted several weeks to the collection of some primary sources on the bomb decision and ran long articles based on their interpretation of these selected documents.[99] While *Newsweek* provided a more even-handed narrative than the *Washington Post*, both publications defended the use of the bomb. As *Newsweek* put it: 'The decision...was understandable, even inevitable, under the circumstances.'[100] During the summer of 1995 the *Washington Post*, the *New York Times*, the *Los Angeles Times*, and the *Chicago Tribune* published a total of thirty opinion pieces (editorials, columns, and op-eds) that dealt at least in part with the bomb decision.[101] Of these, twenty-one took a position on the issue. A remarkable eighteen out of these twenty-one supported Truman's decision, with the *Washington Post* maintaining its pro-bomb margin by seven-to-one, and the *Chicago Tribune* holding a five-to-nothing margin for the bomb.[102] Three of the eighteen pro-bomb pieces were written by historians of the issue. As was the case in 1985, not a single editor or columnist at these four papers took issue with the atomic bomb decision.

Conclusion

During the past five decades, criticism of the decision to use atomic bombs against Japan has never quite abated in the media, as some wartime leaders had hoped it would. Yet while the history of media coverage and commentary reveals some striking instances of establishment dissent, these very moments of occasional yet recurrent rupture tellingly reveal the opportunities largely ignored by the media, in favour of comforting but simplistic narratives of the Second World War. These missed opportunities become all the more unsettling when one considers what knowledge the media have had available to them at specific historical moments: pre-bomb reporting of a tattered Japan offering peace feelers and fearing Russian entry; limited but newsworthy dissent by military leaders in the immediate post-war period; scattered but thematically consistent criticism by various mainstream voices until the mid-1960s (and mid-1970s in the case of David Lawrence); and the development of critical scholarship based on newly released archival evidence in the 1960s, with its occasional by-product, the op-ed or essay that questioned Truman's decision. The media's lack of engagement with the historical issues surrounding the bomb decision no doubt has many facets, among them, the apparently commonsensical—and élite-driven—notion that the bomb was necessary to end the war. But active resistance to questioning the use of the bomb appears to have played a large part as well. This was clearest during the *Enola Gay* controversy: as discussed in the next chapter, the usual near silence about the bomb decision—especially apparent during Hiroshima anniversaries—exploded in 1994 into an aggressive rejection of the very possibility of debate about the relevant historical issues. The media not only failed to feature meaningful debate about the bomb decision for the most part, but sought to undermine several decades of scholarly effort by ascribing unscholarly and unpatriotic motives to such efforts.

The media's own history of dissent has lain largely unclaimed, aside from the occasional challenges of 1995. For the past five decades the media have promoted—through omission and commission, and recently through vilification as well—a conventional wisdom significantly at odds with much of the scholarly investigation of the bomb decision. Our genealogy of dissent shows, however, that a few in the media did challenge Truman's rationale for using the atomic bomb, especially in the first two decades after the Second World War. Equally significant, from the start criticism did not simply rest on moral grounds, but took up, sometimes substantively, the question of military necessity that now occupies scholars. Historians critical of the conventional wisdom that justifies the atomic bombings of Hiroshima and Nagasaki have for years faced an American media and public either unaware of, or largely resistant to, their findings. Historians have rarely pressed their claims outside the academy; but even so, the news media have played a significant role in frustrating the dissemination of a complex, and disturbing, view of the end of the Second World War.

Yet there are some grounds for cautious optimism. As battlefield memories recede, the struggle among historians will take centre stage in future key Second World War anniversaries. In fact, the flurry of pro/con appearances made by historians in the media during the summer of 1995 suggests that the confrontation may have already begun. In this battle of ideas, different kinds of memories and agendas will come into play. Indeed, for many in the media the debate about the Second World War seems to be largely a battle over the meaning of the 1960s. The only remedy for this is for historians not only to assert the importance of the archive, but also to make their voices heard in the public arena. The media can contribute to a fuller, more honest understanding of the decision to use the atomic bomb only if they are willing to grapple with the growing body of historical evidence that challenges the orthodox rationale for its use. At the same time, the media should take the opportunity to reclaim their own rich history of 'legitimate' dissent in order to free themselves for good from the distorting and misleading rhetoric of post-1960s cultural conservatism.

NOTES

1. Portions of this chapter have grown out of a paper presented by Uday Mohan at an August 1995 conference sponsored by the Los Alamos Historical Society, University of New Mexico History Department, University of New Mexico/Los Alamos, and the Union Institute. The argument has been refined and considerable evidence added by both authors.

2. See, for example: J. Samuel Walker, 'The Decision to Use the Bomb: A Historiographical Update', *Diplomatic History,* No. 14, Winter 1990, pp97-114. At the time of writing a compelling historiographical evaluation of the many books and major interpretive essays occasioned by the fiftieth anniversary of the use of the atomic bomb had yet to be published. A thoughtful engagement with some of the new scholarship is Stephen R. Shalom, 'The Obliteration of Hiroshima', *New Politics,* No. 21, Summer 1996, pp153-175.

3. ABC *Nightline,* 5 August 1985, transcript. Although *Nightline* invited three 'experts'—Alvin Cox, Norman Cousins, and Dean Rusk—to discuss the decision to use the bomb after reporting the 'invasion', the guests did not advance any clear historical arguments against the use of the bomb (former *Saturday Review* editor Cousins did challenge the bomb's use, though not very forcefully). The lack of a meaningful debate can be attributed to both the choice of guests and Koppel's continual insistence on framing the issue as a bomb/invasion dichotomy.

4. Walker, 'The Decision to Use the Bomb', p110.

5. Martin J. Sherwin, *A World Destroyed: Hiroshima and the Origins of the Arms Race,* New York, Vintage, 1987, pxxiv.

6. For a more detailed analysis of pre-bomb media coverage see Uday Mohan and Sanho Tree, 'Hiroshima, the American Media, and the Construction of Conventional Wisdom', *The Journal of American-East Asian Relations,* No. 4, Summer 1995, pp141-160.

7. *Newsweek,* 16 April 1945, p56.

8. 'The Periscope', *Newsweek,* 21 May 1945, p30. *Newsweek* added, however, that Japan had never signaled a willingness to surrender unconditionally.

9. 'Heavy Allied Blows, Fear of Reds Make Jap Leaders Seek Way Out', *Newsweek,* 30 July 1945, p29. Also see 'The Peace Offer Stalin Brought From the Japs', in the same issue, p38.

10. 'Fatal Phrase', *Washington Post,* 11 June 1945, p8.

11. 'Mr. Grew On Peace', *Washington Post,* 13 July 1945. The *Washington Post* had a close relationship with the Navy's Psychological Warfare branch during the war. The *Post* was so proud of its editorial efforts on behalf of Psychological Warfare that shortly after the war it published a booklet entitled 'Psychological warfare against Japan: The story of the secret weapon which had Japan ready to yield thirteen days before the atomic bomb struck Hiroshima.' This booklet consists mostly of reprinted *Washington Post* editorials from the spring and summer of 1945 urging clarification of surrender terms for Japan. Thanks to Sanho Tree for bringing this booklet to our attention

12. 'Power v. Statesmanship', *Time,* 16 July 1945, p13.

13. Robert T. Elson, *The World of Time Inc.*, Vol. 2, New York, Atheneum, 1973, pp132-133; Robert E. Herzstein, *Henry R. Luce: A Political Portrait of the Man Who Created the American Century*, New York, Macmillan, 1994, p382, p393; W. A. Swanberg, *Luce and His Empire*, New York, Charles Scribner's Sons, 1972, p235. See also Gar Alperovitz, *The Decision to Use the Atomic Bomb and the Architecture of an American Myth*, New York, Alfred A. Knopf, 1995, p328, pp331-332.

14. 'Attention, Tokyo!', *Time*, 6 August 1945, pp32-34; quote from p33. Luce's publications also increasingly emphasised that: 'The big problem confronting the US with regard to Japan is no longer a military problem; it is now essentially a problem in statesmanship.' 'Japan—An Opportunity for Statesmanship', *Life*, 16 July 1945, p22. See also 'Japan: The Opportunity for Bringing Classic Statesmanship to Bear on Tokyo Still Exists', *Life*, 6 August 1945, p24.

15. 'Is Japan Ready to Quit? New Denials, New Overtures', *United States News*, 3 August 1945, pp13-14; quotes from p13.

16. Only ten per cent of the American public disapproved of the bombings. See George H. Gallup, *The Gallup Poll: Public Opinion, 1935-1971*, Vol. I: *1935-1948*, New York, Random House, 1972, pp521-522; and also, *Public Opinion Quarterly*, No. 9, Fall 1945, p385.

17. 'The Fortune Survey', *Fortune*, December 1945, p305.

18. National Service Board for Religious Objectors, 'Public Reactions to Atomic Bomb', 5 October 1945; cited in Michael John Yavenditti, 'American Reactions to the Use of Atomic Bombs on Japan, 1945-1947', unpublished dissertation, University of California, Berkeley, 1970, pp149-150. See also Janet Besse and Harold D. Lasswell, 'Our Columnists on the A-Bomb', *World Politics* No. 3, October 1950, pp72-87.

19. Paul F. Boller, Jr., 'Hiroshima and the American Left: August 1945', *International Social Science Review*, No. 57, Winter 1982, p17.

20. Lewis, quoted in John M. Muresianu, *War of Ideas: American Intellectuals and the World Crisis, 1938-1945*, New York, Garland, 1988, p368.

21. *PM*, 19 August 1945, p2; quoted in Boller, op. cit., p19.

22. For Chennault see 'Chennault Holds Soviet Forced End', *New York Times*, 15 August 1945, p13. For LeMay see 'Did Atom Bomb Help End War? Generals Differ', *New York Herald Tribune*, 21 September 1945. For Nimitz see 'Nimitz Finds Navy Vital to New Bomb', *New York Times*, 22 September 1945, p3.

23. For a sampling of early American criticisms of the bombings, see Alperovitz, *The Decision to Use the Atomic Bomb*, pp437-445. See also work by Paul Boyer (especially *By the Bomb's Early Light: American Thought and Culture at the Dawn of the Atomic Age*, New York, Pantheon, 1985) and Michael J. Yavenditti (especially 'The American People and the Use of Atomic Bombs On Japan: The 1940s', *Historian*, No. 36, February 1974, pp224-247; and 'John Hersey and the American Conscience: The Reception of 'Hiroshima', *Pacific Historical Review*, No. 43, 1974, pp24-49).

24. David Lawrence, 'What Hath Man Wrought!', *United States News,* 17 August 1945, p38.

25. David Lawrence, cited in 'Atomic Bomb', *Commonweal*, 31 August 1945, p468.

26. David Lawrence, 'The Right to Kill', *United States News*, 5 October 1945, p35.

27. Walter Trohan, 'Bare Peace Bid US Rebuffed 7 Months Ago', *Chicago Tribune*, 19 August 1945.

28. Felix Morley, 'The Return to Nothingness', *Human Events*, 29 August 1945, p144, p146

29. 'America's Atomic Atrocity', *Christian Century*, 29 August 1945, p974.

30. See, for instance, Conrad H. Lanza, 'The Surrender of Japan', *America*, 1 September 1945, pp428-430; 'Editorial Comment: The Atom Bomb', *Catholic World*, September 1945, pp449-452; 'Horror and Shame', *Commonweal*, 24 August 1945, pp443-444; 'Atomic Bomb', *Commonweal*, 31 August 1945, pp468-469; and 'The Bomb and the Peace', *Commonweal*, 14 September 1945, p515.

31. Norman Cousins and Thomas K. Finletter, 'A Beginning for Sanity', *Saturday Review of Literature*, 15 June 1946, p8. Cousins expanded on his analysis in subsequent years. See, for example, 'Hiroshima: Ten Years After', *Saturday Review*, 6 August 1955, pp7-9, pp30-32.

32. Raymond Swing, 12 July 1946, typescript, p3, Box 30, Raymond Swing Papers, Manuscripts Division, Library of Congress, Washington DC.

33. Moreover, prior to Hersey, Americans had learned little about the human effects of the atomic bombing. In fact, photographic evidence of human suffering from the atomic attack continued to be suppressed until 1952, when a number of photographs were finally published in *Life* magazine. See Robert Jay Lifton and Greg Mitchell, *Hiroshima in America: Fifty Years of Denial*, New York, G.P. Putnam's Sons, 1995, pp59-61.

34. Halsey, quoted from an Associated Press dispatch, in Bernard M. Baruch to James V. Forrestal, 10 September 1946, Forrestal Papers, Mudd Library, Princeton University Archives.

35. Norman Cousins, 'The Literacy of Survival', *Saturday Review of Literature*, 14 September 1946, p14.

36. Henry L. Stimson, 'The Decision to Use the Atomic Bomb', *Harper's*, February 1947, pp97-107.

37. For background on and analysis of the article, see Barton J. Bernstein, 'Seizing the Contested Terrain of Early Nuclear History: Stimson, Conant, and Their Allies Explain the Decision to Use the Atomic Bomb', *Diplomatic History*, No. 17, Winter 1993, pp35-72; James Hershberg, *James B. Conant: Harvard to Hiroshima and the Making of the Nuclear Age*, New York, Alfred A. Knopf, 1993, pp279-304; and Alperovitz, *The Decision to Use the Atomic Bomb*, pp445-492.

38. Stimson, 'The Decision', p107.

39. Ibid., p102.

40. According to Barton J. Bernstein, this myth has 'helped deter Americans from asking troubling questions about the use of the atomic bombs' ('A Postwar Myth: 500,000 US Lives Saved', *Bulletin of the Atomic Scientists*, June/July 1986, p40). Military historian John Ray Skates writes bluntly that: '...prophecies of extremely

high casualties only came to be widely accepted after the war to rationalize the use of the atomic bombs.' (*The Invasion of Japan: Alternative to the Bomb*, Columbia, University of South Carolina Press, 1994, p78)

41. For an overall criticism of Stimson's *Harper's* article, based on what is now known about his wartime beliefs, see Alperovitz, *The Decision to Use the Atomic Bomb*, pp458–471; quote from p466.

42. William L. Laurence, 'Truman Used Atom Bomb to Halt War, Stimson Says', *New York Times*, 28 January 1947, p1, 15; quote from 'War and the Bomb', *New York Times*, 28 January 1947, p22.

43. See Alperovitz, *The Decision*, pp473–479.

44. Henry Luce, speech to the National Assembly of the United Council of Church Women at Milwaukee, 16 November 1948; in John K. Jessup, ed., *The Ideas of Henry Luce*, New York, Atheneum, 1969, p297

45. Hanson W. Baldwin, 'Our Worst Blunders In the War: Japan and the Russians', *Atlantic Monthly*, February 1950, p36. Baldwin repeated these claims (in slightly different language) in Hanson W. Baldwin, *Great Mistakes of the War*, New York, Harper & Brothers, 1950, p92.

46. Criticism was largely confined to right-wing publications, but not exclusively. In 1955 *The Christian Century*, a generally politically liberal Protestant weekly, called on the churches to make Sunday 7 August a 'day of penitence and prayer'. This day was not intended merely as a commemoration of a particularly well-known incident of human suffering. Rather, *The Christian Century* contended:

> By its unnecessary act…the United States did far more than incur responsibility for a wanton taking of civilian lives…the bombing of Hiroshima ushered in the era of nuclear warfare….It was an act for which we need the forgiveness of God, to be sought in a penitence which proves the depth of its sincerity by the measure of our commitment to the pursuit of disarmament and peace. ('A Day for Prayer: August 7', *Christian Century*, 13 July 1955, p811)

Some influential Roman Catholic magazines also expressed criticism of the atomic bombing of Japan. In September 1955, for instance, *Commonweal* reprinted 'substantial excerpts' from a highly critical lead editorial published in the *Pilot*, the official newspaper of the Boston archdiocese ('Of Note: 'I Confess'', *Commonweal*, 16 September 1955, p592).

For a study of selected religious periodicals' 1945 response to the bomb, as well as their treatment of the event on five-year anniversaries of its use from 1950 to 1995, see Leo Malley III, 'Hiroshima and Nagasaki: Memory (and Forgetting) in the Religious Press', in Alison M. Scott and Christopher D. Geist (eds.), *The Writing on the Cloud: American Culture Confronts the Atomic Bomb*, Lanham, Maryland, University Press of America, 1997.

47. Forrest Davis, 'Did Marshall Prolong the Pacific War?', *The Freeman*, 5 November 1951, p73.

48. Harry Elmer Barnes, 'Hiroshima: Assault on a Beaten Foe', *National Review*, 10 May 1958, pp442-3.

49. *National Review* evidently believed that some readers might be interested in ordering 100 or more copies of the essay. See the note following Barnes, 'Assault on a Beaten Foe', p443.

50. 'R.I.P', *National Review*, 29 March 1958, p296.

51. Cal Thomas, 'The final insult to honor and history', *Washington Times*, 2 August 1995, pA18.

52. Ken Ringle, 'History Through a Mushroom Cloud', *Washington Post*, 17 July 1995, pD1, pD4.

53. Jonathan Yardley, 'Hiroshima and the Brutal Realities of War', *Washington Post*, 7 August 1995, pD2. Jefferson Morley, grandson of *Human Events'* editor Felix Morley, and himself a *Washington Post* editor, noted in response to Yardley's column that: 'Although my grandfather wrote thousands of articles in his life and won a Pulitzer Prize for his [*Washington*] *Post* editorials, it was his piece on Hiroshima, "The Return to Nothingness", published in *Human Events* in August 1945, of which he was most proud'. (Jefferson Morley, letter to the editor, *Washington Post*, 12 August 1995, pA19).

54. Medford Evans, 'Hiroshima Saved Japan', *National Review*, 14 February 1959, p525. Evans defended the use of the atomic bomb in part for geopolitical reasons: 'Hiroshima was, among other things, a reversal of Yalta' (ibid., p527).

55. 'Was A-Bomb on Japan a Mistake?', *US News & World Report*, 15 August 1960, pp62-76; Byrnes quote from p66.

56. Walter Lippmann television interview with Howard K. Smith, 11 August 1960, transcribed and published in *Conversations with Walter Lippmann*, Boston, Little, Brown & Company, 1965, p21.

57. 'Ike on Ike', *Newsweek*, 11 November 1963, p107. It should be noted that Eisenhower was going over familiar ground here. He had publicly expressed opposition to the bombings in 1948 and again in his 1963 memoirs. See Dwight D. Eisenhower, *Crusade in Europe*, Garden City, NY, Doubleday, 1948, p443; and *Mandate for Change, 1953-1956: The White House Years*, Garden City, NY, Doubleday, 1963, pp312-313.

58. Walter Trohan, 'Ignored Japanese Peace Bids Plague US, West, with What Might Have Been', *Chicago Tribune*, 14 August 1965, p1. Trohan, like some of the other politically conservative critics noted above, believed that Japan could have been enticed to surrender before the Soviet Union entered the war. 'If Russia had been kept out of the war with Japan', Trohan wrote, 'the history of the last two decades would have been different. It is possible that there might not have been any wars— hot or cold.' (ibid., p4). Trohan also provided a moral critique of the atomic bombings, noting that 'Only last week Pope Paul VI described the A-bombs as an 'infernal massacre' and an "outrage against civilization"' (ibid., p1).

59. On the historiographical importance of Alperovitz's *Atomic Diplomacy*, see Walker, 'The Decision to Use the Bomb', especially pp98-102.

60. Ralph E. Lapp, '5:29 a.m.—and the World Was Changed Forever', *Life*, 16 July 1965, p4, 21.

61. For reprints of 'What Hath Man Wrought!', see *US News & World Report*, 12 August 1955, pp108-107; 15 August 1960, p116, p115; 17 August 1970, p96, p95; 28 August 1972, p72, p71; and 21 July 1975, p72, p71.

62. See, for instance, William H. Honan, 'What We Knew Before Hiroshima', *Liberation*, August 1965, pp19-21; David Horowitz, 'Hiroshima and the Cold War', *Liberation*, September 1965, pp26-27; John Gerassi, 'The Bomb, The Cold War and The Presidency', *Liberation*, December 1965, pp29-31; and Barton J. Bernstein, 'Shatterer of Worlds: Hiroshima and Nagasaki', *Bulletin of Atomic Scientists*, December 1975, pp12-22.

63. David Lawrence, 'What Hath Man Wrought!', *US News & World Report*, 21 July 1975, pp72, 71; 'Was A-Bomb on Japan a Mistake?', *US News & World Report*, 11 August 1975, pp51-53.

64. Robert J. Lifton, 'The Hiroshima Connection', *Atlantic Monthly*, November 1975, pp83-88; Richard Rhodes, 'Reunion at Los Alamos', *Atlantic Monthly*, November 1975, pp76-83; Barton J. Bernstein, 'Doomsday II', *New York Times Magazine*, 27 July 1975, p7, pp21-22, pp24-25, pp28-29. Bernstein offered the reader a historian's assessment of the bomb decision, and Rhodes provided in passing the conflicting judgments about Hiroshima of several scientists who had worked on the bomb.

65. Donald R. Cotter, 'How Second World War Really Ended', *National Review*, 23 August 1985, magazine cover and pp22-25.

66. See 'For the Record', *National Review*, 9 September 1985, p11; and William F. Buckley, Jr., 'Hiroshima and All That', *National Review*, 20 September 1985, pp54-55.

67. Jeffrey St. John, 'Another Look at Hiroshima—40 Years Later', *Human Events*, 10 August 1985, p13.

68. 'The Legacies of World War II', *US News & World Report*, 5 August 1985, pp38-52.

69. Time, 29 July 1985, pp32-59; Newsweek, 29 July 1985, pp28-50.

70. *Life*, Spring-Summer 1985, special issue on Second World War. In the first feature, 'America at War: From Pearl Harbor to Victory, A Devastating March', the various stages in the war are chronicled, beginning with Pearl Harbor. The paragraph for Nagasaki begins: 'The US was planning a full-scale invasion of Japan until atomic weapons made it unnecessary.' The paragraph ends: 'Five days later [after Nagasaki] Japan surrendered, and the war was over.' (p14)

71. Walter Isaacson, 'Why Did We Drop the Bomb?', *Time*, 19 August 1985, p72.

72. 'Two Authors Doubt A-Bomb Assertion', *New York Times*, 1 August 1985, p7. This article is perhaps a unique example, pre-1994, of a news item based on the historiographical controversy about the bomb decision. The article largely focuses, though, on the range of casualty estimates for an invasion of Kyushu. The scholarly debate about the decision briefly presented here, however, did not carry over into other articles about the end of the Second World War. A few days later the *Times* ran an article on the planned invasion of Japan without mentioning that Truman faced choices in addition to invasion and bomb: 'Invasion of Japan? Americans Recall Dread of the Military and Civilian Toll', *New York Times*, 5 August 1985, pA8.

73. Opinion pieces were identified by consulting the published indexes of the four newspapers from June to August 1985. In all indexes except that for the *Washington Post*, the relevant articles were listed under World War II. The *Washington Post* index had a separate heading for Hiroshima.

74. One commentator for the *Washington Post* invoked Henry Stimson's 1947 *Harper's* article in order to justify the bomb's use: Philip Geyelin, 'The Search for Another Reason for the Bomb', *Washington Post*, 15 August 1985, pA21.

75. Bush's remarks appeared in an interview with TV commentator David Brinkley (see transcript of ABC's *This Week with David Brinkley*, 1 December 1991. Many newspapers carried Bush's comments on 2 December.

76. Uday Mohan, Gar Alperovitz, and Kai Bird, 'Fact and Fiction: The American Media, Pearl Harbor, and Hiroshima', unpublished paper.

77. A Nexis database search from mid-July to mid-August 1995 turned up roughly three thousand newspaper and magazine items mentioning Hiroshima.

78. Unlike the first two, which are strictly talk shows with an interview format, *MacNeil/Lehrer* offers the news of the day followed by interviews with newsmakers, roundtable discussions on current topics, and lengthy feature stories.

79. Martin Nolan, 'Battle Rages Over WW II Revisionism: Many Defend Victory Against Bomb's Critics', *Boston Globe*, 14 August 1995, p1.

80. Mike Royko, 'Man Not Harboring Pearls of Wisdom', *Chicago Tribune*, 2 December 1991, p3; and Mike Royko, '"You had to be there", WWII veteran says about egghead revisionists', *Albuquerque Tribune*, 17 August 1995, pC1.

81. Donald Kagan, 'Why America Dropped the Bomb', *Commentary*, September 1995, p18.

82. Fox Morning News, 31 July 1995. Thomas Allen is co-author, with Norman Polmar, of *Code-Name Downfall: The Secret Plan to Invade Japan and Why Truman Dropped the Bomb*, New York, Simon & Schuster, 1995.

83. CBS *Evening News*, 31 July 1995.

84. Only historian Barton Bernstein addressed Truman's frame of mind. According to Bernstein, Truman believed that an invasion would be bloody and that the bomb would be justified; moreover, Americans did not foresee the extent of the effects that would be caused by radiation.

85. CBS *Sunday Morning* included an American Legion spokesperson protesting the second-guessing of Truman's decision. However, the news show also highlighted Fred Eaton, a veteran who had flown on the Nagasaki mission, and who insisted on more not less historical examination of the use of the atomic bomb. He was dismayed that the Smithsonian exhibit had been canceled, because, according to CBS, he 'was hoping for an exhibit that would help Americans comprehend the horror that he saw first hand'. The report closed with Eaton saying: 'We're dealing here with memorials. This year is the right year to be talking about this [the dropping of the bomb]...by God, this is the year for this one.' (CBS *Sunday Morning*, 6 August 1995)

86. After this enlightening moment, five individuals with ties to Second World War— Nella Fermi Weiner (Enrico Fermi's daughter), Chester Nimitz Jr. (the son of the Second World War admiral), George Bush, Charles Sweeney (pilot on the Hiroshima and Nagasaki bombing missions), and Hisao Sawada (a Japanese veteran)— commented briefly on the bomb decision. Only Nimitz offered any critical reflections

on the bomb, recalling that his father always regretted it, and that almost everyone in the Navy felt that the war had been won before the bomb was used.

87. *CBS Reports: Victory in the Pacific*, CBS, 3 August 1995.

88. *Hiroshima: Why the Bomb Was Dropped*, ABC, 27 July 1995.

89. 'Vets, historians rip ABC atomic report', *Washington Times*, 29 July 1995, pA3

90. ABC *World News Tonight*, 14 August 1995; transcript retrieved from the Nexis database. Jennings, the usual anchor for ABC *World News Tonight*, did not anchor the news on this evening.

91. Radio showed the same pattern. National Public Radio (NPR), a publicly funded, non-commercial national radio network that conservatives have attacked and tried to de-fund for its supposedly liberal bias, ran five segments on the bomb decision during the summer: one segment replayed an audio-tape of President Truman's explanation of the decision to drop the bomb; two were separate interviews with author Thomas Allen and historian Barton Bernstein, neither of whom questioned the bomb decision; another segment merely acknowledged and briefly elaborated on the debate over the decision; and the fifth was a roundtable discussion about the decision with four individuals—author Richard Rhodes, radio announcer Norman Corwin, professor Rinjiro Sodei, and Thomas Allen—none of whom are known as outspoken critics of the atomic bombings. (The Nexis database was searched for NPR broadcast items that mentioned Hiroshima from June through August 1995. The database contains transcripts of the main morning and evening NPR broadcasts.)

92. 'Sentiment Shifts, 50 Years After Hiroshima More Ask If The Bomb Should Have Been Dropped', *Times Union*, 6 August 1995, pA1.

93. Gerald Parshall, 'Shock Wave', *US News & World Report*, 31 July 1995, pp44-59.

94. Ibid., p51.

95. David McCullough, *Truman*, New York, Simon & Schuster, 1992. For instance, J. Samuel Walker contends that 'Scholars might well be justified in simply disregarding McCullough's arguments as too shallow to be taken seriously' ('History, Collective Memory, and the Decision to Use the Bomb', *Diplomatic History* 19, spring 1995, p327).

96. Parshall, 'Shock Waves', p54.

97. Thomas Powers, 'Was it Right?', *Atlantic Monthly*, July 1995, pp20-23.

98. Murray Sayle, 'Letter From Hiroshima: Did the Bomb End the War?', *New Yorker*, 31 July 1995, pp40-64; John Hersey, 'From the Archives: The Day the Bomb Fell', ibid., pp65-67; Hendrik Hertzberg, 'Comment: The Nuclear Jubilee', ibid., pp6-7.

99. The *Washington Post* indicated that it also utilized some secondary sources, but only one major scholar of the bomb decision, Gar Alperovitz, appeared on the list of sources published with the two *Post* articles. Evan Thomas, 'Why We Did It', *Newsweek*, 24 July 1995, pp22-23, pp25-28, p30; Walter Pincus, 'Truman Didn't Hesitate to Drop Atomic Bomb on Japan', *Washington Post*, 16 July 1995, pA1, pA10, and Pincus, 'A-Bombs Left Top Councils Of Japan Split', *Washington Post*, 17 July 1995, pA4.

100. Thomas, 'Why We Did It', p22.

101. Opinion pieces published between June and August 1995 were located using the official indexes for all newspapers except the *Chicago Tribune*. The indexes listed the relevant items under the heading 'Second World War'. Opinion pieces for the *Chicago Tribune* were located by searching the Nexis database for the word 'Hiroshima'.

102. The *Washington Post* also carried two substantial news and feature pieces defending the use of the atomic bombs. One was an interview with Major General Charles Sweeney, the pilot who flew on both atomic missions: James Webb, 'Was It Necessary' (interview with Charles Sweeney), *Washington Post* (*Parade*), 30 July 1995, pp4-5. The other was Walter Pincus's two-part article noted above.

7 HISTORY AND THE NEWS MEDIA: THE SMITHSONIAN CONTROVERSY[1]

Uday Mohan

In 1994-95, the meaning of the end of World War Two became the subject of prolonged and bitter public debate for the first time in the United States. Stirred out of complacency about the recent past and the role of history in American society—a complacency largely unchallenged outside academia—media commentators, journalists, politicians, war veterans, and outraged individuals with memories of the Second World War fought with critical historians and museum curators for control over the 'truth' about the decision to use the atomic bomb against Japan.[2] This was a battle waiting to happen. Scholarship critical of the bomb decision—and therefore seriously at odds with public understanding of why Truman used the bomb—had accumulated for the last thirty years, though, as discussed in the preceding chapter, little of it had been presented to the American public by the mass media. Moreover, the challenge to conventional wisdom about the atomic bombings of Hiroshima and Nagasaki—in the form of a planned major museum exhibition on the end of the Second World War and its aftermath—occurred in the midst of an ongoing 'culture war': a war of position over the very meaning of the American past, present, and future. In this war, debates about apparently settled history explicitly and immediately became, for conservatives and others, partisan debates about patriotic orthodoxy, rather than about historical matters.[3]

The planned museum exhibition at the Smithsonian Institution's temple of aerospace technology, the National Air and Space Museum, thus collided with the apparent need in contemporary America to call for 'patriotic' thinking and to mark out and eliminate its disturbance. As the noted newspaper and television pundit George Will stated, in his usual tone of reserved but vexed disbelief at those to his left, the people at the Smithsonian responsible for the exhibition script 'rather dislike this country'.[4] Preferring bluntness, Rush Limbaugh simply called the Smithsonian's interpretation of history 'blasphemous'.[5] And just days before Will and Limbaugh warned their audiences about the lack of patriotism at the Smithsonian, twenty-four members of Congress had launched their attack against cultural and historical insubordination at the museum. In a publicised letter to the secretary of the Smithsonian, these Congressional representatives, a quarter of them Democrats, called for the elimination of the 'anti-American prejudice' they believed infected the script.[6] Such charges eventually took their toll and led, despite four successively watered down scripts, to the cancellation of the original plans for an extensive examination of the use and legacy of nuclear weapons. Commenting on the cancellation, Stanford University historian and exhibition adviser Barton Bernstein noted that if World War Two military leaders could voice their doubts and objections 'without having their patriotism challenged, it is dismaying that their judgements have now been deemed too harsh for American eyes and ears'.[7] Earlier, Bernstein had also noted that the patriotism of some of the opponents of the Smithsonian exhibition had a 'retrospective, vengeful quality'.[8] The *Enola Gay* controversy—as the struggle over the planned exhibition featuring the *Enola Gay*, the plane that dropped the atomic bomb on Hiroshima, has come to be known—brought conflict over the interpretation of history to the fore in the culture war. Even though the controversy over the exhibition ended in the spring of 1995, it has become a reference point in ongoing media and academic commentary on the culture war.[9]

It is my contention that the American news media played a key role in the generation, unfolding, and conclusion of the *Enola Gay* controversy. Over the course of more than a year, the media demonstrated an extraordinary devotion to one of the central myths of the Second World War—one that the media themselves have helped to nurture since 1945—that Truman used the atomic bomb simply to avoid an enormously bloody invasion of Japan.[10] The media showed their preference for this simplistic view of the past by allowing members of Congress and organisations such as the American Legion and the Air Force Association (AFA) to become the ultimate arbiters of World War Two history. In their desire to legitimise this history, many in the media placed the *Enola Gay* controversy in a convenient cultural framework, invoking 'political correctness' as a convenient way of labelling the motives of the Smithsonian curators and their initial supporters. By allowing patriotic sloganeering to overtake historical thought, the media played a central role in the eventual cancellation of the original exhibition, an event that led to the forced resignation of the director of the National Air and Space Museum and the cancellation of other, related exhibitions at federally funded museums.[11]

These conservative victories have again postponed American reckoning with the atomic bombings of Hiroshima and Nagasaki. Governmental secrecy, suppression of information, and a general absence of in-depth questioning in the media all have contributed to a simplistic public understanding of the bomb decision—an understanding greatly at odds with the complex history that scholars have told over the last thirty years.[12] The *Enola Gay* controversy revealed a huge disparity between scholarship and much of the popular sentiment about the atomic bombing of Japan, and the tenacity of widespread media myths about the issue. One newspaper editorialist wrote of the 'bizarre explanations' put forward by scholars at the Smithsonian; scholars who 'had to be shoved back into the realm of reason by retired warriors'.[13] A columnist for a major newspaper suggested that scholars who questioned Truman's decision were trying to rewrite 'this country's history to mollify the Japanese'.[14]

The dominant American view of Hiroshima and Nagasaki also owes much to what people felt when they first heard about the bombings fifty years ago. In 1945 many Americans believed the Japanese got what they deserved. Many Americans shared the sentiments voiced by President Truman two days after the bombing of Nagasaki: 'When you have to deal with a beast you have to treat him as a beast.'[15] Far from dying out, such feelings continue to hold sway among some Americans. Writing to Smithsonian secretary I. Michael Heyman at the end of 1994, Republican Representative Sam Johnson and six other members of Congress stated their 'deep displeasure' at the Smithsonian's supposed mishandling of an exhibition that, after all, 'addresses one of the most morally unambiguous events of the 20th century'.[16] It is hardly surprising, then, that President Bill Clinton also supported veterans' efforts to curtail the Smithsonian's plans and that he publicly and unequivocally affirmed the appropriateness of Truman's decision.[17] Nor is it surprising, though it is dispiriting, that no one in the media challenged politicians such as Clinton on this issue. Perhaps what is surprising, or at least new, when discussions of Hiroshima have entered the public sphere in the last decade or so are the rancorous charges of national disservice and disloyalty from those who hold the conventional view about Hiroshima. The atomic bombings appear to have become, in the words of Robert Jay Lifton and Greg Mitchell, America's 'raw nerve' and 'a threat to our national image'.[18] The occasional mainstream dissent against Hiroshima, infrequent but apparent through the 1960s and early 1970s, currently has no analogue in public discussions of the bomb decision. Scholars critical of the bomb decision have been unable to gain the legitimacy that bomb critics of the World War Two generation had in the mainstream media. As older dissenting voices died out over the years, their counter-memory disappeared from the public sphere as well. What has remained overwhelmingly in the media and public discourse is the dubious but culturally useful shorthand that the bomb saved lives by preventing an invasion of Japan, a belief given added weight by media emphasis on what World War Two veterans remember about Japanese brutality.

The Planned Exhibition and its Critics

The Smithsonian Institution's exhibition, originally scheduled to open at the National Air and Space Museum (NASM) in May 1995, was intended to address the gap in public understanding of the bomb decision, as well as to lay out the legacy of nuclear weapons. The controversy began in July 1993 when the NASM issued a planning document calling for an exhibition on the end of the Second World War based on the latest scholarship. The document stated:

> The primary goal of this exhibition will be to encourage visitors to undertake a thoughtful and balanced re-examination of the end of the Second World War and the onset of the Cold War] in the light of the political and military factors leading to the decision to drop the bomb, the human suffering experienced by the people of Hiroshima and Nagasaki and the long-term implications of the events of August 6 and 9, 1945....[T]his exhibit can provide a crucial public service by re-examining these issues in the light of the most recent scholarship.[19]

The decision to place material in historical context was a relatively unusual move. The museum, created after the Second World War to display and memorialise the development of aviation in America, had for years simply displayed without comment iconic objects that marked aviation milestones, such as Charles Lindbergh's *The Spirit of St. Louis* and the Mercury space capsule. As one news account appositely put it: 'In one eye-popping room, visitors see the triumphant roll-call of American aviation'.[20] In the late 1980s and early 1990s, however, the museum began to include more interpretative labels in its exhibitions. This shift away from technological celebration and towards critical scholarship particularly displeased the Air Force Association (AFA), an organisation of about 180,000 Air Force veterans and other individuals dedicated to promoting military aviation.[21]

The plans for an explicitly interpretative look at the end of the Second World War further rankled with the AFA, which in early 1994 began a massive publicity campaign against the Smithsonian. In the resulting controversy, the media reflected not only the version of history established and narrowed over fifty years, but also the extensive public relations efforts of the Air Force Association, vocal conservatism in Congress, and veterans' views as represented by the American Legion (the largest veterans organisation in the United States, with more than three million members). Together, these institutions helped shape the public debate in such a way that a reticent Smithsonian, concerned about its funding (approximately 75% of which comes from Congress), was forced to censor its script and finally cancel the exhibition altogether.[22] As Smithsonian Secretary Heyman reflected, in a column largely focusing on budgetary matters: 'we were uncertain whether the Smithsonian would continue to be cherished in the light of so much negative publicity.'[23]

The Smithsonian's exhibition proposal was brought to the AFA's attention in the summer of 1993 by W. Burr Bennett Jr., a former B-29 pilot who was part of a small group called the Committee for the Restoration and Proud Display of the *Enola Gay*.[24] Concerned that the exhibition would stain the memory of the plane, the group had collected 5,000 signatures urging the Smithsonian to display the plane 'proudly'. Bennett's letter and the enclosed NASM planning document eventually generated a letter of concern from the AFA to the Smithsonian regarding the plan's supposed partisan stand on the 'moral and political questions' raised, lack of acknowledgement of the bravery of the veterans, and depiction of America and Japan as moral equivalents during the war.[25] Through private meetings and letters over the course of several months, the AFA tried to push the Smithsonian towards the prevailing public view of Truman's decision, as well as calling for more evidence of Japanese, rather than American, aggression to be shown in the script. In frustration over the lack of Smithsonian co-operation, the AFA eventually decided to pressure the Smithsonian through the news media and Congress. It issued a press release in mid-March 1994 titled 'Politically Correct Curating at the Air and Space Museum', which attacked not only the planned exhibition as 'politically biased', but noted an almost decade-long trend toward PC curating and the pervasive 'negative attitude toward airpower' that the NASM had developed.[26] The press release also made public a now famous passage—lifted out of context from the first draft—that continues to haunt the Smithsonian: 'For most Americans, it was a war of vengeance. For most Japanese, it was a war to defend their unique culture against Western imperialism.' For critics outraged at the Smithsonian's reinterpretation of the atomic bombings, these two sentences would come to embody the museum's supposedly anti-American, pro-Japanese bias.

The first mass media report that took up the AFA charges came on 28 March 1994, from the *Washington Times*, the conservative alternative to the *Washington Post* in the US capital. The *Times* column, entitled 'Rewriting History', reproduced highlights from the AFA press release, including the offending 'war of vengeance' quote.[27] A follow-up column briefly noted NASM director Martin Harwit's defence of the script.[28] This column apparently pushed the AFA's campaign to the next level, prompting the organisation to make the exhibition script public, something the NASM had asked it not to do. The AFA gave the copy of the script to the *Washington Times* and asked the paper to judge the charges for itself. The *Times* avoided direct judgement and instead quoted remarks of displeasure which a senior Republican senator, Nancy Kassebaum, had expressed to the museum after reading the *Times* reports: 'It seems a travesty that when the *Enola Gay* is finally exhibited, it will be in a manner that many veterans find objectionable.'[29] These early articles in the *Washington Times* established a pattern that remained consistent for the next fifteen months: conservative critics, in this case the AFA, launched charges against the Smithsonian; the media generally chose to reproduce these charges uncritically; the resulting media accounts outraged members of Congress, leading to more media coverage about the irresponsibility of the Smithsonian. But some early media coverage also suggested alternative roads which were not taken in most of the ensuing coverage. A couple of early reports did not reflect a media debate largely favouring or captured by the AFA and like-minded antagonists of the Smithsonian.[30] However, these reports did not feature any historians to anchor a story about history, opting instead for a balance between the views of Smithsonian officials and curators and their non-specialist critics—a balance that would soon disappear.

By May the controversy began to receive national coverage, with AFA charges about the script's unfairness and imbalance published sometimes with and sometimes without countervailing explanations from the Smithsonian. A 23 May Hugh Sidey column in *Time*, for example, simply reiterated many of the criticisms about script bias detailed by John Correll in an AFA article that would be mined often by the media. Sidey also relayed Senator Nancy Kassebaum's indignation at the proposed exhibition. The views of these critics—Kassebaum and the AFA—clearly dominated the *Time* article. The Smithsonian, in the quoted words of John Correll, should 'Just be fair. Tell both sides'. Sidey himself told the other side of the story by limiting a defence of the exhibition script by the Smithsonian staff to two sentences.[31] Again, no historian was interviewed for the *Time* magazine piece.

As the controversy over the draft script grew, news organisations also failed to inform readers that some establishment historians had actually praised the museum for its first script draft. National Park Service historian Edwin Bearss, a member of the exhibition's advisory board, wrote to curator Tom Crouch in February 1994:

> As a World War II Pacific combat veteran, I commend you and your colleagues who have dared to go that extra mile to address an emotionally charged and internationally significant event in an exhibit that, besides enlightening, will challenge its viewers.[32]

Even Air Force historian Richard Hallion, an exhibition adviser, initially offered positive comments about the script. In a February 1994 note, in which some recommendations about script emphasis were made, Hallion and his colleague Herman Wolk wrote: 'Overall, this is a most impressive piece of work, comprehensive and dramatic, obviously based upon a great deal of sound research, primary and secondary.' Hallion added in a hand-written note: 'Again—an impressive job! A bit of "tweaking" along the lines discussed here should do the trick.'[33] As the controversy went public, and the AFA got into the act, Hallion began to reverse his favourable comments.

The media almost never questioned whether the AFA and other veterans groups were qualified to render historical judgements about the bomb decision. The media also never focused on the cultural or institutional motives of these critics. The AFA, for example, as a lobbying arm for air power had a clear interest in preventing the NASM from becoming anything less than a celebratory space for aeronautical technology. Nevertheless, far from examining the AFA's extraordinary role in the *Enola Gay* controversy, the media uncritically used the materials the AFA distributed to them. Not surprisingly, given their narrow use of sources, the media often distorted the contents of the controversial exhibition scripts. In what follows, I aim to demonstrate in detail how the media distorted and narrowed public understanding of the historical debate; misrepresented the planned exhibition; and transformed the desire for wartime commemoration into an ideological weapon in the culture war, attacking the legacy of the 1960s as well as critical evaluation of the end of the Second World War.

Distortion, Misrepresentation and the Culture War

Ironically, the controversy escalated during the summer while the script was being substantially revised in response to some of the charges of imbalance. Initial criticism focused not only on the treatment of the bomb decision, but the overall approach to the war and the bombings. The Smithsonian, according to its critics, was leaving the impression that the Japanese were victims and Americans the aggressors. Given the negative publicity, NASM Director Martin Harwit, concerned about budgetary repercussions for the museum, appointed a 'Tiger Team' in late April to review the script. In late May this team, comprising three retired air force officers, one historian, one NASM volunteer, and the special assistant to the NASM director, recommended forty-two changes to the script. During the next two to three months, most of these recommendations would be implemented—thirty fully, and seven in part.[34] But revisions—inevitable in a first draft—apparently did not matter, especially to media commentators.

It became more important to level charges of bias or political correctness at the Smithsonian. An op-ed in the *Portland Oregonian*, for example, trotted out the 'war of vengeance' quote shortly *after* the quote had been substantially modified. The editorial writer commented acidly: 'That a prominent historical museum could ignore the hard-won lessons of history so easily, and so soon, is appalling.' The op-ed concluded with a call for 'a total review' of the exhibition project—precisely what the museum had undertaken more than a month earlier.[35] Newspapers large and small conveyed the impression that the Smithsonian had revised nothing in response to reasonable criticisms.

As the summer progressed, the infrequent even-handed article about the exhibition became rarer still. The media generally refused to point out how far the NASM was moving to mollify its critics, taking instead the word of the AFA and other opponents that the museum was still being obstinate in addressing criticisms. In fact, by mid-July, several military historians were pleased by the extent of the revisions. The Director for Joint History, Office of the Chairman, Joint Chiefs of Staff, for example, commented that:

> Some attempt has been made to address virtually every criticism raised at [an April meeting]…although in some cases, the fixes have been minor…. Revisionist interpretations no longer dominate discussion of the political and diplomatic issues surrounding the use of the Atomic Bomb…. [T]he script no longer reads as a blanket indictment of the US, casting the Japanese as helpless victims.[36]

Although the latter sentence is a debatable interpretation of the first draft, nothing like this overall assessment, from the top historical branch of the military, could be found in the media. The coverage instead emphasised the disappointment of veterans—including those represented by the AFA—and the simmering anger in Congress.[37]

Several events in June and July led to the widening of the controversy with the help of the media. In June *Enola Gay* pilot Paul Tibbets issued a press release through the Airmen Memorial Museum. He suggested that the *Enola Gay* 'should be presented as a peace keeper' and noted that 'the proposed display of the *Enola Gay* [was] a package of insults'.[38] The latter phrase was widely reported, and picked up about a month later by Eugene Meyer, a reporter for the *Washington Post*. Meyer also used internal documents from the NASM released by the AFA in mid-July to highlight the charges of bias and political correctness levelled at the museum by its opponents:

The critics accuse the Smithsonian of choosing political correctness over historical accuracy.... They charge that the exhibit as planned will portray the Japanese largely as suffering, even noble victims and the Americans as racist and ruthless fighters hell-bent on revenge for Pearl Harbour.[39]

Since Meyer chose to emphasise the critics' charges, readers of the *Washington Post* would remain unaware that several military historians had only recently commented positively on the revised exhibition script.[40] Meyer also offered up the myth of the bomb's necessity in the face of an invasion involving casualties estimated at 'upwards of 800,000'—a version of history which the Smithsonian was going to undermine, according to Meyer's sources.

Inevitably this article, in Washington DC's main newspaper, elicited Congressional outrage. After reading Meyer's piece, Republican Congressman Peter Blute of Massachusetts wrote to the Smithsonian Secretary on 10 August condemning the 'anti-American prejudice' and 'biased' nature of the revised script. The letter, co-signed by twenty-three other members of Congress, echoed the AFA's language and charges, just as news reports had. The lawmakers noted that the script was 'lacking in balance and context', a phrase favoured in virtually all AFA materials. As a mid-summer AFA internal reference sheet for media soundbites stated, 'Our Mantra: The proposed *Enola Gay* exhibit lacks balance and context'.[41] The Congressional letter also repeated the charge made by the AFA, and reported without rebuttal by Meyer, that few of the Tiger Team's suggestions had been incorporated into the script. The letter concluded with a call to 'provide the American people with an objective account of the *Enola Gay* and her mission rather than the historically narrow revisionist view contained in the revised script'.[42] Four days later a strongly worded *Washington Post* editorial criticised the politicisation of the exhibition. 'What the tenor of the debate suggests', insisted the *Post*, 'is a curatorial inability to perceive that political opinions are embedded in the exhibit or to identify them as such.'[43] Again the charge was made that the museum had not followed through with sufficient revisions. In an interview with Tony Capaccio, Congressman Blute's spokesperson said that the *Post* editorial was instrumental in neutralising political support for the museum. Editorialists and columnists around the country echoed the strident *Washington Post* line. Jeff Jacoby, for example, wrote in the *Boston Globe* that the exhibition 'was conceived not as a balanced presentation of how and why the Pacific war ended as it did, but as an emotional attack on the US use of the bomb'.[44] Jacoby suggested that it was the exhibition's anti-American tone that had drawn the fire of critics, including members of Congress, veterans groups, and *Enola Gay* pilot Paul Tibbets. The *Washington Post's* reporting and editorialising demonstrated how the AFA's charges and concerns fed into the media largely unexamined and thus reached Congress. Congress's accusations fed back into the media, further intensifying the debate. By the end of 1994, the AFA had compiled a clippings file of more than 330 periodical articles, and some letters, about the controversy, the majority of them negative. These clippings were bound, and distributed widely as part of AFA's publicity package. The AFA thus attempted to make the negative coverage doubly effective.

The Smithsonian was partly responsible for the lack of countervailing pressure. Museum spokesman Michael Fetters acknowledged in an interview that 'Our own office didn't respond as strongly as we could have so we bear a lot of the responsibility' for the way the coverage turned out.[45] The museum did not prepare a detailed response to the media attacks until 6 September, and then the draft response was never distributed.[46] Moreover, Martin Harwit, the NASM director, did not clearly acknowledge publicly the importance of recent scholarship in understanding Truman's decision. In an August op-ed for the *Washington Post*, for example, Harwit maintained that the controversy entailed generational differences. He did not emphasise the importance of historical interpretation based on archival findings.[47]

Without countervailing pressure, media accounts disseminated factual errors, faulty assumptions, and script passages taken out of context. The accounts fed off each other and further polarised the debate. Perhaps the most glaring gap in the coverage was the failure to challenge the standard assumption—that the Allied forces would have had to invade Japan if the atomic bombs had not been dropped. Typical of the news coverage in this respect were Mike Feinsilber's five Associated Press stories, all of which merely restated or implied the conventional link between bomb, invasion, and the saving of lives.[48] Feinsilber's stories came in January and February 1995, after roughly six months of extensive coverage of the exhibition. Apparently nothing in the coverage—which Feinsilber said he had 'kept an eye on', especially on the *Washington Post*—led him to question the bomb/invasion dichotomy. Despite the historical assumption about the invasion running through his pieces, Feinsilber in an interview felt that the news story 'just wasn't a vehicle for examining the historical arguments'. He added, though, that while he did not feel compelled to write a story examining the historical issues, 'perhaps I should have. Because the current events could have provoked an examination of those issues'.[49]

Other writers also refused to go beyond the conventional wisdom. The syndicated columnist and leading conservative commentator Charles Krauthammer, whose work is occasionally published in scholarly journals, claimed in an interview that before writing a column his assistant calls 'everyone involved in everything…to collect material'. Krauthammer further claimed that he was familiar with some of the written history, which he said strongly supported the conventional view of the bomb decision. Yet none of the scholars whose work he had consulted—Paul Fussell, David McCullough, and Martin Gilbert—are authorities on the decision to use the bomb.[50]

In one of the few attempts to use some of the latest scholarship, *Newsweek* quoted from J. Samuel Walker's 1990 article in *Diplomatic History* to make the point that the bomb was used to avoid a bloody invasion of Japan, a conclusion at odds with Walker's own historiographical appraisal. The *Newsweek* writer conceded in an interview that he had not seen the entire Walker article and based his story on files from other *Newsweek* reporters.[51] Walker's article, at that point the most comprehensive overview of the literature on the bomb decision, crossed the desk of other reporters as well. Historian Kai Bird, for example, sent the article to both Eugene Meyer and Ken Ringle of the *Washington Post*, but neither journalist used Walker as a source in his reporting, or wrote a story on the nature of the historical controversy itself.

It should be noted that the scholarship the Smithsonian included in its first script questioned Truman's decision, but left intact the notion that Truman dropped the bomb to shorten the war. Along the way, though, the script raised the questions scholars are still grappling with: did Truman have more than military reasons for dropping the bomb; was the bomb used to avoid an inevitable invasion of Japan; did the bomb save a million or even half a million lives; what choices did American leaders face?[52] Throughout the sections on these historical controversies, the script reiterated that Truman's options were only clear in hindsight. The fact that the NASM curators ultimately did not 'second-guess' Truman, and that the script fell far short of the challenge to Truman that several scholars of the bomb decision have posed, never became part of the media coverage about the planned exhibition. This simple fact about the script, inserted into news accounts of the curatorial perversion of history at the NASM, could have mitigated the political effects of the more than year-long denunciation of the museum in the media. Such a move by the media would have also introduced audiences to the legitimacy of the controversy about the bomb decision. Other common and significant mistakes in the coverage included the projected number of casualties from an invasion of Japan and the script's supposed impugning of American motives and character. Casualty estimates casually tossed around by journalists ranged from hundreds of thousands—already misleading—to an absurd six million. William Mullen in a *Chicago Tribune* story used the commonly cited figure of one million. Asked in an interview where he got the number from, Mullen admitted: 'I don't know where I got my million figure.'[53]

While very few journalists accurately raised historical issues, *New York Times* reporter John Kifner ably presented all sides of the historical debate. Unfortunately the *Times* piece appeared only after the Smithsonian had decided to eliminate its original plans for an exhibition.[54] But while the *Times* chose to respond to the cancellation with a news story on the continuing and legitimate historical controversy among scholars of the bomb decision, the *Washington Post* only played up and focused on the Smithsonian secretary's statement that the exhibition had been fundamentally flawed in concept.[55] Perhaps the only other instance of a member of the media laying out some of the historical evidence came in a column in the *Arizona Republic* on 6 October. William Cheshire, a senior editorial columnist, criticised the Smithsonian for first going too far in one direction and then backtracking, but failing altogether in promoting intelligent debate about the bomb's use. He then proceeded to show that there were solid grounds for a debate by quoting historian Gar Alperovitz and World War Two critics of the bomb decision, including Admiral Leahy, General Eisenhower, General Arnold, and the US Strategic Bombing Survey.[56] Cheshire admirably demonstrated that a coherent historical challenge to 'orthodoxy' was possible and easily posed. He also clearly demonstrated what most journalists had failed to do. Even when a newspaper published op-ed challenges to the myths about the bomb decision, its own editorials and news reports continued to hold firmly to conventional wisdom. Thus, a newspaper like the *Chicago Tribune* could publish an op-ed by Gar Alperovitz on 9 August 1994, but this made no difference to its subsequent reporting and editorialising. An editorial on 9 September, for example, spoke of the 'tragic necessities' of the bombing and the half-to-one million casualty estimates of a planned invasion.[57]

When journalists were not distorting historical issues, they were misrepresenting the exhibition script. Although by May 1994 the museum had modified the 'war of vengeance' quote that had inflamed veterans, commentators, and the media, the quote was repeated for more than a year in the media by everyone from right-wing presenter Rush Limbaugh to National Public Radio. No one in the media bothered to point out the context of the quote. In the script it was preceded by the following:

In 1931 the Japanese Army occupied Manchuria; six years later it invaded the rest of China. From 1937 to 1945, the Japanese Empire would be constantly at war. Japanese expansionism was marked by naked aggression and extreme brutality. The slaughter of tens of thousands of Chinese in Nanking in 1937 shocked the world. Atrocities by Japanese troops included brutal mistreatment of civilians, forced labourers and prisoners of war, and biological experiments on human victims. In December 1941, Japan attacked US bases at Pearl Harbour, Hawaii, and launched other surprise assaults against Allied territories in the Pacific. Thus began a wider conflict marked by extreme bitterness.[58]

Reprising the quote taken out of this context, a particularly harsh January 1995 editorial in the *Mobile Register* gloated over the Smithsonian's forced retreat: 'The ordinary people who notified the political establishment that the New Deal was over effectively told academia that the New Left has had its day.'[59]

The script was also attacked for its supposed suggestion that American racism had been a motive for dropping the bomb. In a 1 August *USA Today* column, Tony Snow, a newspaper columnist often found on radio and television as well, wrote that the script 'raise[d] a racism charge', and he quoted from the script as follows: 'Some have argued that the atomic bomb would never have been dropped on Germans because it was much easier for Americans to bomb Asians than white people.' Snow then commented: 'No serious historian takes this view but the Smithsonian curators included it.' In fact, the script conclusion was almost identical to that of Snow's: 'The consensus of most, if not all, historians is that President Roosevelt would have used the bomb on Germany if such an attack would have been useful in the European war'.[60] On 29 August the *Wall Street Journal* published one of the most outrageous assertions just as public pressure mounted against the Smithsonian. In an editorial the *Journal* stated that:

> ...it is especially curious to note the oozing romanticism with which the *Enola* show's writers describe the kamikaze pilots....These were, the script elegaically relates, "youths, their bodies overflowing with life".

The next day *Washington Post* reporter Ken Ringle picked up and restated the *Journal's* observation. The quote the Journal attributed to the curators was actually written by a surviving kamikaze pilot, and this was clearly indicated in the script. Both Ringle and *Journal* spokesman Roger May refused to discuss their mistake. May said: 'We don't do post-mortems on editorials.'[61]

Having made an outlandish case against Smithsonian curating, media charges of political correctness came easily and naturally. Apparently, questioning the use of bomb automatically made you politically correct. As the *Tulsa World* put it in an editorial: 'There has been a disquieting move in recent years to sacrifice history on the altar of political correctness.' The evidence the writer put forward to support this claim rested on the charge that some individuals wished to question the notion that the bomb saved lives in a war fought against a brutal enemy. The editorial concluded: 'The bombings...must be remembered correctly and in perspective.'[62] History in this case was simply what everyone already knew, that the Japanese were incredibly brutal and that an invasion of Japan would have been inevitable without the bomb. For some, to suggest that the bomb was not necessary became the sign not only of political correctness, but of psychological problems. As one commentator stated:

> There are among us a few weird and sick individuals. Some strange compulsion inside them causes them to hate themselves, hate their country, hate their heritage, and hate their history. They seem unable to see or to think clearly.[63]

Meanwhile, Patrick Buchanan thought he had uncovered a sinister, un-American conspiracy:

> In all this, friends, there is something less benign than the timidity of academics desperate to be seen as Politically Correct. What is under way is a sleepless campaign to inculcate in American youth a revulsion toward America's past. The Left's long march through our institutions is complete. Secure in tenure, they now serve up, in our museums and colleges, a constant diet of the poison of anti-Americanism on which they themselves were fed.[64]

As the critical coverage wore on, the PC charges turned more specifically into an attack on 'revisionism' as a product of the 1960s and the Vietnam War. In an interview, *Washington Post* reporter Ken Ringle, who wrote the longest newspaper piece on the controversy (pitting a Bataan Death March survivor against the Smithsonian curators of the post-war generation), elaborated on the Vietnam issue his article raised:[65]

> Revisionism was a Freudian effort to undercut the authority of experience...in the sense that children of tremendous achievers, if they can't match those achievements, they try to belittle them.[66]

Ringle and other writers commonly substituted the personal experience of veterans for historical understanding in trying to explain the A-bomb decision, and located the Vietnam War as a turning point toward anti-Americanism. As an op-ed in the *Washington Post* put it:

> …revisionist views of Harry Truman and the atomic bomb sprang from the tragic national division over Vietnam—as did so many other twisted perspectives on the generation that won World War II and designed America's strategy in the Cold War.[67]

Charges of political correctness and the vilification of 'revisionism' in the *Washington Post* were particularly ironic, given the newspaper's wartime role in strongly urging diplomatic, rather than military, means to bring the Pacific War to a close. This was vividly recalled when, on the day of his retirement in 1953, *Washington Post* editor Herb Elliston was asked if he had any regrets. Elliston replied: 'Oh yes, plenty. One thing I regret is our editorial support of the A-bombing of Japan. It didn't jibe with our expressed feeling that Japan was already beaten.'[68]

Most historians were unwilling or unable to do much to put any serious counter pressure on the Smithsonian or the media. Perhaps the reason was reflected in a poll of historians published in the *Journal of American History* in December 1994. The poll showed that only six out of 854 US historians thought that Hiroshima was a 'dark spot in American history', a fact that led the AFA to include the poll among the materials it distributed to the media, Congress, and other interested parties. The Organisation of American Historians did finally speak out in mid-October, passing a resolution that defended the Smithsonian against political interference. A month later some historians, including Gar Alperovitz, Kai Bird and Martin Sherwin, did generate some coverage when they publicly protested script revisions that had entirely eliminated evidence of a historical debate.[69] However, their historical arguments were given short shrift, and they were largely treated as one more contesting group, with no particular claim to expertise regarding the bomb decision. For many in the media, not only was the Smithsonian practising politically correct history, but the practice of history itself became PC because it overrode the experiences of veterans. To compensate for the supposed 'political correctness' of historians, the media emphasised the experience-based identity politics of the veterans in opposition to the Smithsonian's historical intentions.

Desperate to salvage the exhibition and avoid further censure, especially from Congress, NASM's Harwit had agreed to review the script line by line with members of the American Legion in the fall of 1994. The resulting fifth and final script, issued in late October, proved to be a total capitulation to the viewpoint of veterans and Congressional critics. Documents related to the historical debate were excised, casualty estimates for an invasion increased, all photographs of Japanese A-bomb victims except one deleted, and the section on the nuclear legacy of Hiroshima substantially pared down. The AFA, of course, called for yet more revisions. Scholars protested the censorship at the Smithsonian, but made little headway with museum officials. It appeared that the fifth script would be the museum's last word, and planning for this revised exhibition went forward accordingly. In January, however, Harwit made one last change, lowering casualty numbers in accordance with new evidence found by historian Barton Bernstein. The American Legion immediately called publicly for the cancellation of the exhibition and Harwit's resignation. Not wanting to put the NASM and the Smithsonian through further turmoil, Harwit agreed to step down. Smithsonian Secretary I. Michael Heyman then announced that the exhibition as it currently stood would be scrapped and the *Enola Gay* would be displayed practically by itself sometime in the spring.

Troubled by the cancellation of the plans for an extensive exhibition, a few newspapers editorialised about the unhappy outcome. The *New York Times* strongly criticised political interference in the writing of history:

> To reduce the complexities or painful ambiguities of the issue to slogans or historical shorthand is wrong. To let politicians and groups with a particular interest frame the discussion and determine the conclusion is worse.[70]

In an interview, the historian Martin Sherwin commented:

> The part of the story that upset me the most was the demand by the American Legion, supported by Congress—the important support was by Congress—that documents be removed from the exhibit that suggested views critical of Truman's decision....That whole point was missed or ignored by the press. And one reason it wasn't emphasised by the press was that it wasn't emphasised by the Smithsonian staff—Harwit and Heyman. And that's unforgivable. It's unforgivable on the part of the Smithsonian and unforgivable on the part of the press, which more than any other institution in this country should care about open discussion.[71]

As these comments indicate, in general the media refused to discuss this part of the story for what it was: censorship.

Conclusion

In the spring of 1996, a poll taken of Washington journalists supposedly revealed what conservatives have always heatedly maintained: that the American press is liberal by a large majority. 91% of reporters and 67% of editors in Washington, DC—where many national and local media outlets maintain news bureaux—described themselves as either liberal or moderate. The author of the article, the media reporter for the *Washington Post* and a well-known media critic, characterised these numbers as troublesome and even ominous for their under-representation of conservatives. The editor of the *Boston Globe* thought the poll data embarrassing.[72] It is hard to see how media practice bears out these 'troublesome' signs. On the contrary, media coverage of an important cultural and political issue such as the *Enola Gay* controversy reveals self-serving pieties and abject subservience to conservative interests. The picture of the American media that emerges exemplifies the American journalist H.L. Mencken's observation that:

> …what chiefly distinguishes the daily press of the United States from all other countries is not its lack of truthfulness…but its incurable fear of ideas….[O]ne finds only a timid and petulant animosity to all questioning of the existing order, however urbane and sincere.[73]

Even if one takes issue with the comparative part of Mencken's statement, the American media utterly failed, during the *Enola Gay* controversy, to help the nation face an important event in its past. Interestingly, US media coverage was also at odds with recent public opinion polls showing rates of disapproval of the bomb's use in the upper 40% range.[74] A Gallup poll released in 1995, soon after the Smithsonian decided to scale down its exhibition, showed only 51% of Americans approving the bomb's use.[75] This relative fluidity in public opinion about the atomic bombings was lost in the one-sidedness of the coverage and editorialising.

For the Smithsonian at least, the opportunity to close the gap between the history and the public understanding of Hiroshima was frustrated, in large part due to the media's refusal meaningfully to address the critical scholarship on Truman's decision. The media reflected and reinforced a number of obstacles to critical historical examination of the Second World War in 1994-95: the desire for commemoration; the traditional reluctance to question Hiroshima; and the absence of the counter-memory of dissenting World War Two era élites. Furthermore, veterans' memories were transformed by the media into ideological weapons in the culture war. The Smithsonian's timid response and the fragmented and late intervention by historians critical of Truman's decision also contributed to the unfortunate outcome of censorship and, finally, cancellation of the exhibition.

Although those who fought in the Second World War were most concerned with maintaining a positive image of the way the war ended, the media's coverage of the *Enola Gay* controversy did not simply have to nurture and feed off conventional views of the atomic bombings. These media-sustained views filtered out information from an increasingly constrained public debate, further bolstering a narrow patriotism. The public sphere was thus ideologically straitened, as media coverage allied battlefield memory and the official truths constructed in 1945 to the conservative discourse of the 1990s, in order to exclude the critical archivist-historian from public debate, public money, and the public space of the museum—the sustaining elements of a publicly shared history.

NOTES

1. This chapter has grown out of my ongoing research, as well as work undertaken by Tony Capaccio and myself for our article 'Missing the Target', *American Journalism Review*, July/August 1995. I wish to acknowledge Tony Capaccio's extraordinary research for that article; his files continue to be a treasure trove of information.

2. The *Enola Gay* controversy was not the only historical issue to merit widespread media attention in 1994-95. *The National Standards for United States History*— a guide that teachers might use to teach American history in grades 5-12, prepared in widespread consultation with historians and educators—came in for concerted attack from conservative commentators when it was issued in the fall of 1994. The battle over Disney's history theme park, planned for the state of Virginia, also occupied the media spotlight in 1994.

3. Michael Sherry notes that patriotic culture became patriotic orthodoxy when conservatives began to wield a rigid patriotism in response to opposition to and loss of the Vietnam War. He sees the *Enola Gay* controversy as symptomatic of this inward-looking, exclusionary patriotism. See his, 'Patriotic Orthodoxy and American Decline', in Edward Linenthal and Tom Engelhardt (eds.), *History Wars: The Enola Gay and Other Battles for the American Past,* New York, Metropolitan/Henry Holt, 1996, pp97-114.

4. See transcript of *This Week with David Brinkley*, ABC-TV, 28 August 1994.

5. See transcript of *The Rush Limbaugh Show*, WMAL-AM Radio, 19 August 1994.

6. Letter to Robert McC. Adams (then secretary of the Smithsonian), 10 August 1994.

7. Barton J. Bernstein, 'Hiroshima, Rewritten', *New York Times*, 31 January 1995, pA21.

8. See transcript of *MacNeil/Lehrer Newshour*, PBS-TV, 23 November 1994.

9. Recent scholarly publications dealing at least in part with the *Enola Gay* controversy include: Edward Linenthal and Tom Engelhardt, op. cit.; Mike Wallace, *Mickey Mouse History and Other Essays on American Memory,* Philadelphia, Temple University Press, 1996; *Bulletin of Concerned Asian Scholars* Vol. 27, No. 2, 1995, special issue on 'Remembering the Bomb: The Fiftieth Anniversary in the United States and Japan'; Michael Hogan (ed.) *Hiroshima in History and Memory,* Cambridge, Cambridge University Press, 1996; Martin Harwit, *An Exhibit Denied: Lobbying the History of the Enola Gay,* New York, Copernicus, 1996; Philip Nobile ed., *Judgment at the Smithsonian,* with an afterword by Barton J. Bernstein, New York, Marlowe and Company, 1995; Kai Bird and Lawrence Lifschultz (eds), *Hiroshima's Shadow: Writings on the Denial of History and the Smithsonian Controversy,* with a foreword by Joseph Rotblat, Stony Creek, Conn., Pamphleteer's Press, 1997; and Laura Hein and Mark Selden, (eds.) *Living with the Bomb: American and Japanese Cultural Conflicts in the Nuclear Age,* Armonk, NY, M.E. Sharpe, 1997. The book by Harwit, the National Air and Space Museum director who was forced to resign as a result of the exhibit controversy, thoroughly examines and documents the controversy. For continuing media commentary, see, for example, Clarence Page, 'Recent cancellations of exhibits set a bad precedent in Washington', *Hartford Courant* (column; reprinted from *Chicago Tribune*), 7 January 1996, pC7; Paul Goldberger, 'Historical Shows on Trial: Who Judges?', *New York Times* (Arts & Leisure), 11 February 1996, section 2, p1.

10. The literature on the decision to use the bomb is now extensive. For an excellent overview of the scholarship through the 1980s, see J. Samuel Walker, 'The Decision to Use the Bomb: A Historiographical Update', *Diplomatic History* No. 14, Winter 1990, pp97-114. Major new scholarship includes Gar Alperovitz, *The Decision to Use the Atomic Bomb and the Architecture of an American Myth*, New York, Knopf, 1995, and the essays by Barton Bernstein and Herbert Bix in Hogan, op. cit..

11. An exhibition of photographs taken of Hiroshima and Nagasaki a few weeks after they had been bombed was scheduled to open at the American History Museum in Washington DC, in 1995 and was intended to coincide with the *Enola Gay* exhibition. After the Smithsonian controversy erupted, Joe O'Donnell, the Second World War Marine Corps sergeant who had taken the photographs, was notified that his pictures would not be used. See transcript (retrieved through Nexis), *All Things Considered*, NPR-Radio, 28 June 1995. Similarly, two federally-funded museums cancelled a travelling exhibit of Carole Gallagher's photographs of Americans who had suffered from atomic radiation. See Carole Gallagher, '"Nothing Natural Could Have Caused This"', *Technology Review*, August/September, 1995, p65.

12. On the history of the bomb decision, see, for example, Gar Alperovitz, *The Decision to Use the Atomic Bomb*; for more on the cultural and political legacy, see Robert Jay Lifton and Greg Mitchell, *Hiroshima in America: Fifty Years of Denial*, New York, G.P. Putnam's Sons, 1995.

13. 'Revisionists bomb on Hiroshima' (editorial), *Tampa Tribune*, 12 October 1994.

14. Joan Beck, 'Pressure to distort World War II history', *Indianapolis Star*, 21 December 1994. Beck is a columnist for the *Chicago Tribune*.

15. Harry S. Truman to Samuel McCrea Cavert, 11 August 1945, 692-A, Official File, Harry S. Truman Presidential Library. Truman also seems to have expressed some reservations about the atomic bombings. On August 10, 1945, one member of Truman's cabinet recorded in his diary that: 'Truman said he had given orders to stop atomic bombing. He said the thought of wiping out another 100,000 people was too horrible. He didn't like the idea of killing, as he said, "all those kids".' Henry A. Wallace, *The Price of Vision: The Diary of Henry A. Wallace, 1942-1946*, John Morton Blum (ed.), Boston, Houghton Mifflin, 1973, p474. For an overview of American attitudes and a description of one university course on Hiroshima, see Leo Maley and Uday Mohan, 'Challenging America's Hiroshima: Culture Wars and the Classroom', *Interjurist* (Tokyo), forthcoming.

16. Sam Johnson, Peter Blute et al., letter to I. Michael Heyman, 13 December 1994.

17. At a press conference, Bill Clinton said: 'President Truman did the right thing.' See CNN transcript (from Nexis), Clinton press conference, 18 April 1995. Clinton's remarks may have encapsulated his true beliefs or a no-cost attempt to take an easy patriotic stand and offset recent criticisms his administration had received for allegedly wanting to cleanse the term VJ-Day of any references to Japan. The White House denied any such plans to rewrite VJ-Day. During the coverage of this issue, journalists noted that the White House had ducked the *Enola Gay* controversy and had also mollified Japanese feelings over the issue of a proposed postage stamp featuring the bomb. See, for example: Cragg Hines, 'Another Battle Over WW II', *Houston Post*, 22 March 1995, pA1; and Dale McFeatters, '"We Won" is Uncivil in Clintonese' (column), *Rocky Mountain News*, 25 March 1995, p50A. For sarcasm about

'political correctness' over VJ-Day, see Dorothy Rabinowitz, 'A VJ-Day for the '90s' (editorial), *Wall Street Journal*, 5 April 1995.

18. Lifton and Mitchell, *Hiroshima in America*, pxi, pxiii.

19. National Air and Space Museum, *Smithsonian Institution Exhibition Planning Document*, July 1993, p2.

20. Tom Webb, '*Enola Gay* at center of battle even today', *Wichita Eagle*, 24 April 1994.

21. For treatments of the evolution of the NASM, and the AFA's attitude toward the NASM, see Harwit, *An Exhibit Denied*, and the essays by Linenthal, Kohn, and Wallace in Linenthal and Engelhardt (eds.), *History Wars*; also see Stanley Goldberg, 'Smithsonian suffers Legionnaires' disease', *Bulletin of Atomic Scientists*, May/June 1995, pp28-33.

22. A smaller exhibit, focusing essentially on the *Enola Gay* and its restoration, opened in June 1995.

23. I. Michael Heyman, 'Smithsonian Perspectives', *Smithsonian*, December 1995, p20.

24. See Bennett's letter to John Correll (editor of *Air Force Magazine*), 6 August 1993. Bennett's letter and several other documents, including AFA letters to the Smithsonian, Smithsonian responses, Smithsonian memos, Congressional responses, and some historians' views are collected by the AFA in a 'documents package' called 'The *Enola Gay* Debate, August 1993-May 1995'. The AFA updated these materials as the controversy developed and sent them to interested parties, including the press. The AFA also collected and bound news clippings on the controversy and bound the first script. These were also distributed upon request.

25. Letter from Monroe Hatch Jr., Executive Director, AFA, to Martin Harwit, director, NASM, 12 September 1993.

26. AFA press release, 16 March 1994.

27. John McCaslin, 'Rewriting History', *Washington Times* ('Inside the Beltway' column), 28 March 1994, p9A. Very little coverage of the planned exhibition had appeared up to this point.

28. 'Inside the Beltway' column, *Washington Times*, 31 March 1994.

29. John McCaslin, 'No place like home', *Washington Times* ('Inside the Beltway' column), 7 April 1994.

30. See Tom Webb, '*Enola Gay* at center of battle even today', *Wichita Eagle*, 24 April 1994, and Mark Johnson, 'Smithsonian exhibit draws fire', *Richmond Times Dispatch*, 8 May 1994.

31. Hugh Sidey, 'War Remembrance', *Time*, 23 May 1994, p64; John Correll, 'War Stories at Air and Space', *Air Force Magazine*, April 1994. Apparently Sidey had been alerted by a Smithsonian docent unhappy with the exhibit plans. Harwit, *An Exhibit Denied*, p275.

32. Bearss letter to curator Tom Crouch, 24 February 1994.

33. Richard Hallion and Herman Wolk, Comments on Script, 7 February 1994.

34. Edward Linenthal, 'Anatomy of a Controversy', Linenthal and Engelhardt, op. cit., pp44-45.

35. Roger Burt, 'Museum History Imbalanced', *Portland Oregonian*, 3 June 1994, pE9. The quote was modified in the second draft of the script. See the Smithsonian's 'Draft Statement for the Media', 6 September 1994. The second draft was dated 31 May 1994.

36. Memorandum from Brigadier General David Armstrong, Director for Joint History, Office of the Chairman, Joint Chiefs of Staff, to Alfred Goldberg, historian, Office of the Secretary of Defense, 14 July 1994.

37. See, for example, 'Smithsonian exhibit angers veterans', *Nashville Tennessean*, 25 July 1994.

38. Tibbets statement/Airmen Memorial Museum press release, 9 June 1994.

39. Eugene Meyer, 'Dropping the Bomb', *Washington Post*, 21 July 1994, pC2.

40. See also, Capaccio and Mohan, 'Missing the Target', and Tony Capaccio, 'DOD Historians Lauded Revisions In A-Bomb Script', *Defense Week*, 3 July 1995, p1, pp8-9.

41. 'Key Association Messages', AFA, no date (in author's possession).

42. Letter from Representative Peter Blute et al. to Smithsonian Secretary (at the time) Robert McC. Adams, 10 August 1994. Blute's press secretary, Rob Gray, indicated in an interview that Meyer's article had caught Blute's eye. See Capaccio and Mohan, 'Missing the Target'.

43. 'Context and the *Enola Gay*' (editorial), *Washington Post*, 14 August 1994, pC8.

44. Jeff Jacoby, 'Smithsonian drops a bomb in World War II exhibit' (column), *Boston Globe*, 16 August 1994.

45. Tony Capaccio conducted the interview; see Capaccio and Mohan, 'Missing the Target'.

46. NASM, 'Draft Statement for the Media', 6 September 1994; see Linenthal, 'Anatomy of a Controversy', p44.

47. In a reply to the *Air Force Magazine's* April article, Harwit did not elaborate on the historical issues. Harwit letter, *Air Force Magazine*, May 1994; Harwit, 'The *Enola Gay*: A Nation's, and a Museum's Dilemma' (op-ed), *Washington Post*, 7 August 1994, pC7.

48. Four were news stories about veteran and congressional reactions to the Air and Space Museum's January 1995 decision to lower the casualty estimate for an invasion of Japan. The longer wrap-up piece—after the exhibit was cancelled—did in passing raise the question of whether 'Japan would have surrendered anyway, without an invasion', but framed it as a generational issue and then promptly let the matter drop. Feinsilber's five stories appeared on 20, 26, 28 and 31 January, and 21 February, 1995. Feinsilber's approach reinforced the view that Truman had to choose between bomb and invasion.

49. Uday Mohan's interview with Mike Feinsilber, 11 May 1995.

50. Charles Krauthammer, 'World War II, Revised—Or, how we bombed Japan out of racism and spite', *Washington Post*, 19 August 1994, A27. The column appeared in newspapers around the country. My interview with Krauthammer was conducted on 15 May 1995.

51. Bill Powell with Daniel Glick, 'The New Battle of Hiroshima', *Newsweek*, August 29, 1994, p36. Tony Capaccio interviewed Powell on 19 April 1995.

52. The first script was called 'Crossroads: The End of World War II, the Atomic Bomb and the Origins of the Cold War', and dated 12 January 1994.

53. William Mullen, 'WWII airmen gather in storm', *Chicago Tribune*, 2 September 1994. My interview with Mullen was conducted on 11 May 1995.

54. John Kifner, 'Hiroshima: A Controversy that Refuses to Die', *New York Times*, 31 January 1995.

55. Eugene Meyer and Jacqueline Trescott, 'Smithsonian Scuttles Exhibit: *Enola Gay* Plan Had "Fundamental Flaw"', *Washington Post*, 31 January 1995.

56. William Cheshire, 'Why the Government Shouldn't be Entrusted with Writing History', *Arizona Republic*, 6 October 1994, pB6.

57. Gar Alperovitz, 'Loading the Guns of August 1995', *Chicago Tribune*, 9 August 1994; 'The *Enola Gay's* Place in History', *Chicago Tribune*, 9 September 1994.

58. First script, p5. As for what the quote actually intended, its author, Michael Neufeld, offered this explanation in an interview: '[The media] misinterpreted our mindset. It was an attempt to interpret what was in the minds of each side at the time. It's not what we thought the Japanese were all about. We were trying to explain what they thought they were all about.' See Capaccio and Mohan, 'Missing the Target'.

59. 'The *Enola Gay* exhibit a mainstream victory', *Mobile Register*, 6 January 1995.

60. See first script, p15.

61. The mistake was brought to their attention by Tony Capaccio. For May's statement, see Capaccio and Mohan, 'Missing the Target', p25.

62. 'Changing History' (editorial), *Tulsa World*, 31 August 1994.

63. Charley Reese, 'We cannot let museum turn *Enola Gay* exhibit into a guilt trip' (syndicated column), *News Chief*, 24 August 1994.

64. Patrick Buchanan, 'Hose Out the Smithsonian Stables', *Denver Post*, 15 November 1994, pB9. The attack on the Smithsonian as PC was extraordinarily consistent. See, for example, 'Respect History's Truth' (editorial), *St. Petersburg Times*, 19 September 1994, p8A; Marianne Means, 'The Nation's Attic—Historian or Moralizer' (column), *Plain Dealer* (Cleveland), 27 August 1994, p9B; John Leo, 'PC Propaganda at the Smithsonian: More Examples' (op-ed), *Orlando Sentinel*, 4 October 1994, pA7; and Thomas Sowell, 'The Right to Infiltrate', *Forbes*, 11 March 1995, p74.

65. Ken Ringle, *Washington Post*, 26 September 1994.

66. My interview with Ken Ringle was conducted on 10 February 1995.

67. Edwin Yoder Jr., '...Or Hiroshima "Cult"?' *Washington Post*, 4 February 1995. Yoder explicitly endorses this argument, which he attributes to the work of Robert Newman.

68. 'Elliston Reviews *Post*'s Role In Tackling Public Problems', *Washington Post*, 20 April 1953, p7.

69. Kai Bird and Martin Sherwin went on to form the Historians' Committee for Open Debate on Hiroshima, which distributed historical materials to the press and acted as a clearing house for information on public and academic education about Hiroshima.

70. 'Hijacking History', *New York Times*, 30 January 1995.

71. My interview with Martin Sherwin was conducted on 8 May 1995.

72. Howard Kurtz, 'Poll Takes Liberal View of the Press', *Washington Post*, 27 May 1996, pD1.

73. H.L. Mencken, *The Vintage Mencken*, compiled by Alaistair Cooke, New York, Vintage, 1955, p105; quoted in Lindsay Waters, 'Professah de Man—he dead', *American Literary History*, No. 7, summer 1995, p297.

74. A July 1990 Gallup poll revealed that 53% of Americans approved of the use of atomic bombs on Japan (*Gallup Poll Monthly*, August 1990, pp32-33). One in four Americans, however, did not recall that atomic bombs had been used in wartime. The approval rate rose from 38% for 18-29 year olds to 67% for those aged 55 and over. A November 1991 poll showed 50% of Americans willing to apologize for Hiroshima if Japan apologized for Pearl Harbor. Steven Weisman, 'Pearl Harbor Remembered', *New York Times*, 7 December 1991, p26.

75. Kristin Hussey, 'Hiroshima, Nagasaki a Mystery to Americans', *Washington Times*, 3 March 1995. The poll also showed that '35% did not know the first atomic bomb was dropped on Hiroshima', and that a wide gender gap existed: only 29% of women would have dropped the bomb as opposed to nearly two-thirds of the men. 57% of 18-29 year olds opposed the bomb's use, but 55% of those over 50 supported its use.

JAPANESE WAR MEMORIES

John Knight[1]

O n 30 October 1995 a party of twenty-one British former prisoners of war and their families began a two-week stay in Japan. The old soldiers had been interned in labour camps in Japan, and the purpose of the trip was to revisit their former prison camp, known as Iruka, in the village of Itaya.[2] On arrival the former POWs were taken on a tour of Kyoto and Hiroshima, before going on to Iruka, where they attended a local reception, joined in a village festival, stayed with local families, visited the old copper mines where they had worked, and participated in a memorial service with villagers for the sixteen prisoners who died in the camp. The visit received considerable media attention in Japan. This chapter shows how the visit became a media event addressing the vexed issues of remembrance and reconciliation.

The Iruka Story

In 1988 a Catholic priest, Father Murphy, visited a colleague's parish in the Kii Peninsula, in central Japan. When out on a drive, he was shown an unlikely sight by his host. Stopping at a remote village in the mountains:

> …there, in front of my eyes, was a Memorial to sixteen British soldiers who had died, just before the end of World War Two, at a prisoner of war camp here. Two things immediately caught my attention: one was the Roll of Honour with the soldiers' names displayed in bold print; the other was the fresh flowers that had been placed in the receptacles on either side of the monument.

The two foreign Catholic priests were greatly moved by this evidence of the Japanese villagers' enduring concern for their long-deceased former enemies.

> Each year, at the time when the people of Japan remember their dead, a Buddhist priest is invited to come and pray for the repose of the soldiers who died in this place….As we drove back…we talked about the Memorial in that isolated place, and we wondered (indeed, doubted), if a village could be found in any part of the world, where, in similar circumstances, and over forty years on from the end of the war, the people would display such a generous and "Christian" outlook, as the villagers of Itaya.[3]

Father Murphy wrote an account of his visit in a Catholic magazine. The article later came to the attention of a British ex-POW who recognized the place described as none other than his own POW camp—Iruka. He wrote to the priest pointing this out and recalling his own experiences of the camp. Father Murphy then forwarded copies of the letter to the local priest, who in turn passed these on to the villagers. One of the villagers then sent a copy of the letters to her daughter, who had married an Englishman and was now living in Britain.

The daughter, by now a widow, reacted to the old soldier's letter by setting out to get in touch with other former POWs from the camp. She attended a veterans' gathering in London and searched out those who had been interned in her village. She discovered that after the war the Iruka veterans had formed themselves into a group which they called the 'Iruka Boys'. There followed a busy correspondence between the widowed daughter Keiko ('the Iruka girl') and the old soldiers, and the invitation to the former POWs to revisit Iruka developed from this contact. In 1992, 1994 and 1995, the Iruka Boys visited their former place of captivity.

The story of Allied soldiers in Japanese POW camps, especially those along the Burma-Siam railway, is well known from books, television and cinema. Japanese POW camps in Japan itself attract rather less attention. From 1942 to mid-1945, some 35,000 internees were transferred from different parts of Southeast Asia to Japan, where at 100 different sites they were put to work in mining (copper, coal etc.) or in steel foundries.[4] From published accounts, it seems clear enough that POWs in Japan itself suffered. The relocation to Japan, via long sea journeys in which the POWs were crammed in miserable holds for long periods of time, involved considerable hardship. POWs in Japan found that food was in short supply—although this was the case for local people too, since at least half of local harvests were requisitioned by the army. For the most part, moreover, the captives were kept apart from local people, who were told they were dangerous and to be avoided. Prisoners endured (in some cases severe) beatings from camp guards.[5] Yet overall the scale of mistreatment within Japan would seem to have been considerably less than in the South East Asian camps.[6]

When the two foreign priests saw the Iruka graves, they concluded that the dedicated care bestowed on the dead soldiers by the villagers was an unrivalled example of 'Christian' conduct. From the priests' point of view, the villagers had shown a generous, liberal-minded attitude in taking responsibility for the graves of their wartime enemies. Father Murphy entitled his article 'In Japan a Place That is Forever England', as though the presence of the Englishmen's remains indelibly defined that part of the village as English. But there are also reasons to think that, in a certain way, the graves have been incorporated into the village. The conduct which struck the priests as so 'Christian' also makes sense in terms of local norms of grave care associated with Buddhism.

Iruka is a mountain village area in southern Mie Prefecture, where forestry and farming are the main industries. The old copper mine has long since closed, and even if it were still open it seems unlikely that village youth would want to work there. The wartime displacement of the younger village population was followed by a later peacetime displacement of younger villagers from the late 1950s onwards, through migration to the cities of Osaka, Nagoya and Tokyo. The remaining population of the village is largely elderly, and many feel abandoned by their migrant descendants. Remembrance has a particular importance in such a place. There is also a fear of abandonment after death, with older people doubting whether an eldest son in Nagoya or Tokyo will return annually to look after the ancestral graves.

The first obligation of an Iruka family is to tend to the family graves. On the regular attentions of the living (at domestic altar and graveyard) depends the posthumous well-being of the family ancestors. But Buddhism also enjoins the living to direct their attention to abandoned spirits, neglected or forgotten by the world of the living, as well as family ancestors. In many parts of the peninsula, villagers have gathered up old gravestones from the forest or from the sites of former villages and formed mounds within the village cemetery. This act of compassion expresses the village's concern for spirits of the unrelated dead, although such actions may not be totally selfless. For Japanese Buddists, ancestors neglected by their living descendants, or those who die young without reaching maturity, are seen as particularly wretched spirits, whose posthumous suffering makes them ill-disposed to the world of the living. Young soldiers who die before marriage have long been recognized as dangerous in this respect: 'The most numerous occurrences of vengeful spirits are the ghosts of dead soldiers, who are reported in the aftermath of any war in Japanese history.'[7] The British soldiers of Iruka, in their youthful deaths in a wartime labour camp on enemy territory, undoubtedly suffered. The following comments give an insight into the villagers' perception of the soldiers' graves.

> They must have been terribly lonely and very anxious about their future and, together with other reasons, fell ill and did not recover....I imagined the sixteen young British soldiers must have dreamt of a triumphant return. [During the memorial] I could not hold back my tears.

They have not posthumously degenerated to the status of miserable ghosts forgotten and ignored by the living people in their midst. Since the end of the war, the graves have been cared for—cleaned regularly, given offerings of food and flowers, and prayed to—by local people, mostly old women. It is the local Old People's Club which tends the graves, and which sponsors memorial services at the graves on the spring and autumn equinoxes, the traditional time to visit family graves.

Whatever the reason behind the post-war village memorialism directed to the soldiers' graves, it was the belated discovery of this prolonged local expression of compassion which led former POWs to visit their place of past captivity. Some of the Iruka veterans had earlier visited Thailand and Burma, where they had been imprisoned before their spell in Japan. But the story of village memorialism for their dead comrades meant that the Iruka Boys' trip took on a somewhat different character from much of war veteran visiting, especially where this involves Japan. The story of the Iruka Boys' visit was widely covered in the Japanese mass media—on television channels, and in national and local newspapers. The following commentary, based on a survey of press and television coverage, highlights some of the features of the visit that attracted media interest and attention.

Press Coverage

The memorial service for the sixteen dead soldiers received considerable press coverage. The reports included pictures of the former POWs in regimental ties and blazers laying wreaths and offering flowers in front of the large cross over the grave. In one picture the former POWs are neatly lined up before the grave over which flutters a Union Jack. Two or three of the men have walking-sticks, but most are standing to attention, and many bear medals on their chest. While the photographs show veterans moved by remembrance of their deceased comrades, the written part of the report (*Asahi Shinbun*, 5 November 1995) deals with British appreciation of the villagers' dedication to the graves, reproducing the veterans' own words (in translation):

> We are grateful to all of you local people for caring for the graves. The sixteen [dead] soldiers too are happy. Thank you.

In a short editorial piece on the eve of VJ-Day celebrations overseas, the *Yomiuri Shinbun* reflected on the sentiments of a letter sent by one of the former POWs after the 1994 visit: 'There are no winners in war. All it leaves is a river of death and destruction.' By renouncing war in principle, the old soldiers had, in effect, ceased to be soldiers. This ex-POW's words thus call into question the triumphalism of war remembrance in Britain and elsewhere. The same article also favourably compared the words of the Iruka Boys with the apology for the war given by Murayama Tomiichi, the then Japanese Prime Minister (*Yomiuri Shinbun,* 18 August 1995).

Another theme of press reports was the way in which the old soldiers themselves were changed by the visit. Many newspapers reported that the British veterans' lingering hatred of the Japanese had finally been overcome by the warmth of their encounters with local people:

> I hated Japan, but after coming to Japan, this hatred has gone and my thinking has changed. Now I hold no hatred [for the Japanese].

These words were reproduced in most newspapers, often in headlines, such as: 'Hatred has gone on coming to Japan' (*Ise Shinbun,* 7 November 1995); 'Hatred has gone' (*Yoshikuma Shinbun,* 8 November 1995); and 'Through contact, hatred has gone' (*Asahi Shinbun,* 7 November 1995). The theme was reinforced in the photographs accompanying the articles which showed the old soldiers talking to villagers—either children or older people like themselves. One depicted a tall, upright former POW shaking hands with a fragile old village man of roughly the same age—presumably himself a veteran of the conflict (*Yomiuri Shinbun,* 4 November 1995). The horrors of war still disturb in times of peace, it was suggested, but by ending their hatred the old soldiers had found a new peace in themselves.

> For a long time I had nightmares. But when I revisited Iruka [in 1994], and paid my respects at the graves, I was at last freed from the nightmares.

These words were reproduced in a *Yomiuri* article on the occasion of the veterans' visit in late 1995 (*Yomiuri Shinbun,* 1 November 1995).

Press coverage also considered the longer term significance of the visit. This was often illustrated by the example of the Iruka veteran who had died after the war, but whose widow and son had come along in his place to re-visit the old camp. One report went on to conclude that, in this way, the grass-roots contacts occasioned by the former POWs' visit were being continued by the younger generation (*Yomiuri Shinbun,* 1 November 1995). The readiness of veterans to meet with their ex-captors augured well for international reconciliation in the twenty-first century, it was argued: the former prisoners' behaviour was especially laudable given this larger imperative of peace in the future. A seventy-one-year-old reader of an earlier article was moved to contact the newspaper and offer her monthly pension of ¥20,000 (approximately £120) to pay for the flowers offered to the graves by the former POWs. On account of her husband's job, the woman had actually lived near the camp during the war, and remembered seeing the ragged, long-haired veterans pass through the village from time to time. She recalled that, at the end of the war and before they returned home, the British soldiers visited each house in the village to say goodbye. By that time their appearance had changed completely, and they were now neat, clean and resplendent in their uniforms. It was at that moment, she added, that she finally realised Japan had lost the war (*Yomiuri Shinbun,* 8 November 1995).

Television Coverage

Most of the television coverage of the Iruka Boys' visit took the form of short, thirty second reports on breakfast, lunchtime and evening news programmes. What received most coverage was the graveside memorial in which the veterans offered flowers to their deceased comrades. Here the reporting was brief and factual, although sometimes interspersed with short interview comments from the former POWs themselves. There were also some longer, more in-depth reports of the Iruka Boys' visits. One of these was a full ten minute report featured in a New Year's Eve programme entitled *The Outgoing Year, The Incoming Year: A Moment of Contact,* shown by Yokohama TV in association with ten other channels. The first part of the programme, in which the Iruka Boys appeared, was a retrospective look at 1995, while the second part, after midnight, focused on New Year celebrations in different parts of the country. It is worth examining this report in detail because of the range of themes contained within it.

At the beginning of the show, the presenters pointed out that 1995 had been a year in which some terrible things occurred in Japan, such as the Great Hanshin Earthquake and the sarin gas attack on the Tokyo subway. But the year had not all bad, for some remarkable and inspiring things had also happened. The Iruka Boys' visit was then presented as one of the main examples of this more positive aspect of 1995. The report began with a scene showing the old soldiers and their wives dancing at a local festival, as some ten or more young men rhythmically beat drums. The veterans, wearing blue festival coats, were shown mixing with village children. A final camera shot from on-high showed a small, mountain-enclosed village in which a large gathering, of hundreds of people, was taking place. The foreign visitors appeared absorbed by the festival and indistinguishable from the villagers collectively celebrating it.

The second scene showed nine or ten old women cleaning the soldiers' graves and offering new flowers. One woman, bent over almost at a right angle, was shown busily sweeping away leaves from the grave on a bright autumn morning. The women wore old-style, bright-coloured pantaloons, and some had large white aprons. An old woman explained to camera that everybody here—all the old women—joined in with the grave cleaning, and that they hoped that the next generation of villagers would likewise care for the grave. The grave itself had a large, bright metal cross, with a Union Jack and Rising Sun flag either side of it, and seemed crammed with brightly coloured flowers. There followed a shot of all the women, on their haunches, huddled together before the grave, each with her head bowed and hands together in prayer.

The third scene featured the mines where the POWs had laboured. The veterans and their wives were shown carefully walking along the old track in a tunnel beneath the hillside, while the narrator told of the sixteen POWs who had died from accidents and illness there. The next shot was a camera close-up of one of the visiting women crying. This, the narrator explained, was the wife of a recently deceased former POW. This man had wanted to return to Iruka but died before he had the chance, and his wife was there in his place. (This was the same widow featured—along with her son—in the newspaper report above.) Sobbing gently, she carefully placed in the tunnel (leading to the mine-shaft) a small white cross bearing a red poppy. A close-up showed her late-husband's name written on it.

There was then another sudden change of scene and mood: the 'welcome party' held for the Iruka Boys by the villagers. This featured music and dancing, a shot of a veteran looking intently at—and possibly a little alarmed by—the spectacle, and then successive pictures of veterans and their wives talking to, smiling at, and laughing with villagers old and young. The report then showed the end of the party, an emotional parting scene of the old soldiers and villagers, hands joined together in a large circle, all singing Auld Lang Syne. The narrator introduced this as 'music from the country of the Iruka Boys which reverberated across into the hearts of local people'. The soundtrack was a discordant mix of English and Japanese singing—for the villagers sang the Japanese version of Auld Lang Syne, *Hotaru no hikari* (The Light of the Firefly). The Japanese lyrics have strong wartime associations, recalling the parting of village sons for the war—here they were seeing off a very different group of soldiers.

The following scene featured a village household in which the family of one of the Iruka Boys were being hosted. The two families were seated on the rushmat floor, gathered closely around a small table having dinner. The exception was Alex, the former POW himself, who was seated on a stool in the corner. His village host, a forthright, plain-speaking man in his fifties, recounted to the interviewer the suffering that his friend Alex had endured. Alex had been so badly beaten on his lower back by the Japanese camp guards—even now the scars remained, Alex had shown them to him—that he could not sit down to eat with the rest of them at the table. Suddenly, in a loud, emotional voice, the host then declared in Alex's direction 'I would really like to offer a deep apology'. Cut to a smiling Alex, who, against a background of noisy laughter said (with Japanese subtitles): 'This [dinner party] is wonderful. It really gives the flavour of what people are like in their own homes.' Although, on his host's own admission, Alex had good reason to hate Japan and the Japanese, in fact the old British soldier bore no grudges and appeared happy and relaxed in the company of his village friend.

The next scene was a school gymnasium where the Iruka Boys and their families were seated together on small fold-up chairs. Behind them was a large banner bearing the words (in English) 'Think of Peace Meeting'. In front of them were perhaps a hundred dark-uniformed high school students seated on the floor. The narrator explained that this was an opportunity for the students to learn about the veterans' war experiences and about the importance of world peace. One or two students were shown asking the old soldiers questions in slow, nervous English. 'Do you have any pleasant memories of Iruka?' A veteran thoughtfully responded: 'There was many a pleasant conversation and many a small friendship between civilians and POWs which grew up in the dark corners of the mine.' Then, before the camera, the narrator reflected, slowly and solemnly, on history, war and hatred, concluding from the Iruka Boys' experiences that: 'War is also a form of human encounter, but one which leads to hatred. Although it is not possible to erase history, it is possible to erase hatred.'

Back in the studio, the two presenters of the New Year's Eve show, a middle-aged man and woman, looking greatly impressed by what they had seen, concluded by stressing the value of 'private diplomacy' rather than inter-governmental diplomacy. The male presenter asked the reporter (still visible on the screen behind him) to confirm that the initiative was a local one and not a government one, and then went on to marvel that a 'depopulated village' could have carried out the programme of exchange all by itself:

At the government level, Japan is always challenged by others, especially other Asian peoples, but what the Japanese really feel about the war is represented by those villagers we just saw. If only this could be more widely known.

The female presenter then took up the theme and remarked that: 'even though the language is different the feelings are the same.' She was particularly impressed at how determined the villagers were to instruct the younger generation. In this dark year of 1995, with the terrible things that have happened, she suggested, this example of contact between people gave great hope for the future.

Themes of Coverage

There was, of course, considerable overlap between the press and television coverage of the visit. A recurring theme of the press coverage was the transformative power of human contact—even between old enemies. Although motivated to visit by their gratitude to villagers for care of the graves, the former soldiers were naturally apprehensive about revisiting their old enemy, even fifty years on. But by the end of their visit, the old men appeared different: the war has finally ended for them. Contact was also a dominant theme in the television reports. The explicit theme of the larger programme in which the item discussed above appeared was again that of human contact: the visit was presented as an example of past enemies coming together. As the programme title indicated, the temporal 'contact' of one year with another on New Year's Eve was a metaphor for the contact between people. At a time of so much violence, destruction and division in the world, this programme set out to show examples of the good things that were happening, of enmities being overcome and new friendships being forged.

Where the television coverage went beyond press reporting was in highlighting the role of the village as sponsor of this international event. The tone of the coverage was lightly ironical. While it is the metropolises of Tokyo or Osaka which are usually considered to be in the vanguard in Westernisation and the take-up of new or foreign trends, here it was the village, often considered a bastion of conservatism, parochialism and insularity, taking the lead in the all-important matter of international reconciliation. It was, moreover, a remote village, itself the location of a wartime captivity and forced labour, which was reaching out. The simple honesty of rural people was seen as more effective than the posturing and machinations of politicians and diplomats.

Some aspects of the visit were neglected. In recounting the background to the Iruka Boys visit, the efforts of Keiko, the Iruka girl, were duly referred to, but her well-known devout Christianity was not mentioned even though it was arguably this which drove her to bring about reconciliation between the old soldiers the villagers. This makes for an intriguing irony. While Father Murphy attributed a 'Christian' character to memorial behaviour wholly consistent with folk Buddhism, Japanese media coverage neglected the actual role of the Christian spirit—personified by Keiko—in the process of reconciliation. Instead, the Iruka Boys' story became a tale of the power of village sincerity, along with the spirit of the old soldiers, in overcoming their feelings of hatred. Just as Father Murphy found the 'Christianity' of the villagers' care for enemy graves an edifying lesson in the generosity of spirit, which ought to be communicated to Christians throughout the world, so the Japanese print and television media saw the visit of former enemy soldiers to the small village of their captivity as exemplifying a reconciliation that did not dishonour the memory of the Japanese war dead.

Conclusion

It is not only war itself which divides, but also memories of war. Despite the formal post-war peace, Japan continues to be embroiled in 'memory wars' with supposedly friendly countries.[8] Public anger over Japanese 'war amnesia' was manifest in Britain in 1995 in the lead-up to VJ-Day. British war veterans' organisations mounted a sustained public campaign calling on the Japanese government to apologise for wartime misconduct and to offer financial compensation to former POWs. Throughout the summer of 1995 British press coverage of the forthcoming VJ-Day anniversary stressed the failure of Japan to repent fully for its wartime past. Japan was presented as stubbornly refusing to accept its full guilt. Prime Minister Murayama's 'apology', disclosed by the British Prime Minister John Major in advance of VJ-Day, was itself greeted with disappointment. 'This apparently is intended to be the apology for which so many people in Asia, Europe, Australia and America have waited for half a century', was the response, bordering on bewilderment, of the *Times* correspondent, who doubted that it really was 'a request for forgiveness' (16 August 1995).

The International War Crimes Tribunal's interpretation of the war—'a war of aggression in violation of international law and a criminal act involving inhumane conduct contrary to the rules of war'[9]—is widely known in Japan and not without some popular support. However, many Japanese remember their nation not as a simple aggressor, but as a belligerent which, while badly led, genuinely feared for its own security at a time of Western imperial expansion in Asia. Moreover, the Japanese memory of the war is dominated by the atomic bombing. As John Dower puts it:

Hiroshima and Nagasaki became icons of Japanese suffering—perverse national treasures of a sort, capable of fixating Japanese memory of the war on what happened to Japan and simultaneously blotting out recollection of the Japanese victimisation of others'.[10]

It is against this background of polarised war remembrance that the visit of the Iruka Boys is of particular interest. Existing uneasily between the two dominant memories of the war on each side, it is reducible to neither. Arguably, this could potentially make the Iruka Boys' story a challenge to both dominant war memories. However, as the Iruka Boys' trip received scant media coverage in Britain, it had little effect on the impression of the wartime Japanese as the cruellest of captors. It is rather on the Japanese side that the Iruka Boys' visit engages war memory, though in a complex way.

In the 1990s there have been many visits to Japan in connection with the war including the visit of the so-called Korean 'comfort women' and British veterans of the Burma-Siam Railway. All went demanding recognition of, and often compensation for, their wartime suffering at the hands of the Imperial Army. Given the media coverage they have received, the effect of these various petitions by different groups of claimants may well be to alter the popular Japanese consciousness of the war from the preoccupation with Japanese suffering to a recognition of the suffering inflicted by Japan on others.[11] As veterans of Japanese camps in Burma and Japan, the Iruka Boys could, of course, be viewed as another instance of this trend whereby past victims confront their victimisers, and thereby induce a revised remembrance of the war. The surviving Iruka Boys are a living reminder of Japanese wartime excesses, and their presence in Japan can help to teach younger generations of Japanese about the realities of war.

The visit of the Iruka Boys is not, however, a neat, clear-cut part of this process. They differ from many of the other visiting victims in that they have not—at least in the first instance—come to remind their former captors of past suffering, much less to seek compensation. If they bear enmity due to past captivity, they also feel gratitude for the posthumous care given to fellow prisoners by ex-captors. For other wartime victims, the reference point is the war itself, and the suffering associated it. Post-war neglect has only compounded their wartime suffering and the feelings of bitterness they hold towards Japan. By contrast, the Iruka Boys are joined to their former captors by a continuous (if only recently revealed) post-war history of compassionate memorialism for dead comrades. While fifty years on from the end of the war Japan continues to be condemned for its 'war amnesia', the village of Iruka finds itself the object of admiration and affection for its dedicated remembrance of enemy soldiers. The Iruka Boys come to give thanks rather than to apportion blame.

One might expect Japanese media coverage to focus on the Iruka Boys' story not just as an instance of reconciliation, but also as a means of combatting the charges widely levelled at Japan for wartime conduct. Were the media to highlight Iruka amity, this could conceivably serve to offset the censure usually directed at Japan over POW camps. Does not the warmth of the Iruka Boys' visit, and the fact that their memories of captivity are not all bad, indicate that internment in Japanese POW camps was not as unrelentingly bad as is often portrayed? Yet in the television programme discussed above a villager offered precisely the kind of wholehearted apology that the Japanese Prime Minister was criticised for not making. Of course, the occasion on which this apology was made was one of obvious convivial warmth between a village family and an former POW family. In this instance, reconciliation preceded apology—indeed made it possible. Perhaps it is in this respect that the Iruka Boys' story may prove to be of larger significance.

NOTES

1. The author would like to express his thanks to Toji Isao, president of the *Kinan kokusai koryukai*, and to the newspaper *Kinan Shinbun* for assistance in obtaining videotaped television news reports, press cuttings, and other materials on which this chapter is based.

2. Itaya is the name of the hamlet, while 'Iruka' refers to the municipality of which it formed part. In the 1950s Iruka was merged with other municipalities to form the larger municipality of Kiwa-cho. Hence the place-name of 'Iruka' is no longer commonly used.

3. Cyril Murphy, 'In Japan a Place That is Forever England', *Far East*, 1988. Reproduced in Holmes *et al. A Little Britain*, an unpublished catalogue of letters and photographs.

4. Hugh Clarke and Colin Burgess, *Barbed Wire and Bamboo: Australian POW Stories*, St. Leonards, NSW, Allen and Unwin, 1992.

5. Ray Parkin, *The Sword and the Blossom*, London, Hogarth, 1968; and John Fletcher-Cooke, *The Emperor's Guest*, London, Hutchinson, 1971.

6. Olive Checkland, *Humanitarianism and the Emperor's Japan, 1877-1977*, London, St. Martin's Press, 1994.

7. Gregory Barrett, *Archetypes in Japanese Film*, Selinsgrove, Susquehanna University Press, 1989.

8. Geoffrey M. White, 'Memory Wars: The Politics of Remembering the Asia-Pacific War', *Asia Pacific Issues: Analysis from the East-West Centre*, No.21, 1995.

9. Ienaga Saburo, *Japan's Last War: World War II and the Japanese, 1931-1945*, Oxford, Basil Blackwell, 1979.

10. John Dower, 'The Bombed: Hiroshimas and Nagasakis in Japanese Memory' in Michael J. Hogan (ed.), *Hiroshima: History and Memory*, Cambridge, Cambridge University Press, 1996, pp116-142.

11. Ibid and see also: Tachibana Seiitsu, 'The Quest for a Peace Culture', in the same volume, pp168-186.

CONTRIBUTORS

Daniel Ben-Ami has worked as a journalist for ten years and has written for several national newspapers as well as numerous specialist publications.

Phil Hammond co-ordinated the London International Research Exchange's Images of Japan project, and is co-author (with Joan Hoey) of the Exchange's report, *History as News* (LIRE, 1994). He has taught media, film and sociology at several universities and colleges, and currently works at Buckinghamshire College.

John Knight is a Research Fellow at the International Institute for Asian Studies in Leiden, the Netherlands.

Leo Malley III is a graduate student in history at the University of Massachusetts, Amherest. He holds degrees from Bucknell University and Wesley Theological Seminary. Before returning to graduate school he researched American responses to the use of the atomic bomb at the National Center for Economic and Security Alternatives in Washington DC, and taught a course on Hiroshima in the Honors Program at the University of Maryland, College Park.

Tessa Mayes is a director of the London International Research Exchange. She works as a television journalist.

Uday Mohan is a doctoral student in the history department at American University in Washington DC. He has published several articles, presented papers and taught a course at the University of Maryland on the shifting ways American media and memory have dealt with the atomic bombings of Japan.

Gina Owens graduated in Philosophy from Sussex University. She has worked in education for twenty years, both for the Inner London Education Authority, working on projects to provide education and support for Traveller children, and as a teacher.

Lynn Revell is a doctoral student at the University of Kent at Canterbury. She has worked for the Commission for Racial Equality, and as a school-teacher. She is a contributor to Suke Wolton (ed.), *Marxism, Mysticism and Modern Theory* (Macmillan, 1996).

Megan Rowling graduated in Japanese Studies from Cambridge University. She is a writer/researcher for the London International Research Exchange, and works as a reporter for the Jiji Press News Agency, Japan.

Paul Stirner is a freelance writer specialising in education and runs his own consultancy DSM Partnership.

INDEX